When Angels Die

When Angels Die

The haunting memoirs of a clairvoyant blessed & cursed with the ability to 'see' through the eyes of missing & murdered children.

Jeanne Marie Antoinette

Writer's Showcase

San Jose New York Lincoln Shanghai

When Angels Die

The haunting memoirs of a clairvoyant blessed & cursed with the ability to 'see' through the eyes of missing & murdered children.

Writer's Showcase
an imprint of iUniverse, Inc.

For information address:
iUniverse, Inc.
5220 S. 16th St., Suite 200
Lincoln, NE 68512
www.iuniverse.com

ISBN: 0-595-21486-X

Printed in the United States of America

To my children Joel & Harmony
To all those who have so graciously participated in my life
and my work,
Thank you.
Jeanne Marie

Contents

Introduction

Before you begin to read this story, you should understand that it contains many painful memories. For me they are things that have already been. They are my history and as such they are a familiar place, a part of me. But once you open these pages, once you enter the reality of my world, they will also in some way become a part of your memory and as such a part of you. This may open some unsettling thoughts. It may answer many questions, and it may open many more. I only warn you in this way, to be prepared. Do not open these pages, unless you are truly prepared to see all that they contain.

I write this for my children, my family and my friends. I write this for many reasons. Including a heart-felt desire to give each person who has participated in my life some insight, even if it is only a small glimpse into the other side of my somewhat unusual internal life. I may not ever have the opportunity to sufficiently explain the strangeness of my life, the distance of my thoughts or the intensity of my feelings. It is important to me however, to express my gratitude to all those who loved me in spite of these things, in spite of myself. Also, I am compelled to shed some light on the shadows of these unusual events. As I know that one-day one of my children may follow in my footsteps and I do not wish for them to walk blindly into this dark world.

Ironically, it was this very blindness in myself that has always led me to the extraordinary experiences in my life. And, it may well be the same blindness that brings it all to an end. Perhaps I will finally have an ending. I have lived so many endings, so many deaths. But I have also found more than my share of beginnings. Such is my path. A life of endings and beginnings, a life of deaths and births, a life path the ancients know as the 'path of the living dead'. It is a somewhat shadowy existence, but not really quite as ominous at it sounds. I have come to know its ways. I now understand its meaning and have come to appreciate its wisdom. I have come to terms with my life, such as it is.

I am a clairvoyant by birth, and a Santera by choice. For those who are unfamiliar with this term, a Santera is a priest in the Afro-Caribbean religion of Santeria. Santeria is a word meaning 'the way of the saints'. There are many saints in this world, and diverse are their paths to sainthood. All of the saints however share in one indisputable prerequisite, death. For a Santera, this death is traditionally a symbolic one. It is a death of their old way of life. But for me, this death has many meanings. For me, death has become a way of life.

For some reason, I was chosen to share the deaths of so many innocent victims of this world. Understandably, sharing the final moments of someone else's tragic decent from life is hardly something that a child grows up wanting to do in this world. I was no different. I did not choose to become a clairvoyant. I do not know how it was decided that this particular ability would be given to me, but I did believe strongly that if it was, it should be used to help others. I worked for many years peering through the eyes of missing and murdered children. Watching helplessly from their eyes, feeling their pain and sharing their deaths, all in an effort to identify their murderers or find their bodies. Who can ever know if I used this ability, as it was intended to be used? For that matter, who knows if it should ever have been used at all? I do not have those answers. I can only tell you what happened to me. I can only recount to you how those terrifying visions began. I can share with you all the extraordinary events that led me to 'the work'. I can explain to you in vivid detail how I used those unbidden abilities, but I cannot tell you if any of this should have been. I can only tell you that it was, and how it all began.

1

On distant Shores

I t was the early sixties in Southern Germany. I lived with my family on a military base, in a small town called Erlangen, just outside of Nurenberg. World War Two was still a fresh memory in Germany, and the artifacts of war still littered the countryside. We were all warned about these dangers, but we were children. As such, our curiosity and innocence often betrayed us.

The woods were forbidden playgrounds for us, but those dark wooded forests were magical places. They were a secret place where my brothers and I spent many hours huddled in snowy thickets, searching for some obscure truth we suspected the Grimms Brother's had hidden in their tales.

I grew up with four brothers. Of the five children in our family, Raymond was the oldest. I was second, the only girl. Sometimes I thought about wishing for a sister, but more often, I simply wished I had been a boy so I could be like the others. I was a healthy robust tomboy with short hair and dirty nails, and what I lacked in size, I made up for in sheer determination. I was confident that short of urinating for distance I could do anything the boys could do and probably better. It was usually the three of us, Raymond, Jason and I who snuck out and into the forbidden forest. The two younger brothers were far too little to tag along with us on these outings.

I do not recall the month, as the winter months in Germany are all still frozen somewhere in time for me. I do remember it was late in the morning on a cold winter's day. My brothers and I were crouched down in the snow under a very large evergreen tree. The trees grew so thick in that area the sun could barely penetrate through their dark green branches. These were dense woodlands. They were known as the Black Forest. And it was, through the dark womb of a small thicket, in the midst of this Black Forest that our childhood myths were born.

"Be still Jeanne Marie," Raymond warned me. "These woods are crawling with wolves, and they're always looking for food."

"Well no wolf is going to eat me for lunch," Jason assured him.

"I wouldn't be so sure Jason. You remember the story of Red Riding Hood, and Hansel and Gretel?" I asked.

"Yeah," he answered his eyes growing wider.

"Well it was two brothers who wrote those stories. They were called the Grimms brothers. It was a long time ago, but they were from this country. As a matter of fact, I think they lived right around here. Probably right on the other side of these very woods, the same woods we're sitting in right now." My teeth were chattering from the cold but my eyes got the point across.

"So," he said. "They're just stories."

"Jason," Raymond jumped in. "They call em stories, but that's just because they don't want to scare the little kids too much."

"That's right," I agreed turning to Raymond. "There's got to be some truth to all those stories. They've got to be more than fairy tales, otherwise, why would they still be telling them? What do you think Raymond?"

"Well I think about it this way, those stories are old, maybe even a hundred years old. Now there must be hundreds of wolves living here, maybe even thousands. And how many kids do you think have come wondering into this forest, kids, just like us, huh? Hundreds, maybe thousands right? But, have you ever heard how many of em never came out again?" Raymond suddenly stopped and raised his hands gesturing absolute silence from us. Jason and I both froze and watched Raymond as he cocked his head to listen.

"Did you hear that?"

"I heard it," said Jason.

"I did too," I agreed. "What do you think it was Raymond?"

"You know what I think," he said. "I just hope he's alone, and he's not too big."

"You mean a wolf. How big do you think they are?" Jason asked.

"Well you can't be too sure," Raymond explained. "But I heard those German Wolves are really big. As a matter of fact, they might just be the biggest ones in the whole world."

"I can believe that," I agreed. "Remember Red Riding Hood? In that story, one wolf was so big he ate Red Riding Hood and her grandmother, in a single meal." I pulled at the strings on my own hood, until I felt the knot securely under my chin. "I'd say that's a pretty big wolf."

"That's a big one alright," Jason agreed.

"Yeah, you wouldn't even be a snack for him," Raymond taunted. "And speaking of snacks, I'm hungry."

"Yeah me too," Jason piped in. "Hey if those stories are really real, what about Hansel and Gretel? You know, what if there's really a gingerbread house out here?"

"Oh would I like to find that. All that candy, I'm so hungry I think I would eat the whole roof." Raymond patted his stomach and smiled. "And it would be made of pure chocolate, the best chocolate in the whole world."

"I'd take the candy canes," Jason said. "And lemon drops, I'd eat all of those."

"Yeah, well before I started eating, I'd be looking for the old witch who lives there." I said. "And she's not going to be too happy when she finds out you ate her roof either Raymond!"

"Oh that fat old witch, she couldn't even catch me," Raymond said confidently. "I could outrun her any day of the week."

"Me too," Jason said reaching over to shake the snow from the small branch. "I'd grab that candy and run so fast. She could never catch me."

"Yeah, well witches may not be able to run so fast, but they have brooms. What if she grabbed her broom and flew after you?" I said.

"I could still out run her, and I'd eat all her windows too! I bet they'd be made of the best rock candy you ever tasted.

"Yeah, well Hansel thought he was pretty smart too, and you know where he wound up?"

"Where?" Jason asked.

"In a cage," I said. "He got to eat all the candy he wanted, but it was just a trick to fatten him up. The old witch was planning on eating him!"

"Did she?" Jason's eyes widened. "Did she eat him?"

"Naw," Raymond assured him. "He got away."

"Only because his sister pushed the old witch into the oven and let him out," I added.

"Yeah, well the only reason she did is because her brother told her how."

"He did not," I argued. "Without his sister, Hansel would have been dinner!"

"No he wouldn't, and he didn't need some dumb girl to help him either. He could've gotten away any time he wanted to. Besides, Miss I know everything, why would he want to leave when he was getting all the candy he wanted? Huh?"

I shook my head and let out an audible sigh. "He was living in a cage dummy."

"Who cares anyway, all that candy is making me hungry. I haven't eaten since breakfast and I'm starving," Raymond declared standing up and brushing the snow from his pants. "Let's go home and get something to eat."

It was a long walk home and we were all cold and hungry when we arrived. My mother was on the phone when we came in. We knew it must have been a serious conversation because she didn't even yell at us for tracking in the dirt and snow. She hung up the phone, then without a word she picked Jason up and sat him on the chair in front of her. She untied his scarf and began peeling the frozen gloves from his hands. Then she grabbed him and just started hugging him.

Finally she released him and turned to Raymond and I. "I want you all to sit down she began. That was Major Grayson's wife on the phone. There's been … an accident. Raymond and I sat down. My mother looked up at the empty ceiling and then back down to us. "You all know little Billy Myers," she began.

Billy was seven, the same age as Jason. He lived on the same street. We all played together at the playground. "Was he hurt?" I asked.

"He was killed," my mother said softly.

"How?" Raymond asked.

"You know how your father and I always tell you not to go into the woods alone."

"Was it wolves?" Jason looked to Raymond for assurance.

"No sweetheart," my mother said. It wasn't wolves. Billy was playing, in the woods. He found an unexploded grenade. He picked it up, and it blew up. Right in his little hands," her voice cracked and she tried to recompose her words. "It just exploded, and Billy was killed, just like that, just that fast." My mother looked away. "It's just so hard to believe."

"It's okay mom," Jason interrupted. "We know what hand grenades look like, and we won't pick any of em up, even when we're in the woods."

My mother directed her attention to Raymond and I. "Do you understand how dangerous these things are?" She looked at Raymond and I. "When your father and I warn you not to do something, there's a very good reason for it. Do you understand?"

We both shook our heads in agreement and we felt bad, partly because we had disobeyed, but mostly because Mom was so upset. Billy was dead. For us that meant he went to heaven and wouldn't be on the playground anymore. Of course this did not stop us from sneaking off to the woods in search of wolves and gingerbread houses. One time we actually saw a timber wolf. It wasn't very big. Raymond told us it must have been a baby and we believed him, mostly because we wanted to. We all knew that Billy just didn't know any better. He was just a little kid, but the army sent Billy's parents home anyway, to someplace called America.

We were American children, or so we had been told. We were military children. Many of us had never been to America but all of us had lived in other foreign places. Foreign to us was the world at large. We had always been foreigners in foreign lands where the world was not really so different from place to place. There were always children to play with and language for us was never a barrier. A smile, a touch or a simple motion was enough to convey your interest in exploring the new territory and making new friends. Our lives were filled with changes, and changes always brought new things. Growing up, the only things we knew would remain constant in our lives were the immediate family, and the many uniformed men who protected and took care of the world we lived in.

The children we played with were like the seasons. They came into our lives but never for too long. They were sent on to other places, where they would meet other friends. We learned early that part of friendship was letting go. Living with four brothers was not easy, but it was consoling to know that they would always be there. I would always have someone to play with. Wherever we were sent in this world, we would all be sent together.

We all waited anxiously for the school week to end. Finally it did, and it was Saturday. Like most Saturdays we got ready to play. We usually played war. It was my favorite game. There were rules in the game of war, a chain of command, strategy and honor. War was filled with death, but it was also filled with courage and heroic men. My father had been one of those heroic men. He had fought in two wars. He had taken life and he had risked his own to protect his family and their world. He was a hero with many metals that decorated his uniform.

I was born from war, my mother told me that. I was born nine months after my fathers return from Korea. She said something good always came from terrible tragedies like that, and I liked believing that I was one of the good things that came from that war.

It was early November. The weather was cold and the ground was hard, but we were soldiers and we were ready for battle. We all had bits and pieces of army supplies. Whatever our fathers had not donated to the cause, we raided from the storerooms. I had on my utility belt and a canteen heavy with water hung on one side. A pouch filled with emergency supplies; candles, matches, bandages, a cereal bar and a little aluminum can opener hung on a clip on the other side. Raymond carried the knapsack filled with K rations and Jason carried the first aid kit. He was usually the appointed medic. The Applebee brothers were already waiting for us in the small clearing near the front gate and Jerry was not far behind. We threw rocks at the fence and kicked dirt until the rest of the gang arrived.

Marc showed up with his little brother again and he made a face that was half apologetic and half resignation. We all knew that when sides were chosen there would be a fight over the fairness of having to contend with a little kid who couldn't keep up. There were usually a few heated disputes and try as we may; this battle often over shadowed the one we planned to fight. Everything had to be divided fairly before the game began, supplies, area boundaries and the number of players. It was rarely an equitable division.

The first obstacle was getting past the guard and on to the battlefield. We had access to the fields where the soldiers trained for battle. It was filled with tank tracks, empty shells and foxholes ready for the taking. The only way in was through a small hole in the metal linked fence. None of us knew how the hole got there, we all assumed that some earlier generation of kids who lived on base had cut the fence and we were all grateful to them. The trick was to get through without being seen by the guard, we all knew that the fields were absolutely off limits. While the opening itself was not easily detected, the area of the fence was in clear view from the gate. We usually set up a diversion on the other side of the gate. A couple of the boys would start a mock fight and when they got the guard's attention the rest of the troop slipped through the opening in the fence. The last two had to wait for a vehicle or some other momentary distraction of the guard's attention. When the last person arrived safely on the field we all celebrated our first victory.

Predictably an argument ensued over the Marc's little brother and it was finally resolved by giving the side with the kid first choice of territory. Sometimes we played capture the flag, but today we were there to hold the line. Three of us huddled in the foxhole while the other two went on a mission to search for the enemy. I stayed in the foxhole with the older Applebee brother and Tom. I loved to hide in the foxholes. It was dark and warm like a tiny womb within the earth itself. Sometimes we lit candles and told ghost stories. Of course it was a prime time for a sneak attack by the enemy. We had been blown up or taken prisoner more than once that way, but it was all part of the game. If you couldn't win, at least you could always die valiantly.

We were lucky today. The scouts had returned to tell us where the enemy camp was. We would be the aggressors now. We were going behind enemy lines. We crouched down in the dirt, and as soon as we had them in sight we crawled slowly forward on our elbows. Then, just as we got close enough, Jim yelled the battle cry and we all jumped up for the charge. Our weapons were made of wood or they were invisible. It was sound effects alone that constituted a hit or an explosion. A couple of our men were shot down in the charge but Tom was able to throw an invisible grenade into the foxhole and got them all. We started chanting we won, we won, and soon the dead got up and we all collected our things for the long march home.

The only way out was the same way we had come in, so Tom and Raymond volunteered to sneak out first and divert the guard once again. But when we reached the fence we could see that the guard was already distracted. There were several cars at the gate waiting for permission to enter. We all crawled quickly through the fence to see what was going on at the gate.

Nancy and Alice were standing on the other side of the street when they saw us emerging from the field. They crossed the street to greet us. They seemed to know what was going on. The cars were all very official looking and an officer who had just arrived in a jeep with an MP got out to talk to the guard.

"Look in the back seat of the second car," Nancy whispered to me. "You see the girl, she was raped by an American GI."

I didn't know what rape was. I didn't even know what sex was yet. I was eleven years old. All I knew was that rape must be a terrible thing because this girl was being paraded through the town for some kind of confrontation. There were both German and American officials involved.

I stood on the curb to get a closer look at the girl in the car. She looked to be about twelve or thirteen, very thin with strawberry blond hair. Her skin was white, an unnatural kind of white, like translucent porcelain. Then I saw her eyes. They were motionless, like when you stare off into space, but different even from that. I couldn't take my eyes off her. I knew it was rude, but I just couldn't stop looking. She appeared so strange, so empty. That was it, her face was empty, and her eyes were hollow. I wondered if she was dying.

I thought about her when I went to bed that night. I said a prayer for the thin pale girl with the hollow eyes who had been raped by an American soldier. I prayed for the governments, that they wouldn't fight over what had happened. I prayed there would not be another war.

Weeks passed and it was now mid December. I fidgeted in my seat along with the rest of the children. It was almost three and we all waited impatiently for the bell. School would be out soon and this was the last day before Christmas vacation began. My desk was cleaned out already and I eyed the coat rack for my jacket. There it was on the first hook by the door, bright red with a white fur trim around the hood. I loved red, even my boots were red they were dark red leather and scuffed up around the toe, but they were red and I wore them everywhere. I played with the coins in my hand, five of them. I had saved my milk money all week for this. Today as soon as school was out I was going to the candy store and this time I was going alone.

The candy store was outside the base. I would have to go through the back gate and that was not a familiar guard post. I had gone through that gate once with Raymond. He went off base often, but he rarely took me. He would go and buy candy for us sometimes, but he usually took half of it for making the trip and made us beg him to do that. I told him it wasn't that big a deal and that next time I would go there myself. He had laughed at me. "Oh please," he mocked, "please buy some candy for me Jeanne Marie."

I wasn't sure why Raymond was always like that to me. I thought it must have been because I was a girl, and it seemed the older we got the worse he became. The very worst of it however, was when my parents weren't home. Whenever they went out it was Raymond who was left in charge. "Because Raymond is the oldest," my father would tell me. But the moment my father was out of sight, Raymond took advantage of that status. I remembered one time spending the entire afternoon hiding out on the roof until my parents got home. They had gone into town shopping. I stayed in my room hoping Raymond would find something other than tormenting me to occupy his attention. But as soon as they drove off he was on his way upstairs with the three younger boys in tow. He stood in front of my bedroom door. "Oh is the little princess playing with her Barbie dolls again?"

"Leave me alone Raymond. I'm not doing anything to you."

"Come on Jeanne Marie, I just came up to play with you," he said.

"Why don't you just go down stairs and raid the refrigerator or something."

"I will, but before I do that, I just wanted to play with my little sister. Is there anything wrong with that?"

"Come on Raymond, why don't you just leave me alone?"

"What fun would that be? Besides, I want to see what Barbie looks like naked."

"Yeah," Jason joined in and grabbed my doll. Then he handed it to Raymond.

"Oh my, I think she wants to be naked. Don't you think so Jason?"

"Yeah I think so too," he agreed.

"Well, since she can't do it herself, I guess we'll just have to take her clothes off for her. Won't we Jason?" Raymond said as began pulling her dress off.

"Stop it, and give me my doll back before you rip her dress." I grabbed for the doll but he held it up over his head so I couldn't reach it. "Give it to me," I demanded.

"But how are we going to play if you won't even share your precious dolls?" He taunted.

I jumped up on the bed to try and rescue my doll, but I wasn't quick enough. He threw it to Jason. Jason laughed. I instinctively jumped down and knocked him to the floor but once again Raymond grabbed the doll. I went after him.

"Oops," he said tearing the dolls head off in front of me. "I think Barbie just lost her head." Then he threw the head across the room. I punched him in the stomach. He doubled over, but I knew he wouldn't stay that way long. I had only knocked the wind out of him. As soon as he was able, he would really hurt me. I looked for somewhere to run.

"Don't let her get away Jason," he said holding his stomach. Jason stood in the doorway. The two younger brothers just watched. Then I saw the window. I jumped up on the bed and climbed out onto the roof. It was steep and covered in ice and snow. I was scared but I made my way around the dormer and secured myself on the other side of the window peak.

Raymond poked his angry head out the window looking for me. I made myself flat against the peak so he couldn't see me. "She's out there," I heard Jason yell.

"Oh, Jeanne Marie," Raymond called out the window. He waited a minute and called out again. "There's only one way back in, and it's so nice and warm in here. I can wait a long time." He waited a few more minutes. "Oh well, I sent the rest of em down to get some snacks. So I think I'll just sit here on your bed, eat some goodies and wait. Mom and Dad won't be back for hours." Finally he got bored and yelled one last threat at me. "There's only one way in Jeanne Marie, and the window of opportunity is closing, right about now." Then he slammed the window shut.

At first I thought I might freeze to death. There hadn't been time to grab my coat. I pulled my arms inside of my woolen sweater. Under my cotton tee shirt I wrapped my bare arms around my warm belly. It was filled with the heat of anger. I would survive. I would out last him, and in the end I would show him who was the strongest. It was several hours before my parents got home. I got into trouble for climbing out on the roof. How was Raymond supposed to know I was out there when he closed the window? I knew better than to tell on him. It would only have made it worse the next time. Brothers were like that.

Yes, I smiled today I will bring you candy. Rock candy, I knew it was his favorite. Raymond thought he was so tough, but I would show him. Someday, I thought, he will be asking me to buy rock candy for him. I would buy his candy first, and then I'd pick out anything I wanted. I couldn't spend too much time at the store though, it was a long walk home and I could not risk being late. I had to be in the house by five o'clock or I would be grounded.

Everyone on base had the same curfew. There was an old cannon in the middle of the base and promptly at five o'clock every evening the cannon was fired. The flag was lowered and trumpet played taps. The sound of the gun was heard throughout the base. If you were unlucky enough not to be inside by this time, you had to stop wherever you were, face the flag and sweat bullets until the trumpet finished and the flag was folded. You and whomever you were with were grounded. There were never any disputes and certainly never any excuses. You were caught by the cannon and had the duration of the ceremony to accept it. When it ended, you went home and served your time.

The bell rang, at last. I dashed for the coat rack, and while everyone else loaded on to the bus, I made my way to the back gate. The guard was inside the little house and I wasn't quite sure how I was going to slip through when I saw the cleaning woman approaching the gate. By the time she reached the gatehouse window, I was out, and onto the other side. I walked quickly. It was freezing and the snow was piled high on the banks of the road but I was on my way. Raymond would be surprised. I couldn't wait to hand him the rock candy. He would be asking me to go get it for him one day.

As I came to the end of the second block I hesitated for a moment. The road had ended and I really wasn't certain, which way the store was. I stood at the intersection and looked up and down the street, but everything was covered in a blanket of white. Nothing looked familiar. The snow began to fall again, and I stretched my arms out to catch the snowflakes. Snowflakes were so beautiful, no two alike and no one more beautiful than another. I threw my head back and watched them fall. As they swirled through the air I twirled along with them, sticking my tongue out, hoping to catch one.

Then a voice came out of nowhere. "Are you lost?"

It was a man's voice. I stopped, startled and a little dizzy from the swirls. "No," I answered instinctively. There was a black car in front of me, not that I was paying much attention but I hadn't seen it arrive.

"Are you American?" He asked me. I looked at him now, he had dark hair and dark eyes, his face was not frightening, but he was a stranger.

"Yes." I nodded my head. "I am an American." He would know now that I was the daughter of an American soldier that my father and the entire American army protected me.

"And, where is it on this very cold day that you are going?" His German accent was obvious, but his English was perfect.

"To the store," I replied.

"The one on Kalb Strasse?" He seemed to be genuinely interested.

"Yes, that's the one. I am on my way to buy something for my brother." I added proudly.

"I am on my way there as well. I am going there to pick up my little sister," he volunteered. "Do you speak German?"

"Yes, a little," I replied in German. "I understand more than I speak though."

"My sister speaks English very well," he told me. "But she rarely has the opportunity to speak English with anyone her own age. Perhaps you would meet her?" He opened the car door now. "Come, it would be my pleasure to drive you the rest of the way."

The car was black, inside and out. Suddenly I was inside, with a man I did not know. The car sped away, quickly. Too quickly I knew to stop at the store, too quickly for me to jump out. I was frozen now like the ice on the windshield. Everything was visible, but blurred and motionless. My father could not help me now. He did not know where I was. I did not know where I was. No one knew where I was.

I do not remember getting out of the car. I do remember entering the dark stairwell. The stairs led only down. They were narrow and steep. The man stood behind me now like a great dark shadow and I descended stoically to my fate. When we reached the bottom there was a small forked passageway. One side led to the furnace room. I caught a glimpse of the metal grate that covered its fiery mouth. Then I saw the tools they used to feed it, big shovels and iron pokers, all black with soot. On the other side of hall way there was a small room lit by a single bulb that hung on a wire from the low ceiling.

He took my hand and led me to the small room. I was numb. I could not feel anything, and I was so terrified that I could not do anything. I knew I could do nothing now, nothing more than observe my fate. There was a bed on one side of the room and an old wooden table and chair on the other. He led me to the bed covered with a dark woolen blanket.

He laid me down and began to take my clothes off. As he undressed me, I stared up at the blackened ceiling. My body stiffened and I thought again of the ice on the windshield. I would become like that ice. It was hard and fragile at the same time. It was still and peaceful. When you looked through it, the world was visible but blurred and wholly unrecognizable. Unless of course, you knew exactly what it was you were looking at. Then you saw it twice. First the way you remembered it, then the way it really was. But if you looked without remembering, without knowing, it was only the way it appeared to be. It was only a vision, with beautiful undefined forms, like a kaleidoscope filled with shifting colors.

I heard his voice. He spoke in gentle tones. He did not want to frighten me. He did not know that I was far beyond fear, and that I was far beyond his touch. As he removed my panties, he expressed some surprise that I had no pubic hair. I did not know why, children did not have pubic hair. He tried to put his tongue in my mouth. Here he would not penetrate. I gritted my teeth until they turned into iron, like the metal grates on the furnace. I thought about the furnace in the next room. I wondered if he would feed me to the great fiery furnace when he was finished. I wondered if I would become black soot and rest forever on the ceiling, looking down at him. Perhaps there were others, looking down at me. I stared up at the swirls of soot on the ceiling. I watched the shadowy faces from where I lay. Some were sad. Others were frightened, but they were all looking down, through the same helpless eyes.

From the darkness, my first sensation was the cold itself, then something hard but smooth against my face. Stones, I could not see them, but I recognized the texture. They were cobblestones. I moved my fingers a little. They stung from the cold but I wiggled them into the crevice between the stones. I tried to trace their form, to make sure they were real. I dug my fingers deeper between the stones. They were the right size, and I knew what they were. There was something strangely soothing in knowing what they were. Old stones warn smooth from the passage of time. Gray stones covered with dirt and soot from the chimneys. I was feeling a familiar thing from total darkness, they felt good and even in their hardness they became soft and comforting.

I felt voices from behind the stones. I could not actually hear them, but I knew my ear must be pressed to the stone, even though I could not feel it. I stayed very still, hoping to hear what the people were saying beneath the stones. One voice grew stronger. I heard first the voice of a boy and then a young girl. Somehow I knew it was his sister.

"It's okay," she told me softly. "There are many children here. We lived here before; we played too, until the soldiers came. My brother tried to run, they thought he was a man, but he was only a boy. There was so much blood. It ran down between the stones. He called to me to stay, but I ran too. Then I fell down beside him and my blood too ran down under the stones. We are not alone here, and it did not hurt. Do you hurt?"

No, I thought I don't feel anything, only the cold against my face and the stone on my fingertips. I knew my lips did not move, that I spoke somehow without words. I also knew that it did not matter. "Am I raped?" I asked.

The brother's voice answered, "We are all raped. We are children who have lost our blood. We are the lost children who live beneath stones."

"You can walk now," the girl's voice gently assured me. "When you are able to get up, go to the corner up ahead. You will see bullet holes in the wall there, some of the pieces are missing, but beyond that there are many people on the street. Don't be afraid if they do not see you though. Many people will look at you, but they may not ever see you again. People don't seem to notice lost children. Maybe you can speak to them though, maybe they can help you find your way home."

I don't have a home, I thought. I want my mother. Where is my father, where are the soldiers? No one came to protect me, no one came to save me. I began to cry and with the tears came breaths of icy air. Awareness began to slowly creep back. I tried to open my eyes now and I began to move within my numb and half frozen limbs. I looked down and saw my red leather boots on my feet. My clothes were on. My red jacket was buttoned up and only my head was not covered. The hood with dirty white fur now hung down my back and I realized that I was curled up in a little ball lying on my side, on a cobblestone street. I looked up and saw the soft ember glow of streetlights.

I tried to stand up but my legs were not wholly cooperative, and as I straightened up the part beneath my belly seared with pain. I began to cry more tears, but they only formed an icy trickle on my frozen face. I thought I must have been bleeding somewhere. I looked down but I couldn't see any blood. Maybe it was only on the inside, maybe the blood had not come out yet. Perhaps it was a hurt that no one could see.

I took a few steps, and looked back to see where I had been lying. I was just inside the walls of the old city. I knew of this place from a school fieldtrip. The walls had been built in medieval times. It had stood for centuries protecting the city from invaders, but this was all I could remember. Now I knew only one thing more, the great stone walls had not protected the children. Children had been raped and somehow they had fallen through the cracks of the old cobblestone streets. The gate was only a few yards away, but no one was there. It was dark and no one had seen me. I was lost, and no one had noticed.

I dragged my hand along the building as I walked and as I reached the corner I saw the places where the stone had been blown away. I saw the holes left from the soldier's guns and felt the empty spaces with my frozen fingers. I peeked around the corner. There were many people, twinkling lights and beautiful music. It was Christmas time, and the streets were filled with rosy-cheeked people walking briskly up and down the sidewalks preparing for the holidays. Carolers lifted their voices like angels to heaven and sang the somber lyrics of *Stile Nocht*, Silent Night.

I pulled my red hood over my head, wiped my eyes and thrust my hands into my pockets. I would find a mother. She would know I was a lost child, a foreign child, an American child. She would help me find my way home. I ventured onto the street and the first woman I saw had a small chubby child by the hand. She carried several small packages neatly wrapped and tied with string. She wore a dark woolen cape like most women wore in town. As I approached her the child looked at me with a strange fixed interest. The woman did not seem to see me so I gently tugged on the sleeve of her cape.

"Please," I tried to say. It was strange, I knew German but I couldn't remember any words. Only English came out. "Please I am American." She finally looked at me, but she wanted no part of me. She pulled her child closer to her and they marched forward and away. She didn't understand. She didn't know. I would find another mother who would know what to do. I tried to speak to several mothers. None of them understood. They did not help me. Perhaps they could not see me. The girl in the stones, she had been right no one noticed lost children. I had to ask her why. Maybe she would know what to do. Maybe she could help me. I walked listlessly back around the scared corner and scrunched down on the cold stones against the wall. I pulled my hood back and held the old stones with my fingertips as I placed the side of my face down on the stones below me.

"My brother said you must speak to them," she said. "He told me you could come to us, but you could not stay. He will help you get back."

Why couldn't I stay? I am raped. I am lost. Surely my blood is lost too. I wanted to stay. I wanted to be under the stones with them. I knew it was dark but I wasn't afraid I wanted to be inside the earth. I wanted to be safe. I started to cry again, and involuntary sobs kept forcing me to breathe. I lifted my head as I gulped more air and through the blur of icy tears I saw the shadow of a man standing at the corner.

"Don't be afraid, he is not a man, he is only a boy. Go with him," the girl said softly.

I lifted my head from the stone, leery of leaving the friendly voice in the midst of the dark night. I wiped my eyes and stood up. Then I looked at the figure again. He was only a boy. Maybe fourteen, but he was tall and full-bodied. He motioned for me to follow him and as he turned the corner I began to run. I was afraid he would leave before I could catch up with him. When I turned the corner, I could see him up ahead. Then he stopped on the next corner and waited to make sure I had seen him. Suddenly he stepped to the side, and he was gone. I ran to the spot where he had been only seconds before. Then I stopped, and tried to catch my breath. I looked from side to side, but he was nowhere in sight and I was still lost.

I looked around again for something recognizable, something that I could touch through the darkness. But I did not recognize anything. I leaned back, allowing the building behind me to support my head and back. I stared up into the darkness and wondered if I was invisible to God too. Maybe that's what happened to the others, the one's that lived under the stones. Maybe God just hadn't seen them. How would he ever find them to take them to heaven? Somehow I wanted him to know they were there. "If I ever get back," I whispered. "I'll pray. I promise. I'll tell him where to look."

I don't know how long it was, but eventually, it occurred to me that there was light emanating from something behind me. I turned to see what it was. It was only then that I realized I was standing in front of the window of a small shop. The little store was filled with soft yellow light and in the window was a magnificent display of Christmas Angels. They were the Nuremberg Angels. I remembered the story our teacher had told us in school.

There was a man long ago, a woodcarver from the town of Nuremberg, who had lost his only daughter. The father grieved inconsolably for his lost child, and for a long time he refused to see or speak to anyone in the town. The lonely woodcarver just stayed inside his little shop and worked. Day and night he worked, but no one knew what he was working on. The people of the town were all curious, but none could bring themselves to approach the grief-stricken father.

Then one cold December day just before Christmas, everyone gathered in the center of the town. They all stood before a giant evergreen tree gazing up in awe. There, all of the people in Nuremberg saw for the first time what the woodcarver had been working on for so long. On the very top of the tree, he had placed the most beautiful Angel anyone had ever seen.

Soon everyone began to look around to congratulate the woodcarver on such fine craftsmanship, but he was nowhere to be seen. Then, one by one the villagers began to recognize the face of the magnificent angel. The entire town began to remember the face of the child who had been lost and almost forgotten. From that time on, every Christmas the Angel of Nuremberg was placed on top of the tree in the center of town so no one would ever again forget her face. Later many artists would carve the beautiful girl who had become an angel and everyone, even now, so many years later still know her face.

I wondered if she had been able to tell her father that she was a lost child. If she had told him how sad it was that no one could see her when she tried to find her way back again. Somehow her father had known. He had understood. I wondered if he had found her now and they were together again. It had all happened so long ago.

I looked around at the place now where the boy had disappeared. He was gone, but where he had stepped to the side was a pay phone. There were coins in my pocket. Coins intended for the candy store. One of my younger brothers answered the phone. "Get mommy," I couldn't seem to speak words anymore, but he had heard me. He put down the phone and announced that it was her all right. My mother got on the phone, she had that stern tone that said you're in trouble young lady, but all she said was, "Where are you?" My heart sank. I didn't know. I couldn't answer. "I can't hear you, where you are you," she asked again.

"I am lost." At last some words came.

"Lost where?" My mother asked again, she sounded angry.

"I don't know." I began to cry. "I was going to the store off base, now I am lost."

"Look around you." Her voice was strong but reassuring. She knew what to do. "Is there a street sign near you?" I read the street signs to her. "She is near the Kauf Hauf," I heard her tell my father. "Just stay where you are and we will be there in a minute, don't move from there," she commanded.

I stood still in front of the window looking at the tiny faces of the Nuremberg Angels as I waited. Somehow I thought my parents would know, but they did not. They did not know what terrible thing had happened. No one knew. There would be no political confrontations over the American child who had been raped by the German man. One German girl was lost and now one American girl joined her. There was no need for a dispute. The score was even. There would be no war.

I wondered now if they had told the German girl too that she could not live among the lost children. That she would have to go and live among people who would look at her, but not see her anymore. I wondered how much blood she had lost to make her skin so pale. I wondered if her eyes were empty because it was not of much use to look at people who could not see you. I wondered if I saw her now if she could see me and know there were others. There were many others. They had all been raped and they had all lost their blood. Some lived beneath the stones deep in the earth and some walked among the people unseen, unnoticed.

I was grounded for several weeks. I did not mind. I would not have left anyway. Christmas came and went. I no longer played with my brothers or the other boys. I no longer lived in their world and I would never again fight in their wars. I was quiet now and I began to read books of ancient times. I read about history and lost cultures. I no longer wore bright colors. I vowed I would never again wear red. I began wearing only neutral tones, the colors of old photographs and images of people who lived long ago. Faded browns and yellowed beiges these were the colors of dying. The colors of things that are in the process of passing from life to death, flowers, fruits and people. Not until the change was complete could they turn into rich dark browns and black. Those were the colors of death, and I could not wear them because I was not dead. I only lingered in this world, somewhere in-between.

My mother began to notice the change. I heard her talking to father one night. "She doesn't go out to play anymore," she said. "And none of her friends come over. She just sits in her room and reads. I'm worried about her."

"She's growing up," my father assured her. "She'll be out there soon enough. Then we'll both have something to worry about."

"I don't know Leo. I just can't help feeling something's wrong. She's twelve years old now, that's an age when girls are inseparable. She should be giddy and boy crazy, I know I was. I've tried to talk to her, but I don't know. I just can't seem to reach her."

"Do whatever you think you have to do," my father resigned.

I knew then I had to make some effort to appease her. Otherwise she might start asking questions. The next morning I got on the school bus and looked over all the girls I knew. They were silly, and all they talked about lately was boys. I had no interest. Janie was sitting in the front as usual, with her face buried in a book. Janie was black, and a little chubby, but she was always dressed perfectly. Everything always matched, even her shoes. She was smart in school, but she didn't talk much to anyone, so I sat next to her.

"What are you reading?" I asked.

"Charlotte's Web," she replied not looking up.

"Is it good?"

"Yeah," she peeked over the top of her book and our eyes met. "Have you read it?"

"No, but I like to read too." I volunteered.

"What do like to read?"

"History, mostly mythology, you know about gods and goddesses."

"You don't believe in them do you?"

"No, I just like the stories," I said.

"Good. It's blasphemous you know."

"What?" I asked.

"Believing in more than one God. My mother said you can go straight to hell for that."

"Maybe for believing," I shrugged. "But not for reading."

"No, I guess you're all right there," she said.

Janie and I became friends. I brought her home to meet my mother and she brought me to her home to meet hers. When we went to her house, she showed me her closet. "Wow you really do have a pair of shoes for every outfit. How many pairs of shoes do you have?"

"I don't know, I never counted them." She said.

"There must be at least a dozen pair of them in there," I exclaimed.

"Outfits are supposed to be coordinated," she said. "My mother says everything should match. It shows you know how to be tasteful."

"My mom thinks shoes are there to keep your feet warm, she doesn't bother much about the colors." We got one pair for school and one pair for Sundays. Janie was an only child and her mother had been a nurse before she was born. She seemed to know a lot of things. Janie said she went to school a long time to learn them.

When I went home I couldn't wait to tell my mother about Janie's shoes. "You wouldn't believe it," I said. "She has a whole closet full of them. One pair for each outfit."

"Janie is an only child sweetheart," my mother attempted to explain. "Every year before school starts your father and I buy ten pair of shoes. In our family we just have to divide them up a little bit."

"I wish I didn't have so many brothers then."

"Well, which one of your brothers would you like to give up then?"

I thought about it. Raymond and Jason were both good candidates. They were always in trouble anyway. But without them diverting all the attention away from me, I would be in the center stage. I wouldn't trade the little ones. I liked them most of the time. "Never mind," I said. "I don't really need the shoes."

One day we were at the playground, sitting on top of the monkey bars talking. One of the boys got underneath and looked up our dresses. I climbed down and chased him, but he caught up with his friends before I could catch him. My brother Raymond was with them. "I don't know why you think it's such a big deal to see our underpants anyway," I yelled. "Boys are all stupid."

"Sex," Eddie yelled back. Then they all laughed and ran away."

That night I asked my brother what the word meant. "Don't say it out loud again," he warned me. "Especially don't ever let Dad hear you say it, cause it's a dirty word and you'll get in a lot of trouble."

"Okay, I won't. But what does it mean?"

He rolled his eyes to the ceiling and took a big breath like I was stupid for not knowing. "All right, when a boy puts his thing into a girls thing. It's called sex."

"What thing?"

"You know," he pointed to his penis.

"Why," I asked. "Why would a boy want to do something like that?"

"They just do, that's all. Well, it's also how you make babies."

"No it's not Raymond. That's disgusting."

"No, it's the truth. I'm telling you that's how babies are made."

"Mom and Dad would never do that. I don't believe it."

"Yes they did. I'm telling you they had to. That's the only way you can make a baby. I swear it." He held his hand up. "I swear on a bible it's true."

I finally believed him. "What a terrible thing to have to do. Mom must have really wanted babies bad. I guess she had to have done it at least once," I said.

"Five times," my brother corrected me. "There's five of us kids in the family. They had to have done it at least five times."

That meant every woman who was a mother had done it. What a terrible secret they kept. I could understand why they didn't want to tell us about it. What girl would ever want to get married? I told Janie about it the next day. She looked at me skeptically but didn't say anything right away. By the next day she said she had asked her mother about it. "It's true," she confirmed. "That's how a man plants his seed in a woman. It's like a little egg that comes out of his penis and goes right into the woman's womb. That seed grows into a baby."

I tried to forget about it after that. But I had not forgotten about my promise. Every night I prayed that God would not forget about the lost children who lived under the stones. I told him where they lived, and I prayed that he would find them soon. I was sure they belonged up in heaven with him. He needed to make them angels, but I was never really sure he heard me. I prayed extra hard on Sundays. All the children on base went to the same church. Services for all denominations were held in the same building. At nine it was Catholic, eleven it was Protestant and on Saturdays it was Jewish. I went to them all. I wasn't sure which one God liked best, but the Catholic Mass was my favorite. I loved the Latin prayers, the rituals and the saints. I especially liked the saints.

I learned that God had a whole army of deceased souls he had recruited to help the people on earth. Every saint had a specialty, and each one had an individual assignment. For every problem you could ever imagine, there was a saint to call on, a saint to protect you. I was impressed. It seemed like such a good system. I only wished that I had known about it earlier.

I read everything I could about them. I knew there had to be one who specialized in lost children, and as soon as I found out which one it was, I was sure the whole dilemma would be resolved. I read first about the saints who were assigned to help children in general. The first one I found was about a bishop named Nicholas. He was from some far away place called Myra, and he lived long, long ago.

Nicholas grew up in a well to do home with good Christian parents. They both died when he was still a young man. He devoted himself to the church. They educated and encouraged him in his 'thirst for sincere and true religion'. Nicholas used his whole inheritance for works of charity. One day, he was told of a man in town who recently lost all his money. At home he had three daughters he could no longer support, and because he was too poor to pay a dowry, the girls could not marry. So, their father decided to give them over to prostitution. Upon hearing this, Nicholas waited for the cover of night. Then he took a bag of gold and threw it into the father's house through an opened window. In this way the eldest girl received her dowry and was soon married. Nicholas did the same for the next child. But when he came to rescue the third daughter, the father was waiting for him. When he discovered who the benefactor had been, the father overwhelmed Nicholas with his gratitude. Nicholas had saved all three of his daughters from a terrible, terrible fate.

On another occasion, three young boys were murdered. An innkeeper had killed them and hidden their bodies in a brine-tub. When Nicholas found out about the atrocity, he immediately went to see if he could help. Nicholas brought all three of the little boys back to life and his holy day was celebrated every since by rewarding good children with presents. It was the Dutch who brought this story to America, they called him Sinte Klaas, and we pronounced it Santa Clause. The books said that all Christians, young and old, men and women, boys and girls, should revere his memory and call upon his protection. That his favors, which knew no limit of time, would continue from age to age to be poured out over all the earth. Why did we only know to ask Santa Clause for toys? Why didn't they tell us we could have asked him for protection too?

Saint Nicholas was a great saint for children, but somehow I didn't think he was the right candidate for the job at hand. I spent many hours looking though the gilded pictures of long dead martyrs, the beautiful and the grotesque. I read about the virgin Saint Lucy, who preferred to tear her eyes out and carry them on a silver plate rather than marry. I wondered what made her decide to rip out her eyes. Had God really asked her to, or had someone told her about the sex part? I looked for a clue as I studied the picture of Saint Lucy. She was holding the silver tray where she displayed the bloody eyes she had just torn from their sockets, but her expression gave no hint as to why she had done this painful thing. The book didn't give much of an explanation either. It said only that she martyred herself in order to remain faithful to God.

Then there was the beautiful maiden Saint Barbara. Her father locked her in a tower until she was old enough to marry. One day her pagan father came to inform her he had found a husband for her. Barbara told him it was too late. She told her father that all those years she had spent trapped in the tower were spent reading books and studying Christianity. She had secretly dedicated herself to God. Consequently, she would never marry.

Her father grew angry and beat her, but this did not sway her. Next he threatened to turn her over to the authorities. This was dangerous as Christianity was illegal at the time, but Barbara still refused. Even under their torture she would not give up her faith. The father was then ordered by the authorities to put Barbara to death himself. Her father obeyed and killed his own daughter. He chopped her head off with a sword. No sooner was this done, when a huge bolt of lightning came down from the sky and struck the pagan father dead. Barbara was noted as the patron Saint of lightning, artillery and War. I knew none of those things related to the lost children, but there was something about her. Something strange that both drew me in and repelled me at the same time. I copied down her prayer and put it in my bible at home, just in case I ever needed her. You could never be too sure about wars.

All the books said the Saints lived in heaven, I wondered why. Why did they live so far away from the people who needed their help? Saint Michael lived in heaven. He visited the earth on occasion, but it never said how often. Michael was magnificent; he was not just a saint. He was an angel, a powerful angel who used his sword to fight evil in the heavens and the earth. Death was listed as one of his territories, but the literature never elaborated on this. He was beautiful, with long flowing hair and piercing eyes. Saint Michael was above all a protector. He was also one I would keep at the top of my list of saints to call on.

There didn't seem to be any specific saints for the dead. The ones who did not go to heaven, all those who slipped through the cracks like the children beneath the stones. Maybe, I thought, they were not really considered dead unless they left, both body and soul. But if they were not dead, and they were not alive, what were they? Perhaps religion didn't know about them. The little girl had told me they were forgotten, but surely God had not forgotten them. Incredibly, I could not find any reference to them in the books. I read about ghosts, but I did not think they were ghosts. They were not tormented souls who rattled chains and haunted the living. They had their own world, and they didn't seem to have much interest in ours. Perhaps the Greeks were more informed, they at least knew of them. They called them shades and they lived in a place called the underworld. They knew of the shadows who lived beneath the earth, but I could find no saint for these shadows to call upon. I closed the books and returned them to the library shelf. It was nearly four and I had to get home.

At the dinner table that night, my parents announced that we would be spending the summer in Spain. "We'll be staying right next to the ocean," my mother said. "The beaches there are beautiful and it's sunny and warm there. You can swim everyday if you want to."

"As long as we don't have to stop at all those churches on the way like we did in Italy last year," Raymond complained.

"I like the churches." I said.

"I like church," John the second to the youngest repeated.

"See, John likes them too." I said.

"Yeah, well you've seen one you've seen them all and I've seen more than enough of em." Raymond said reaching for a second helping of mashed potatoes.

"They're not all the same, and maybe if you paid a little more attention you'd know that."

"That's enough," my father commanded.

"Were going to Spain to have fun," my mother said looking at my brother. "And," she said looking me. "We will stop at some historical sights along the way." Raymond and I both made faces that said; see I told you so, across the table, not daring to say anything else out loud.

My mother had always read voraciously. She said it kept her sanity in tact. She could read a book, listen to the news on the radio and carry on a conversation all at the same time. The commotion of five kids never seemed to faze her. On long car rides she read to us. My father would map out the trip and pack up all the provisions, while my mother collected all the appropriate reading materials to keep us occupied along the way. The books were always about the new people and cultures we would encounter on our excursion. This was seasoned with the local folklore, history and places of interest. My mother always encouraged us to question and discover. My father reminded us that being a guest in a foreign city was like being a guest in someone's home. We were to conduct ourselves accordingly.

We saw a bullfight in Madrid. I was feeling sorry for the bull until he gored the matador. It was bloody and I wanted to cover my eyes but I didn't dare let Raymond see me afraid. The boys thought it was great. They talked about it all the way to the southern coast. We got in late at night. I couldn't wait to get up in the morning so I could go out and look around. After breakfast I took off to explore the area. We were in a wooded area, with the whole Mediterranean Ocean sprawled out before us. I walked out to the woods, just to be alone. I found a river and sat down beside it. It was beautiful and peaceful, and I liked the sound of the water flowing. It was really flowing too. It was not a lazy river. Then I heard someone coming up behind me.

"What are doing?" Raymond asked. John was beside him swinging a little stick at the tall grass.

"Just looking, where's Jason?"

"He went with mom and dad to the bakery. Mom said we could go swimming when they get back."

"I'd like to go swimming right now," I said wistfully.

"There's the river," he said. "Go ahead, jump in." I looked at the water and threw a leaf in. The river carried it rapidly downstream. "No, I don't feel like it now."

"Bet your scared aren't you?" He taunted.

"I'm not sacred. I could jump in if I wanted to, but I don't want to."

"That's cause you're a girl, and too chicken to do it." He looked at me and smiled. "I dare you to jump in the river."

"Fine," I took off my shoes. "Watch me." I dived straight into the river. The water was cold and when I surfaced I proceeded to swim to the side to get out. I had proved my point. But the water was strong and I was swimming against it. No matter how hard I swam, I could not reach the side. It was caring me too quickly downstream.

Raymond could see what was happening. "Oh shit," he yelled. "If you drown Dad's going to kill me." He was pulling off his shoes as he ran beside the river. Little John watched as Raymond dived in after me. Then he pulled me out, cursing the whole time. "Now were both in trouble," he said catching his breath. "We weren't supposed to go swimming until mom and dad got back."

"Come on," I said still breathing hard and trying to sit up on the riverbank. "We can go sit on the beach. Maybe we'll dry off before they get back.

"John you won't tell on us, will you?" Raymond asked.

"No," he shook his head.

"See, John and I are buddies. Aren't we John?"

"Yeah," he said proudly swinging his stick.

"Look," Raymond pointed to the mouth of the river. "That's where it was going. You could have been carried right out to sea."

He was right, but I didn't say anything else about it. "Hey, look at that," I said pointing to some huge white columns partially covered by the sand and water. "I'll bet they're Roman. Wow, what do you think they were?"

We all ran down to look. They were ruins of some kind, resting there, just as they had fallen who knows how many years ago. "Yeah, you're right," Raymond said examining them. "They're Roman all right."

"I'll bet it was a temple," I said. "They loved to build temples." I sat in the sand and dreamed about ancient temples and beautiful long robed goddesses. Raymond and John rolled their pants up and waded in the water knee deep. When we thought we were dry enough, we went back for lunch. John never told on us, so we didn't get caught.

When the summer ended, we were back in Germany and off to school again. There was only one American school for junior high and high school students. It was a half hour away in Nuremberg. It was my first year there. Janie and I sat together at lunch "You want to go next door before the bell rings?"

"Why," she asked. "There's nothing there but a bunch of ruble."

"My brother said they go over there all the time. Did you know that Hilter used to give his speeches from there? It's supposed to be real famous."

"And real off limits. I think it's dangerous. They bombed it out a long time ago, but you never know."

"No, there's no bombs over there, but there might be some ghosts," I said.

"Ghosts?"

"Yeah, Raymond said a lot of Nazis died there. They were generals too. He said they hung them right there. He said his friend saw one of them, and he got so scared he wet his pants. I told him if I saw one I wouldn't be scared. I'm not scared of ghosts."

"I am," she assured me. "And I'm not going over there. You couldn't drag me over there."

"All right, I'll go by myself. Just don't tell anybody. I don't want to get into trouble."

"I won't tell on you, but you better come back before class starts."

"I will." I ran through the gate and quickly climbed over the rocks before anyone spotted me. I found a clearing where the boys hid out and smoked cigarettes. Part of the foundation was still in tact and I could see the floor had been inlaid with different colors of marble. I couldn't tell what the pattern had been. Other than a few pieces of mangled iron, there was nothing but piles scorched stones and ruble. I sat on one of the larger stones and put my ear to it to see if I could hear anything. I sat very still and listened. I could hear the faint sounds of engines. Then I recognized the sound, airplanes flying overhead, explosions all around me, then fire. Fire was everywhere, screams and cries from terrified people. I pulled my head up. I did not want to see anymore. There were no ghosts, only the sounds of terrible memories. I went back to school.

Raymond wouldn't talk to me at school or on the bus. He always had a pack of cigarettes rolled up in his sleeve and was usually too busy cursing with his friends to be bothered with me. When we got home, I told him I had gone over there. He didn't believe me until I told him about the clearing where I knew he had been smoking with his friends. I told him there were no ghosts there. He said it was probably because he and his friends had already scared them all away. I told him I didn't think ghost were that afraid of boys who wet their pants when they saw them. Raymond threw his shoe at me.

Just before Halloween Janie told me they were moving. Her father got orders and they were going to back to the States. I would miss her. She was my best friend. Who would I talk to when she was gone? But it was not too long before my father also received his orders. We would be leaving in January. It would be our last Christmas in Germany. My father was retiring. We were going home, they told us, back to America where we would live forever. I would go back to America, but part of me I knew would forever be left behind. My parents talked excitedly about going home, to Miami where everything was new. There would be sunshine, white sandy beaches and grandparents I had never known. I could not imagine a city without a past.

I did not choose to leave Germany, the place where the lost children lived within the stones. But the ancient walls refused to hold me and the old cobblestones had refused to keep me. I passed through the gates often those last few months. I walked on the old cobblestone streets and I visited shadows of the lost ones who came before me. They were children, but they were not young. They had been there for a long time and there were many who came before them. They knew many things and they spoke without words. They told me I must leave this city, and that I could not stay among the stones. They said I no longer belonged there with them. "You must go home," they told me. "You will find other lost children in the new city. There are many lost children in this world."

2

The New Foreign World

I was no longer a child. I had forgotten how to play long ago. I was no longer an American here in America. I did not belong. I left Germany, where the Brothers Grimm would forever tell their tales. Where Hansel and Gretel, and Red Riding Hood would live for generations to come. Germany, the place where storybook castles still stood along the Rhine and cobblestone streets marked the passage of lost children. We had been sent home, home to the new world, home to America, to a place I had never known.

We landed in New York City, where we would wait several days for our car to arrive. My father had bought a new Mercedes to drive home in. We were in the tallest building I had ever seen. My brothers and I rode the elevator up and down an endless number of times, mostly for entertainment, but it eventually got us to the lobby. In the lobby we watched television, in English! We watched it until it was time to go to bed.

It was a long drive to Miami, and we all cheered when we finally reached the Florida turnpike. We stopped at the first rest stop and all of us ran in. Raymond was the first one to spot the water fountains. There were two of them, one said white, and the other said colored. We all ran to the colored one to see what color the water was. Jason got there first and pushed the button. The water shot up where we could all see it. "It's just clear," he said. "It's not colored, look." We were all disappointed.

After we were back in the car, my mother tried to explain to us that we shouldn't touch the colored water fountains. It seemed that things

37

were not the same in this country. Here colored people and white people did not use the same bathrooms or water fountains. They didn't even go to the same beaches. "Then how can you be friends?" I asked. "I mean if you can't even swim together. How can you hang around if you can't even go to the same places?"

"Well," my mother tried to explain. "You can be friends, but just not as close. Most people here just don't understand anyone who is different from themselves."

"But they're not different, they're Americans just like us."

"I know sweetheart, but here things are a little different. In the military things are one way, everyone is treated the same. But this isn't the military any more. People here haven't learned to live that way yet."

"You mean if the Johnson's lived next door to us here, you and dad couldn't go out with them," Jason asked.

"Here they have separate neighborhoods," my father said. "White people and colored people live in different parts of the city."

"I don't believe it," I said. I thought about Janie and all the other kids we knew. I guess when they got to America they all found out just like I did. We'd probably never see each other again in this country.

But that was only my first disappointment. I hated Miami. The sun was garish. The buildings were boxes. The land was flat and there was only one season. Why had they allowed me come to such a horrid place? I was angry and alone. There were no others here. How could there be? Everything was new. I longed for the old city, the ancient stones and the lost children. The structures here had no bones. The buildings were made from empty cinder blocks and thinly covered with stucco veneers. The streets had no soul. They were an ugly mixture of seamless tar and crushed gravel that stretched on forever. The streets here were made for the wheels of machines, not for the touch of the people who traveled them.

I spent the next two years studying. Like Saint Barbara, I would live in my own little academic tower. I focused on nothing but finishing high school so I could get to the university where I could really learn something. I graduated early, just after my sixteenth birthday. Then I was informed that there was an age requirement. I would have to wait until my seventeenth birthday to attend the University. I was disappointed at first, but it was just as well. I knew I would have to pay my own way through college. My parents had too many mouths at home to feed. Besides, I was a girl and anything beyond high school was little more than an indulgence for girls. Boys were different. They needed an education. Someday, they would have to support their wives and children, while all I had to do was get married. I knew I would have to get a job and save my money. It wasn't too likely that Saint Nicholas was going to throw a bag of gold coins through the window for my education.

My first job was as a waitress in a local restaurant. I didn't mind the job, but the manager was a fat greasy bald man who was constantly trying to trap young girls in the back room. I found another job, as a bookkeeper in a small office downtown. I lied about my age, there didn't seem to be much choice in the matter. Everyone seemed to have the same diluted concepts of age and time.

I knew I would have to wait for my seventeenth birthday, but while I waited, I decided to explore the city. On my days off I took the bus to different parts of Miami. Even if it was a new city, it had to have a soul, somewhere. I would search for it, and I vowed to find it however long it took. I would uncover it however deeply it was hidden.

Miami Beach was intriguing. It was a city filled with beautiful old Mediterranean mansions on small private islands. Sadly, they were inaccessible, too many guards and too many gates. It was totally inaccessible. I could not touch their walls to see if their former inhabitants still lingered within them. South Beach however, was within reach. I frequented this old beach with its crumbling hotels and dim eyed aging tenants. The young did not come here. South Beach was for the old. It was for the Northerners who came south to die in the sun. It seemed like such a strange contradiction to me. Surely they knew they were dying; yet they feared death. They hid from death in frightened anonymity, leaving their homes and families behind. They left everything familiar hoping that death would not find them on the sunny southern beaches of Miami. Yet death was the only thing that could release them from the painful processes of dying. The logic perplexed me. They were old but not wise.

At last I was disenchanted by South Beach. It was not an old place. It had no old and noble soul. Originally, it had been a pastel fantasy built in the late twenties, but like most fantasies, by the late sixties it was no more than a decaying illusion where people still lived.

I had worked all week. I had patiently waited and it finally came. It was Saturday. I could hardly wait to get across town. Two buses later I was on my way to Greynolds Park. I had finally run across something encouraging in my search. I had found a reference to the oldest building in Miami, a monastery. A very old monastery, built of stones from Ireland. Precious old stones brought here in pieces from the old world. I couldn't wait to get there, just to see it, to touch the ancient rock. Perhaps I would finally find others who would speak to me again through the stones.

The monastery was a tourist attraction, but it still served as church where a priest said masses on Sundays. As soon as I arrived, I was sure I had found the place I had been searching for. It was a sacred place. I saw the priest, taping a brochure on his thigh as he spoke to an older couple standing on the other side of the parish. I peeked though the open archway. It was not elaborate like the cathedrals in Europe. It was a simple stone structure with few embellishments, but it was authentically ancient.

I decided to walk around to the back of the building where I would be alone. The walls were nearly covered with green vines and drooping purple blossoms. Eyeing a small clearing in the foliage, I knelt down to touch the stones. I caressed them with both hands and pressed my face against the sacred stones. I ached for them to touch me. I spoke to them as I had long ago without words, through the common language of feeling and thought. I felt the resins of ancient life within them, but they did not speak. I begged them to answer me, but they would not speak. I waited for what seemed like forever, but they would not respond. I was heart broken and alone. Tears welled up and I knew it was no use. There was nothing more I could do.

The sun cooked the moist air while the humidity thickened it, creating a vast invisible primal soup. I breathed in the heavy mixture. It was a calming elixir and as I left, walking slowly through the old stone archway, I could see that great old oaks draped in Spanish moss shaded it. There were several trails that led from the old monastery grounds into the park itself and I wondered without direction down one of them. The ground was soft from the decay of fallen leaves and the rich decay was covered in lacy dark green ferns. There were not many oak trees in Miami, especially old ones. Hurricanes swept the flat land clean every few years and the city had to grow anew perpetually. I was grateful to be among these old oaks. They had lived through much and survived gracefully. The scent of tropical earth mixed with the green foliage rose up with the heat and I breathed in the residues of its life force. It was good. It felt familiar like a mother's warm embrace. It felt old, not old like medieval walls, not ancient like Roman ruins. It was older still, older than civilization itself.

I continued my stroll through the park. Forgetting now the disappointments I had suffered earlier. I was just beginning to return to serenity when I heard laughter up ahead. Gentle laughter like the laughter of happy children. I meant to walk by as I always did unseen, unnoticed. Before I could pass by however, one of the girls addressed me. "Hello," her voice was sing songy but not insincere. "Are you here all alone?"

"Yes." I stopped now and looked at the small gathering. They were flower children. One was bearded with a leather band tied around his forehead. He had on a long white cotton shirt with brightly colored embroidered flowers around the neck. The other young man wore a purple felt hat with a great white plum that waved gently as he moved his head. One of the girls sat cross-legged in a plain white peasant dress and she stared oddly, not at me but past me. The girl with long blond hair who had spoken first now took a yellow flower from the pretty wreath she wore in her hair. She got up and placed it in my hair. "You are not alone anymore," she said. "We are all brothers and sisters here. My name is Sunny. What's yours?"

"Jeanne Marie," I smiled. Then I thanked her for the flower and spotted the clearing in front of me. Just beyond the clearing was a hill. I was delighted. I did not know there was a hill in all of Miami. And it got even better. On top of the green hill was what appeared to be an old stone fort. I couldn't believe it. I began to run and as I reached the top of the hill I stretched out my arms and turned around and around. I danced like I had in the snow so very long ago.

I was so completely self absorbed that I hadn't realized there were others on the hilltop. Not only were they there. They were actually beginning to join me. Soon there was a whole group of us, twirling around on the sun-drenched hill. I laughed through the dizzy whirls and finally allowed my body to drop, from the heat or exhaustion. I looked up. I had stopped but the world continued to spin. It was a beautiful blurry mass filled with fuzzy colorful spinning forms. There were others. Perhaps these were the children I was supposed to find.

When I looked up from my daze, the girl who had given me the flower was reaching down to pull me up. "Come on, there's music on the other side."

I followed her lead towards the music and the next day we made plans to meet there again. Sunny was a poster flower child. Her only offense to nature was secretly covering the freckles across her nose with Cover Girl's liquid concealer. She was a pretty girl, petite but not fragile, with gray blue eyes and a great mane of golden hair reaching almost to her waist. The unruly strands were bleached daily by playful afternoons in the sun. Sometimes, Sunny's hair had a halo effect, appearing to be lit from within. I thought she was beautiful and she thought I was smart. We became the best of friends.

Weekends in the park had become a ritual. Sunny and I followed the others to all the "in" places in Miami, Sunny Isles and Coconut Grove. The flower children were peaceful happy children, content and grateful to play in the parks. They laughed, sang and danced. I was usually with Sunny. She was the outgoing one, so I was not required to speak too much. I was fairly comfortable. Most of these children felt, touched and understood, and what they did not understand they accepted. For me this was blessing. I had largely forgotten my verbal skills. It seemed like I had been alone for such a long time. In public, I spoke few words and only then when it was absolutely necessary or required of me out of politeness. Luckily it was all excused beneath the umbrella of shyness.

As the summer went on, many of the flower children wondered about glassy eyed with vacant stares. I knew the look. I recognized the hollow eyes and I knew well the feeling of lingering between two worlds. I knew many would not long remain in this one. I tried to reach them. I spoke to them, like the old children in the stones had spoken to me. I spoke in the language beyond words without sound, but they did not understand and I did not know why. I knew they longed for comfort, like the comfort beneath the stones. I knew too that they would not be allowed to stay, for they like me had not lost their blood. I wanted to share with them that I knew. I wanted to tell them how seductive the longing for finality could be.

I thought of the hollow eyed girl in Germany. I had always thought she would have known me. That she would have seen her American sister and known that we had shared a fate between two worlds. Then again, it may not have been after all. Perhaps it was only in those rare moments when one was firmly present on either one side or the other that the ability to communicate was available. I did not know.

Darkness fell on the park and a boy walked through a lingering crowd blowing his trumpet to the setting sun. I remembered the soulful sound of the trumpet playing 'Day is Done' on the old base in Germany. I remembered the old cannon as the sun and the American flag went down in the square where the soldiers marched. But, this was a different time, and a different country. No one froze to attention here. No one saluted or carefully folded the flag. Instead it was cut up and sewn into clothing. It was used for blankets to sit on and occasionally it was burned in protest. That was all a bit too sacrilegious for me. I watched, but I would not participate. Even if this country disillusioned me, I would always honor my father and the soldiers who died protecting it.

The Viet Nam war was not a memory. It was a current event, and daily people lost their fathers and brothers. So many young men were sent away and killed in the war. Many were boys, but they were shot as men. I watched the brothers and the sisters who were left behind. Many in sympathy tried to follow. They were not so fortunate as their dead brothers. The process of dying was not a quick or painless one. Here they used needles to shoot themselves, and I watched as they were seduced by the promise of oblivion. I saw them scale the walls of ecstasy and held them and rocked with them as they plummeted back down to reality. It was temporary. I tried to tell them that it was all so temporary, all so futile, but they did not understand.

"Come on," Sunny took my arm. "Doug and I got a place, right on the beach and you have to come see our new little pad. It's great, and you can't say no, you have to come because… okay, you remember Mark don't you?"

"Mark?"

"Yeah, Doug's friend, the one from Berkeley, he's staying with us for a few days and I think he likes you."

"Mark, with the little wire specs. I don't even know him."

"Oh come on, he's cute and he's smart like you. Besides…" she stretched the word for effect. "It's time you got a boyfriend, and guess who's going to get you ready for that. Come on, I have the perfect outfit all picked out."

I had to laugh, she made everything, even this transparent set up date, seem fun. We were pretty much the same size so we often borrowed and traded clothes. Of course they always looked better when she wore them. And they were always so much more 'hip' on her. But, I resigned to let her dress me up anyway.

The 'pad' was a run down hotel room on North Miami Beach, not far from Sunny Isles. On the small sagging bed, she had spread a blue cotton blanket with fringes and a white wheel of the zodiac woven in the center. The lamps were artfully draped with tie dyed scarves and the room was generously filled with multicolored candles in various shapes and sizes. The ashtrays were full with incense and ash covered matches, but other than that it was neat and clean, she had made it her home.

"The guys won't be back for while, wait till you see this top." She pulled on the one remaining knob to open the drawer. The clothes swelled up, and before they could spill over she grabbed the blouse out. It was brightly printed with geometric shapes and swirls. She held it up for me to see. It was nothing more than a silk triangle. "What do you think?" She waved it as she asked. "Sexy, huh."

"So how does it work? Sunny, I can't wear that," I protested. "I don't have boobs like you do. Look at me, what am I going to hold it up with?"

"Oh stop worrying," she laughed. "It just ties in the back, I swear it won't fall down. Show a little skin, you'll look great. There's a pair of white hip huggers in the bottom drawer. Pull em out while I find the earrings, I have the perfect ones." She walked into the dimly lit niche harboring a sink and partially tarnished wall mirror and began rummaging through a red lacquered jewelry box.

I opened the drawer, and spotted the white pants, but as I pulled them out, something in a rolled up cloth fell out on the floor beside me. I reached down without thinking to put it back, but as I grabbed it, a hypodermic syringe and a yellowish rubber tube slipped out of the piece of fabric. Sunny looked over her shoulder and realizing what I had uncovered she began walking towards me. I looked up at her.

"Are you using that shit?"

"No, I'm not using… look, just forget it, it's Doug's."

I grabbed her arm in disbelief. "Forget it? There are marks on your arm; you've been using a needle. Why, why would you shoot up?"

"If you ever felt the high…" She lifted her chin and threw her head back allowing her silky blond hair to fall freely down her back. She continued moving her head, sweeping her back and her shoulders with her hair as she spoke. "If you were high you would know, you would understand and you would never, ever ask me why again."

"I don't need to be high to know Sunny. And I don't need to shoot myself with a needle to hear voices from the other side. I have heard them…and I've answered them more than once."

"Oh, Jeanne Marie, I love you, but you don't know the first thing about it. In a few months you're going away to school, and you should because that's where you need to be. But you know me. Where am I going? My own mother threw me out for having sex with my boyfriend. I'm sure her latest old man put her up to that, mainly because I wouldn't have sex with him. Now that I'm thinking about it, this new ass hole may actually be an improvement over the last one. At least he understood the word no."

She turned around and continued her search for the earrings. Plucking out the first jeweled accessory, she went on. "Thank God I have Doug, because I don't know where I would be right now without him… Yeah, I do. I'd be right on those streets down there, your lucky Jeanne Marie, you have a real family and you know where your going, but you don't know anything about those streets."

"Your right Sunny. I don't know anything about those streets, but I do know about other ones. They might have been old and made of cobblestone, but they were streets. I know what it's like to give up, to not want to live in the world you're born in and choose another one that you can't stay in. I have been on the streets Sunny, face down."

"Then you should understand why. You shouldn't have to ask why I get high."

"Of course I know why," I said. It's wonderful when you get there. It's warm and soft you can just sink into... nothingness, oblivion. It makes you forget all the hard and ugly things that living in your body subjects you to. Your somewhere where no one can touch you, no one can hurt you anymore, you're free." I looked at her waiting for some kind of objection.

"And that's bad?"

"No, I never said it was bad. It's just that it makes you want to stay there. You don't want to come back anymore. It's oblivion, and it can give you whatever illusion you need. Oblivion gives you whatever you want while your there and it asks nothing of you."

"I think you've been holding out on us all," she said accusingly. "Your not really quiet and shy little Jeanne Marie. You've been getting high all the time, haven't you?"

"No, not high, not with drugs, but it's not so different. There's more than one way to get there but that's not the point. What I'm try-ing to tell you is, that oblivion... it's a trick. The trick is you can't stay. It's only that tiny little place between life and death, and you can't stay because it's only a passageway. It's not really a place at all. It just makes you think it is. You think it's oblivion calling you, but it's not oblivion, it's nothing, it's nowhere."

"It's death that's calling," I tried to explain. "Beckoning you from the other side. Don't you understand when you get there; it's so easy to get confused. It's so easy to forget the way you came in and you don't really know the way out. You forget which world you live in, because you just want to stay in oblivion, so you don't choose either one. Then you're stuck, between two worlds, the one you belong in and the one that will not allow you to stay. It's non-existence."

"Only when you leave," she said.

"I just don't want anything to happen to you. I'm going away to school soon. Who else is going plead with you to stay? Be silly, be pretty, be stupid, be anything Sunny, but be here. Your alive and you can be anything you want to be, but you can't keep going there.

Sooner or later you won't be able to get back. Oh, God, who else is going to tell you all the stuff you don't want to hear?"

"Doug will. Don't worry, you know he'll take care of me."

"Doug, your in great hands." I said as I re-wrapped the little bundle and put it away. "It's up to you, Sunny. Doug won't be there with you in oblivion. It's a narrow passage, a one-person ride. You can only go through it alone and you hate to be alone. Promise me you won't forget…" My voice began to crack. "And when you hear it calling you'll remember who it is… promise me you won't answer."

"I promise," she said. "I've only done it a few times. It's not like I'm hooked or anything. Besides, I'm not the one that's leaving. You are, and I'm going to miss you." She hugged me and began to cry. We both hugged and cried together until we were interrupted by a knock on the door in the corridor. Luckily it was down the hall and not on our door.

"Oh my God, look at us," she said. "The guys are going to be here and we both have mascara running down our faces. You look like an owl."

"Yeah, go look in the mirror. You should see how you look," I said. We both laughed and ran for the tissues and a glimpse in the mirror to wipe our smudged eyes.

Doug and Mark got there just as we were putting on the final layer of lip-gloss. Doug seemed irritated, maybe rushed was a better word. He set a six-pack of Pepsi and two joints down on a wobbly three-legged end table. Sunny, took out the bottles and began serving her guests. Doug picked up one of the joints, ran it under his nose and gestured an overly dramatic inhale. "Nothing but the best." He lit the end and drew a mouthful of smoke before passing it on to Mark. Mark held it between his fingers for a few seconds before he indulged. He was giving me the 'you dressed up for me and I think I like it' eye. I tried to hide, folding my arms in front of my belly, covering my bare skin.

"So, what do think of Jeanne Marie?" Sunny asked, embarrassing me further.

"Is that you Jeanne Marie? Wait a minute let me take these shades off. Hum, sometimes clothes do make the woman. Looking good." Doug said with a whistle.

"You look ex-cep-tion-ally beautiful," Mark added, emphasizing every syllable of the long word.

"Thank you." I said, trying hard not to divulge my self-consciousness and ruin my new image. "But, we must give credit where it is due, wardrobe and makeup by Sunny." I waved my arm, gesturing for her to take the center stage.

Sunny curtsied for them as they applauded, and everyone including Doug seemed to relax a little. "All right, now that everyone's feeling good, we've all had our refreshments, a little smoke, some friendly chit chat... the plan is this; since my beautiful lady here, and I would like to have a little private time, to do some little private things." He smiled at Mark. "I think that Mark and Jeanne Marie might enjoy a nice walk on the moon lit beach maybe...hum? Sound about right? And... we'll meet up with you a little later on the pier. Some band is supposed to be jamin there later."

Mark took my hand and kissed it. "Would you care to accompany me to the beaches, my dear."

I giggled a little, Sunny smiled and winked at me, and we left. Mark and I walked along the beach, listening to the band whail in the background. Then we sat down in the warm sand and talked. He was interesting, and we must have been in some deep conversation for a long time when we heard a siren. We could see the lights of the ambulance as it pulled up in front of the hotel where Doug and Sunny were.

There's always a sort of shock that runs through you at those moments, a series of jolts that tell your head, "it did not come for someone else this time". It could have been for anyone, there were a lot of people there, but I knew whom that ambulance had come for. Mark grabbed my hand and we both broke into a run. By the time we got there, they had blocked the hallways. Police were there.

"What's going on?" Mark asked one of the uniformed officers who guarded the doorway.

"Another O.D. You and the young lady got some business here?" He asked.

"I'm staying here with a friend." Mark said.

"What's the room number?" the policeman asked, taking out his two-way radio.

"306." Mark answered.

"You two wait right here." He told us.

Everything after that was in fast forward. They carried her out on a stretcher. She was covered, all but the top of her golden head. A few strands of her long hair hung limp off the side of the stretcher, sweeping the ground, as they rolled her lifeless body through the crowd. Doug just stood there, pale, vacant eyed and hand cuffed. I glared at him. Sunny had always loved everybody. I wondered if anybody had ever really loved her?

Somehow I got home. It wasn't until then that I realized I was wearing her clothes, her earrings and whatever was left of her makeup on my swollen tear stained face. I took off the little top and smelled it. It was all that was left of her, a faint scent on a silk kerchief. Her young life had been reduced to two letters. The policeman's words replayed in my mind, "another O.D." I hated those initials. Oblivion and death began with the same two letters. I hated them too. I wasn't sure which of them was worse. They had both conspired to take Sunny away from life. Together they had succeeded.

Oblivion was so much subtler than death. It had no guardians at its gateway, only a great gaping entrance into a hungry void. There had been no one there to warn her, no one there to send her back. It had led her to believe that she could stay, knowing all the while that she could not. Temptation offered boundless heights and God rarely intervened. It was the lowly spirits I suspected, the shadowy ones who hovered close to the earth who were the first to show. It was the ones who had known life first hand, who were there to offer help. But if you went too high, they couldn't help you, because they could not reach you. Sunny was in oblivion. I knew she could not hear me anymore. She had gone too high. I prayed she would somehow escape from the mouth of oblivion and fall down into the safe arms of death. There would be others there, and she would not be alone.

So many lost their lives. Some only lost their minds. Their bodies would remain behind to be cared for by grief stricken mothers. Bad trips were commonplace. I saw Tom, after they released him from the hospital. Tom's brother and my brother had been friends. His family lived two blocks away. Tom had been the high school valedictorian. He too had been waiting this summer to attend the University, until LSD the great mind opener had expanded his mind into eternal oblivion. His mind was gone, permanently. His eyes were fixed in a blank stare. His mother now buttoned his shirt to keep him warm, and wiped the drool from his mouth. He would never even know she was there. I could not wait to go away. Somehow I thought the university would be my deliverance.

A few days later, the phone rang. It startled me from my sleep, "Raymond, Raymond is that really you?" It was my brother and I could hardly believe it. He had been away for over a year now. He was a real soldier in the U.S. army. I had just been dreaming about him. I dreamed he was holding this beautiful little Japanese doll, and he told me he was bringing her home for me. I couldn't figure out why it was a Japanese doll when my brother was stationed in Korea. "Are you back?"

"Yea, it's really me and I'm really here. I'm back and I'm at the airport." He was excited. "Don't tell anyone, I want to surprise mom. I have a surprise for you too." He told me where to pick him up and to hurry.

"So, where's my surprise?" I asked as soon as we left the airport. "If it's still in your suitcase, I'll pull over so you can get it out."

"No, it's not that kind of surprise," he said.

"What, you didn't bring me anything? You get me out of bed at this hour, I drive all the way to the airport and you didn't bring me anything."

"It's not a thing, it's a her," he said.

"A girl, where is she?"

"Slow down. She's back in Korea, but not for long. Her name is Kim and I'm going to bring her back and marry her."

"Jeanne Marie, she's beautiful. Her father was Japanese. She looks like a little doll."

"How did I know that?" I couldn't help but to smile. "Raymond I can't believe your here, you weren't suppose to be here for another four months."

"Yeah, well the army can shove their four months," he said. His left knee bobbed involuntarily and he pressed it down with the palm of his hand. "You have no idea what it was like. The only thing worse is Nam, and I'm not all too sure about that. At least they've got some good weed over there."

"Not to mention all the free morphine they give after you get shot. Are you kidding? What about Kim? You just told me you found the love of your life there. What happened?"

"Nothing, nothing you could possibly understand. I just don't belong in the army, that's all. I am so glad to be back in the states. Out of uniform and back to bare feet, strolling through good ol' Miami, drug paradise of the free world."

"Yea, it's a real candy store." I knew he had no idea what that meant to me. I also knew that there was nothing else I could say at that moment.

I suspected my father had something to do with my brother staying out of Nam. My father was an old soldier. He knew war and he knew his son. Raymond would not have survived it. Even as children playing war games in the German fields, it was evident that my brother lacked most of the basic skills. He did not have a mind for strategy and he had very little self-control. Much to my father's disappointment, Raymond was not a soldier.

Raymond wanted to spend the day at Greynolds Park. I had not gone back since Sunny's death. It was all too fresh and far too painful. I did not want to go there. "Oh come on," Raymond begged. It'll be just like sneaking off to the fields in Germany when we were kids. It'll be fun, Jason's going to come too."

"Raymond, you don't understand. A lot has happened since you've been gone."

"Oh, come on, just this once. I've been gone for a long time, and I don't know anyone anymore. It's only one day. I'm your brother, the only older brother you've got."

What else could I say? I tried to make the best of it. My brothers and I were going to play together again. Jason brought his little medical bag. It was filled now, not with Band-Aids and iodine, but drugs and paraphernalia. Raymond and Jason both shared in an unbridled fascination with drugs of all denominations. I smoked the dark herb with them. It was one of the few social rituals I participated in. Marijuana I knew brought you to the gateway of oblivion, but it could not take you too far inside. For my brothers, it was not far enough. They had heard the song of the sirens, and they believed they could go and stay forever.

They had forgotten about the witches who hid in the forest, always hungry for children, tricking them with their sweets. It was a bribe, a gingerbread house illusion but they had tasted her sugarcoated promises. They had followed her into the deep woods, and soon they would be trapped and eaten. I tried to explain this to them, but they did not understand. They had gorged on her sweets and they no longer cared.

By the end of the summer Greynolds Park of the peaceful protesters was not so peaceful anymore. The unknown rock musicians cranked up their speakers and played an electric version of Star Spangled Banner as two policemen tried to make their way through the crowd. There was some sort of scuffle on the other side. I could not see what was happening. Words were whispered from one group to the next. Like the old game of telephone by the time it reached us it had been distorted into some kind of drug bust by the pigs, who had maliciously beat up on some poor peacenik. By the time we left, a crowd had gathered and began turning the police cars over in anger. Aspirations of peace I began to believe were just another part of the grand illusion, part of the sweet dreams, where mankind could not remain in forever.

It was the following week, on a Friday afternoon. I sat at my desk in the corner of the small office, checking the clock several times as I copied numbers into the ledger. I was beginning to dream of numbers when I went to sleep at night. The clock finally raised both hands and pointed to twelve. It was lunchtime, and I knew I could at least escape for a little while. I jumped up and headed straight out the door, and onto the busy downtown street.

Around the corner was a small boutique. I liked to go in and look around. I couldn't really afford to buy anything, but looking was free. As I walked in I noticed the new display. It was a red crushed velvet pants suit with an intricate chain belt set with colorful shinny stones. The belt looked like something from a Medieval artisan. Something one of the ladies from King Arthur's court might have worn. I was admiring the belt when I heard a soft male voice asking me a question. "Do you like it?"

I turned to see who was talking. It was a young man with curly dark hair and big mustache. His shirt was open in the front. He was dressed a little flashy but very hip. "I like the belt," I said.

"What about the clothes?" He asked.

"Oh, the fabric is beautiful."

"What about the design? Is it something you would wear?"

"No," I said.

"Why not? Don't you like it?"

"It's not that I don't like it," I said. "It's not my style."

"What is your style?"

"I don't know," I said. "But I know it when I see it."

He held up an electric blue outfit. "What about this one?" He asked. "No, that's not me either."

"I know," he said. "Wait here, one minute. I'm going to my car. I have the perfect one for you."

I tried to tell him I wasn't even going to buy anything. I didn't want him wasting his time but he just ran out so I waited. When he came back he had a dress still hanging in plastic. "Wait till you see this one," he said unwrapping the outfit.

It was a beautiful white dress, with soft folds at the shoulders that draped around the neck and it had a fabric sash with delicate white fringe at the ends. "Oh, that could definitely be it. It's beautiful," I said. "But I have to be honest with you. I can't really afford anything in here. I can't buy it."

"Oh, don't worry about it. I'm not trying to sell it to you. I sell these to the stores. I design clothes. I just wanted to know if you liked them."

"Oh, in that case I have to tell you they're all nice, but this one's exceptional."

"Then please, accept it as my gift." He said handing it to me. "After all, I think it was made for you."

"No, I couldn't do that. I don't even know you."

"Joseph, my name is Joseph. I live on Miami Beach. My family manufactures clothes there. My parents came here as refugees from Cuba. I'm a Cuban Jew. What else do you need to know?"

"I don't know," I was suddenly too shy to say anything.

"Then accept the dress as payment for helping me with my marketing study. And… will you have dinner with me? You don't have to say anything but yes."

"I couldn't help but to smile. He was charming. "Yes."

We went out a few times, in his car on real dates. Then one night he took me to his factory, to show me his latest designs. The factory was closed. We were the only ones there. It was dark and a little spooky, but it was fun, and also a little forbidden.

Joseph turned on the light in the small office and went back to lock the main door. "What do you think?"

The window of the office overlooked rows of sewing machines and empty seats. There were several large tables and bolts of fabric stacked on metal shelves. It looked eerie, lit only with the glow from the room we stood in. I had not answered, but Joseph did not seem to notice.

"This is what I wanted to show you." He said rolling in a rack with several dresses hanging on it. "These are brand new. Come here." Joseph held the dress under my neck. "This one looks like you, would you try it on?"

"Try it on?"

"Yeah, there's a dressing room right behind you. I'd like to see it on you."

I was flattered to be asked to model for him, but shy about undressing, even in the next room. "I can't do that," I said pushing the dress away.

"Why not? We're alone here. You're not afraid of me are you?"

"No, I'm not afraid of you. It's just…"

"Just what," he said pulling me closer to him. Then he kissed me, first on the mouth then gently all around my face.

"Okay," I said catching my breath and pushing him away. "I'll try it on."

It was a soft knit fabric, in a deep cranberry color. It wrapped around the waist and tied on the side. The folds in the front came down too far. It was made for a woman with larger breasts. I tried to pull the folds over a little before stepping out.

"What do think?" He asked.

"I think it's a little big," I said still tugging at the opening.

"Come here," he said. Then he pulled the shoulders up and the knit clung to my breast revealing my tiny hardened nipples. "That's how it should look." He said turning me around to face the mirror. "Come here," he said. "I want to show you the rest of the factory. Have you ever seen one before?"

"No," I said following him out into the darkness.

"Those are the sewing machines over there. During the day this place is filled with women sewing. You should here the noise from all those machines, all going at the same time. You see these tables. This is where cutters work. They cut layers of fabrics at a time." Then he lifted me up and sat me on the edge of the table.

"What are you doing," I laughed. He pulled himself up and sat beside me.

"I used climb up here and go to sleep when I was a kid. My parents worked day and night to build this business. When they first came to Miami, they had nothing. They left everything but me behind in Cuba. My father washed dishes when he first got here. A lot of time we ate scraps from other peoples plates, but we weren't alone. Miami is full of refugees, especially from Cuba." Then he reached over and pulled me close to him.

"Was it lonely being an only child?" I asked him.

"No, I don't think so. I don't think I ever remember feeling alone, until lately. Lately I've been feeling alone. I think about you, and when you're not here, I feel alone."

"Really?"

"Really," he said kissing me once more on the lips then gently laying me down on the table. "I think about you all the time," he said kissing my face and then my neck. "I want us to be together," he said undoing the tie of my dress. Then he lowered his head and gently kissed each of my breasts. My body was completely exposed. There was only the thin lace of my panties to secure me. The small light from the next room illuminated the whiteness of my small form.

"My God you're beautiful," he said removing the nylon panties. "I want to make love to you," he said softly slipping his own clothes off as he spoke. "I'll make it beautiful for you, I promise. Don't be afraid. Making love is beautiful."

I felt it go in. It didn't hurt. When it was over it was wet and sticky, but there was no blood. "Jeanne Marie, you're wonderful," he said pulling me closer and I felt his chest warm against mine. "Your just so beautiful, tiny and fragile like a little kitten. Are you okay? I mean I didn't hurt you did I?"

"No." I said a little surprised by his concern. "I'm okay." There was something about it I liked, not the sex, but the attention, the gentleness and the concern. Making love had not been exactly beautiful, but it was not painful and the truth was I felt relieved. There had been no virginity for me to lose. The only thing I had to lose was fear, and I did. Sex did not hurt. I didn't want his tongue in my mouth, but the other part didn't seem to matter. He seemed to really like it. I couldn't imagine why, but there didn't seem to be too much to it and I felt good knowing that. It was as if some great weight had been lifted from me. I was free.

I tried to pull away, but he held me with both arms and pulled me closer to him. My face was pressed against his neck. It was then that I first noticed it, a scent, his scent. It's hard to describe. It was neither pleasant nor unpleasant. It was not a perfume or a sweaty odor. It was simply a scent that was exclusive to him. It exuded somehow from the pores of his skin. I burrowed my face under his chin and inhaled the earthy elixir. It was a scent I knew I would always remember.

We had an uncanny link Joseph and I. It was beyond the physical, beyond anything I had ever known before. He did not need to ask what I thought, and all I had to do was picture him and he called. "But how did you know?" I would ask.

"I felt you," is all he would reply.

One day we sat on the beach. There was an elderly man under a large blue umbrella in front of us. He was shriveled and drawn with age. Joseph drew circles in the sand with his fingers as he spoke. "Jeanne Marie what do you believe happens when we die?"

"We leave this world and go to another one," I said matter of factly.

"You mean like heaven?"

"No, well not the fluffy angels and the pearly gates heaven anyway."

"I don't believe in heaven," he said erasing his drawings in the sand.

"So, what do believe in?"

"That when we die, the only thing that keeps us alive is if someone remembers us."

I thought for a minute. "What happens when everyone you know has died?"

"I'm not sure. Maybe that's why people put their names on tombstones, or pass their names onto their children."

"Maybe," I agreed. "A lot of memories are preserved in history because they were written down." Then I remembered the face of the woodcarver's daughter in Germany. She would live forever, as a Christmas angel.

"Would you remember me Jeanne Marie? I mean even if we weren't together anymore. Do you think you would remember me?"

"I'll always remember you Joseph. You don't have to worry about that."

"I want you to have this." He unhooked the silver chain from around his neck and placed it on mine. On the chain was a small silver and blue enamel Star of David. "Someday, I'm going to make time stand still for you."

"What does that mean?" I asked. "Time doesn't stand still."

"I can't explain it. But promise me you'll remember it, and you'll remember me." He kissed the little pendant that now hung from my neck.

I promised, even though I had no idea what he meant. A few days later I found out that Joseph was getting married. There was a picture of his intended in the newspaper with a short article about the wedding plans. Joseph came over that night. He swore that his family had arranged the marriage. That he was not in love with the girl, but he would have to marry her. It was only a business arrangement he assured me. I cried, and whether I believed him or not was of no consequence. I was devastated.

The year was about to come to an end. I had turned seventeen and another form of learning would soon begin. I soon discovered that college too was like a candy store. I gorged on the vast assortment of educational treats. I loaded myself down with every course that peaked my interest and I was in love with learning.

I was still living at home and working part time to pay my tuition. The school I attended was a local community college. My dream was to go away to school. A real school with ivy covered walls, old professors and antiquated traditions. But I was a girl, and legally too young to leave home, my parents assured me, for any reason other than marriage. I knew the only reason they allowed me to go to college at all was because they hoped I would find a husband there.

I met Vic at school. We worked together tutoring foreign students in the English department. Within six months we were married, and with my parents blessings I was finally on my way to a real university. Vic was seven years older than I. He was a student, an aspiring writer. He had been in the military, stationed in Germany before we met. He would use the GI Bill to attend the University in the fall. I saw him as a mature and worldly man. Vic was twenty-four.

Somewhere inside I knew, even then I knew, that I had betrayed the saints. I thought of Saint Barbara, how she must have known what a coward I had been. No one had beaten, tortured or even threatened me. In my heart I knew I had simply taken the easy way out. Vic's family was devoutly Catholic. Before we married, I formally became a real Catholic, but it was a small consolation in the scheme of things.

Vic wrote for the school newspaper and was politically active in the college revolutionary scene. He strongly supported the anti war movement and we spent a good deal of time marching in protest. We sat in an endless number of sit ins and met with the long-haired militants of the day. Everyone cursed the establishment and in general fought a war against the war. Some sat barefoot and preached peaceful solutions while others acted out their opposition in violent confrontations. I watched in silence as the protesters for peace threw stones and turned over police cars.

I had been at Kent State when national guards shot and killed several students. It had begun for most of us, a game. Students lined up, sides had been chosen, left and right, protesters and guards. The battle began with shouts and taunts and ended with gunfire into the crowd. Everyone ran mostly from the noise. No one believed the bullets were real, until it was over, and the dead did not get up. The reality of that moment was captured in a single photograph, which appeared in every newspaper, magazine and TV network in America. The photo of a young girl kneeling over the lifeless body of the Kent State student shocked everyone. Guns, soldiers, death and war were real. They had invaded our campuses. They were not just words on protest signs anymore, not just stories from a distant country on the six o'clock news. They were real, and everyone was a participant in one way or another.

We were back in Florida, enrolled at U.S.F. and still busy protesting the inevitable. The plan was to block Dale Mabry, one of the major streets in town. The protesters had gathered. They angrily waved their signs, and then proceeded to sit down in the middle of a busy street and wait for public attention. I sat quietly as the national guards marched in wearing gas masks and carrying guns with bayonets pointed at us. Vic was on the other side of the street carrying a friend's little blond haired boy on his shoulders. The three year old held a sign that read: Will I have to go war someday? I listened as the radicals jeered them on to shoot us when it suddenly occurred to me that this was not a cause I wished to die for. I had for the first time I could remember discovered a cause I truly wanted to live for. Mothers, I knew might not be able to protect their children from war, but I would do my best to provide my child with at least a safe place to grow. I picked up my bag and stood up to leave. The only safe place I could offer was inside me. I was carrying the seed of a new life.

As most pot smoking, freedom loving hippies of the day, Vic was not overjoyed with the impending birth of responsibility. Roe had not yet versed Wade, consequently there were no choices of whether to be, or not to be pregnant at that time. The seed had been planted, it would grow and responsibility would be born. A child according to Vic was a burden, a frightening one at that. He claimed it was a chain and anchor that would hold him to the bottom of the sea of life. It was a cumbersome weight he could not endure. His passionate idealism soon turned into angry outbursts. He became temperamental and violently unpredictable.

For me, the child was a miraculous new life form that was subtly growing inside of my own body. The birth of my son was my initiation to womanhood. Blood flowed from my darkest most secret place and spewed forth a separate new life. I had experienced creation. I knew then, as only a woman can know, that life and death were two sides of the same coin. They both spewed forth from the very same source.

In less than six weeks, Vic was somewhere touring the country in a blue Dodge van and I was headed back to Miami with a backpack and a newborn child. I moved back home with my parents. Where my mother who knew everything there was to know about motherhood tried in vain to share this experience with her daughter. Unfortunately I knew only the momentous experience of bringing life into the world. I knew nothing of caring for it once it arrived. I had never cared much for my own life, how would I be able to care for another. A baby's first instinct is to survive, and survival requires care and nurturing. My mother exuded these virtues. She had given birth to five children and took in numerous others along the way. I paled in comparison and when my child reached out, he reached for the experienced mother. He did not reach for me. I quietly went to work to support him.

I was twenty-one, going on a hundred and twenty-one. I was never quite sure whether I was living in the wrong century or on the wrong planet. I tried to reconcile with God. I asked the Saints to forgive me for getting married, even though I was grateful for my child. I decided to become a teacher. I taught religion at a parochial school, where I attended Mass daily.

It was almost time for Christmas vacation and I was on my way home. My thoughts were filled with the encroaching holidays. It would be my son's first Christmas. I was within a mile from home when my car was suddenly consumed broadside into the belly of a massive semi.

I had no idea what miracle had taken place until I was helped out of the car and saw the accident from the outside. My car had been crushed like a tin can. The police reminded me of how incredibly lucky I had been to escape with my life but I still could not quite grasp what had happened. The actual moment of impact is always such a strange moment. I heard so many people talk about their lives flashing before them, but that did not happen. It was a still moment, the kind of moment when time just stops. I don't really know how long that still moment was when I remembered to check my own physical inventory. Gratefully there was no blood. The windshield was smashed and my head hurt. I had dislocated my knee, but I didn't have a cut on me and I said a prayer of gratitude before the ambulance arrived.

I was taken to the hospital, whereupon they tested and observed me. I was released in a few days and told that it had been only a minor concussion. Everything was perfectly normal, they told me. I smiled; my life had never been perfectly normal before the accident. I couldn't imagine what made them think it would change now, but it did. I lost my car, my concentration and my job. I figured it was all part of my penance and it was not so bad. I was left with a small financial settlement, and another marriage proposal.

Steve had professed his undying love for me. He swore his deepest desires were for a wife, a home and children, all my parents had ever wished for me. I wasn't sure if it was love, but who could ever be sure of that? I longed to be a real mother, and I wanted to have another child. It seemed like the right thing to do. I was sure I could be a good wife.

There was something about Steve that reminded me of Joseph, although I was not sure exactly what it was. When I met his family, they were less than thrilled with our impending marriage. I thought it was because I had been divorced and came with a child. Perhaps they thought it would not be easy for their son. This was unfortunate, but completely understandable. I tried to tell Steve that I understood their concern. Taking on a readymade family may not be so easy for him. It was Steve who finally broke it down for me. We were driving home from a dinner with his parents. "Steve I know your parents are not crazy about me. And can understand their concern." I tried to reassure him. "But I'm not really sure what I can do about it. Is there something? Something I can do I mean."

"No," he said smiling as he spoke. "Jeanne Marie. It's nothing you can do or not do. Nice Jewish boys don't marry non-Jewish women. What did you expect?"

I wasn't sure how to respond to this. No matter where I was, it seemed, I was a foreigner. I did not belong. I thought of Joseph. I wondered if Joseph's family had believed this too. Perhaps they really had forced him into an arranged marriage. Would it happen again? "You mean because of the religion?" I asked. I looked out the window, hoping he would notice the tears welling up in my eyes.

"Look, it's not that my family is very religious." He assured me. "They go to temple once a year and they do all the dinners for the holidays. That's about it. It's really more of a cultural thing. So, have you ever thought of converting?"

"No, Steve I can't say that I have. But if it's not religious, why would it matter?"

"Who knows, but it would make a big difference to them." He said tapping his fingers on the steering wheel. "And it would make life a lot easier for us."

A week later, I met with the Rabbi to discuss my forthcoming conversion. "So, you know a little about our religion I understand."

"Yes, I studied Jewish history for two years at the university."

"That's a good start." He nodded approvingly. "And what about your beliefs? Do you believe in Jesus Christ?"

"Ancient history was one of my majors. I'd be a little hard pressed not to believe, don't you think?"

"Yes, well there's no denying he existed," the Rabbi lowered his head and peered over the top of his glasses. "I mean do you believe he was the Son of God?"

"I thought for a minute. "Yes I do. I also believe that as human beings we are all sons and daughters of God. Is there a conflict?"

"Do you feel any conflict or regrets about becoming a Jew?"

"I don't think so. I'm looking towards Judaism to help me discover my roots. I studied Judaism because I wanted to understand the source. I mean Judaism is the root of Christianity, Islam too for that matter. You see I love religions, all of them. For me, religions are divided by culture and politics, not by God.

I believe we all pray to the same God, and the words and rituals we use in those prayers are simply things that are familiar and comforting for us to do. We reenact things to bring back memories of sacred moments that link us with past generations. For me every sacred act is a connection to the people before me, and every prayer is dialogue with God. There is no language he cannot understand and no people, past or present he does not love." I took a breath, suddenly unaware of where all those words had come from. I shrank back in my seat a little embarrassed.

"A difference of opinion maybe, but a conflict? No, I don't think we have a conflict. With the rest of the world, maybe," he smiled. "But, what else is new?"

Steve and I were married in the temple. It was a beautiful wedding and I looked forward this time to a real marriage, a home and a family of my own. My son reluctantly came with me. He refused to call me mommy and swore that he had been in my mother's stomach, not mine. There was no convincing him otherwise. He loved me but he thought of me as his sister and I didn't think he would ever forgive me for taking him away from the real mother. I brought him to 'Grand-mas' often.

I was left with terrible headaches after the automobile accident. They were frequent and when they raged, I was left immobilized. I was grateful my mother was there. The doctors had given me every imaginable painkiller and I feared taking them because I knew oblivion still lurked somewhere out there.

My mother had gone back to school after the baby and I left. She had studied hypno-therapy and now worked with people who were diagnosed with chronic pain. The concept hadn't thrilled me, it seemed valid but I really didn't believe in it. The pain seemed to get worse and nothing helped. I finally consented to being hypnotized by my mother. At the time I would just as easily have consented to a guillotine had there been one available. My mother proved to be quite talented in the area of hypnosis. I went out like a light. I remembered nothing, except the sound of my mother's voice as she brought me back from the deep sleep.

"I am going to count now from one to five Jeanne Marie, when I say five your going to wake up refreshed, calm and relaxed. Feeling like you've had a wonderful nights sleep. One, two, three, coming up now, four, eyes opening, five wide awake."

I was still in a kind of dreamy state when I came out of trance, but I felt good and painless. "Jeanne Marie, why don't we go into the other room and I'll make us a cup tea before you drive home. Sometimes it takes a few minutes to wake up, especially when you go that deep. Are you sure your okay?" My mother asked.

"Oh, yeah, yeah I'm fine. A cup of tea would be really good." We walked into the family room and I sat down, still dazed at the amazing results of the secession. The headache was completely gone. My mother walked into the kitchen to prepare the tea and I gazed at the television as it played the afternoon news. A picture flashed on the screen, it showed a young Latin man who had been murdered the night before. The broadcaster asked that anyone who could help, by giving information should contact the Hialeah Police Department.

The face of the young victim etched itself in my mind. I literally fell into his eyes and before I knew what was happening, another film played right before my own. The room he had been murdered in, the fear he felt, the very thoughts he thought. I knew somehow of the men who had been there that evening, their names, the bar they frequented. I saw the cars they drove. My god, I knew where they lived! Suddenly I opened my eyes to my mother's puzzled face as she calmly suggested I needed to relax and explain what was happening.

I was scared that the bump on the head had jarred my brain loose. I wasn't sure if I was hallucinating and I was more than a little frightened that I was losing my mind. I started telling my mother what had happened. She began taking notes and asking for details. I told her everything I had seen, everything I had felt and as I spoke I began to feel something different.

She was listening. She heard and somehow understood what I spoke about. For the first time in many years, we were actually communicating. I was fine, alive and conscious, for some reason I began to feel giddy. I knew my mother loved me, but I also knew that she was acutely aware that somewhere between childhood and adulthood she had lost her daughter. She had always been out going. She was free spirited and loved people. She could not understand what had happened to her daughter. I knew she must have often wondered how the child she had known and loved had become so silent, so strange and so incredibly unreachable.

She put the pad down and we drank the tea in silence. The pad was like an unopened letter and curiosity was getting the best of her. "You have to call them." She handed me the phone.

"No, I don't think so. Maybe there's some other way to find out."

"How? This could be important. What if it's all true?" She asked.

"And what if it's not? What if it's just some kind of hallucination from the hypnosis?"

"I don't think so Jeanne Marie. I think it's some kind of phenomenon. You know like Edgar Casey. When they put him under hypnosis, he just knew things. Things that no one to this day can explain how he knew. He was a clairvoyant, but only under hypnosis."

"Do you think that's what this is?"

"It could be," she said tapping her pencil on the pad.

"But I wasn't under hypnosis," I argued.

"Well you weren't quite out of it either. I think you were still in a heavy beta state. It made you receptive to the news announcer's request for information. He asked for help, and you responded."

"How? How could that happen?"

"Some people are very suggestible. Look how easily you went into trance. It didn't take much effort on my part. You might just be a natural clairvoyant, the hypnosis only opened it."

"Even if that's true Mom, I don't really know if we should be getting involved with this."

"How else are we going to know?" Her voice was questioning but firm.

"I'm sure they'll catch the murderer eventually. We'll know then."

"What if all this information turns out to be true Jeanne Marie. What if it prevented someone else from being murdered?"

"I don't know Mom. Call if you want to." I resigned.

The next thing I knew, I was on the phone to homicide. "I think I might have some information on a murder, does the name Orlando mean anything to you?" Within fifteen minutes there were two homicide detectives knocking at the door. I regretted the call, but my mother was so excited by all the possibilities. How could I disappoint her?

I tried to begin with something like, "I know you're not going to believe this." Not only did they not believe it, but they also weren't even the slightest bit amused. My mother handed over the notes while I was being interrogated on my whereabouts on the evening of. I was still too amazed to be frightened. It seemed that the locations I had given were under surveillance. They knew of the cars, the bar and the ridiculous names. I didn't know what to say. How could I explain how I knew those things? I did not know myself.

That's when my mother came up with another idea. "I can hypno-tize her again, and you can ask her questions," she told the detective. "She is obviously clairvoyant under hypnosis."

I could not imagine how she was even familiar with the term, much less the procedure. It was not a popular concept at the time. I was not sure if she was kidding or not and I was hoping I was still sleeping in some hypnotic trance in the other room. I was hoping I would soon wake up to find that I was only dreaming this whole bizarre situation.

I have no idea how she convinced the detectives to participate in this little experiment, but she did. I must admit she was a good hypnotist. I went out immediately, and the detective began to ask questions. "Jeanne Marie," he spoke to me in a low but not unpleasant tone. "Tell me what my house looks like?"

I looked through my eyelids and there was a house. So I began to describe it. "It's white, with green trim. There is a woman and two children, two boys standing in front of it. There is something new inside, red, curtains, they must be new drapes."

"Do you have two sons?" My mother asked.

"Yeah, and I live in a white house with green trim. My wife just bought new curtains," his voice trailed off.

"Is there something else you want to ask her?"

"No, wake her up," he told my mother. "I've heard enough."

When I woke up, I was sorry I had missed the expression on his face. My eyes were closed, but I could tell it must have been a combi-nation somewhere between doubt and amazement. The detective looked down and shook his head. "We'll need those notes," he said pointing to the pad on the table. The other detective confiscated the notes and they left without a word. I sat with my mouth open, but my mother was ecstatic. She could not wait to get started. For her the ave-nues of adventure were endless.

The ensuing weeks were spent on an endless array of experiments, myself being the guinea pig. I had always known the other world, the deep one where the living did not venture, but she did not. My mother was a great and radiant life force, her interest in the dark was only to bring it to the light and share it with others. My main focus at that time was to join my mother, even if I could not stay. Through hypnosis, she taught me to position myself firmly in one world at a time. For this I would always be grateful. I would learn in this manner to communicate with life.

My mother's exceptional reading abilities went into high gear. She now devoured every book in print on the subjects of hypnosis and parapsychology. It was a good exchange. She learned from one side, and I learned from the other. We always seemed to meet somewhere in the middle. We went exploring into the depths of the great unknown, without maps or compasses. We found that the harder we looked for information to guide us the less we found. Looking back it was probably the most fortunate thing that happened. She was convinced that the mind was unlimited under hypnosis. Not knowing any different I believed her. I never questioned her. I simply answered the questions without having the slightest idea of how or why.

She must have read about the phenomenon of psychometry, because our first experiments were conducted with objects belonging to various friends and family members. At first it was a game to identify the owner of the object in hand. The visual images were vibrant and filled with details.

"Take this Jeanne Marie and tell me what you see." My mother said placing a small ring in my hand.

"A girl, in a maroon uniform. Looks like high school. Oh, God, it's you. You look pretty funny," I laughed out loud to see her as a sixteen year old in a band uniform. This game went on for weeks. I was getting bored with identifying the objects when one day she handed me a piece of hand made ceramic.

"A little girl, a brand new baby. Oh, she's beautiful, the most beautiful baby girl I have ever seen. Who's is this, someone's going to have a baby."

"Open your eyes," my mother said. "Guess who it belongs to."

I looked down. It was a piece of pottery Steve had made in an art class. I looked down at my stomach. "I can't believe it." But it was true; I was pregnant with my second child. By this time my headaches had completely disappeared and I was making great progress learning my new skills. Meanwhile, my mother was busy stirring up interest with her professors and scouting out the local supernatural talent pool.

These adventures began long before Shirley McClain went out on a limb, before Dr. Weiss met Katherine and prior to the New Age enlightenment era. This pool of supernatural talent was filled with a bizarre lot of strange and curious characters. Some were unusually talented. Others were just unusual. I watched like a child at the circus. This was definitely the sideshow, the one that peeked people's curiosity with the peculiarities of nature.

It was about this time that my mother met Sandy. Sandy, like my own mother had raised five children. One of who would later marry my younger brother. She had tried to keep her sanity throughout her child rearing years by following her own spontaneous brand of spirituality. Sandy was honest to a fault and had a heart of gold, but she had a tendency to walk right past limits of reality. I was beginning to wonder now if the number of children one bore was in direct correlation with the degree of sanity a woman was left with in her later years. Between she and my mother, they had produced ten children.

Sandy was queen of the sideshow spiritualists. She knew everyone in town. The woman had a wonderful childlike faith, conversing with spirits like they were next-door neighbors. She wanted to share everything and everyone she knew with us. Sandy introduced us to a whole world of underground places and strange people. There was a whole world of weird and wonderful experiences right here in Miami and she knew exactly where to look. We would explore many of these other worlds without ever leaving the city. Perhaps, I would find the soul of this city after all. I was thrilled. I was about to see the world now from the ground up. I was about to meet others for the first time in my life that spoke out loud of the world below.

One of our first encounters took us to the streets of Opa Locka, an unusual little town in the North West section of Miami. Opa Locka was an experience in itself. The whole town was fashioned after an Arabian Nights fantasy. The town hall was a hot pink mosque complete with turban-capped towers. It conjured visions of magic carpets, brass lamps and Aladin's hidden treasures. The theme ran true throughout the architecture of the town. It seemed appropriate, a real Arabian adventure right here in Miami. I couldn't wait to see what magic would be conjured. We drove up to a tiny aqua stucco house not far from Ali Baba Avenue.

The yard was a jungle of weeds and the windows were all open to the midday heat. Sandy said she would wait for us in the car. I wondered what she knew that we didn't. She just smiled and instructed us to just go up and knock on the door. My mother led the way and I trailed after. An elderly woman answered the arched shaped door, "Rev. Gilman will be right with you, please come in and have a seat." It took a moment for our eyes to adjust from the bright sunlight outside, but we were led to the sofa and sat down. The elderly lady walked into another room and soon returned to tell us that the Reverend was ready. I prepared to be nudged to go first, when my mother stood up to go. I knew it was a protective gesture. My mother was a lot of things, but above all she was a mother.

As I waited I looked around at my surroundings. The house was old with faded furniture covers. It had no light save the natural light of the open windows and the room was filled with clutter. It was incredibly cluttered; clothing, stacks of old papers, assorted everyday articles just filled the tiny room. I sat patiently waiting, while I imagined what it would be like to meet someone who for many years had perfected her communication between the two worlds.

My mother emerged from the dark hallway, smiling to assure me that all was safe and well. At last it was my turn. I followed the lady down the dark corridor to an even darker room at the end. "Rev. Gilman is blind," she explained. "She can see outlines of images sometimes but not much more." That explained the darkness and the clutter that was stacked in various heights throughout the house. I wondered how on earth she ever found anything. I was directed to a chair placed in front of the window and as I sat down I saw Rev. Gilman.

She was ancient, short and plump with thin strands of hair pulled back into a knot on the back of her head. Her cane hung on the arm of her chair and she looked straight at me with her faded blue eyes. "I'm mostly blind," she began. "I can only see the light that comes round people anymore. You make yourself comfortable, and I'll call my guides. I got Indian guides. They're always close to the spirit. Soon as they get here I'll start talking. You just listen, you understand?"

"Yes." I sat wide-eyed, ready to listen.

"Chief says he's ready, we start now." She rapped the cane on the floor a few times. "You were blessed with a sister from the other side of the world. And I'm talking about this world not the next. The two of you have a lot in common. You'll learn from one another. You got a long time to come. She's the eldest, but things will follow you.

You got a strong willed little boy. He's a hard headed, but you'll be glad someday. He's gonna give you a tough time though. You're gonna wonder if he'll make it some times. But he'll grow up. They all do. You got a lot of talent. But don't be lazy about it. What God gives you he means for you to use. And don't be chasing the ones who promise you short cuts down side streets. Every street may lead to the center eventually. But you'll waste a lot of your time and efforts while your let em lead you down back alleys. You ask spirit to lead you. You got lots of protection from spirit. You got your purse open. It'll be filled with money. But it won't mean nothing to you, cause you'll be taken on the work. Person's gotta be born for that, but you are.

You'll be working with the children, the lost ones. There's lots of em out there. You got a lot to learn. You ask spirit. Spirit'll guide you. And start writing, cause you got books to come. They talkin about a little boy, maybe a lost child. You'll write about him first. All this'll come later, but you start writing now. And don't be lazy. You get out there and do what you're supposed to do. Cause there's a lot that needs to be done. You know what I'm talking about, don't you?"

"You pick up that piece of paper on the table next to you," she said motioning the location with her chin. "It's on the top of the stack. It's got an address on it. You come there next Thursday night, I don't teach everybody, but you got a lot to learn. Chief says that's enough for you now."

I thanked the good Reverend and the Chief, picked up the piece of paper with an address and time scrawled on the top and made my way back through the dark tunnel. We emerged from the tiny stone house only to be blinded by the bright light of the midday sun. Sandy was stretched out across the front seat of the car with her head buried in a romance novel. She was unaware of our presence until the car door opened. When she looked up, she grinned. "Well," she asked stirring to consciousness. "What do you think?"

"I don't know," I said. "What she said was probably right, but it was kind of like a riddle. I haven't figured it all out yet. But she invited me to come to a class or something on Thursday."

I climbed in the back seat while Sandy and my mother chattered happily all the way home. I quietly contemplated the day's event while I fumbled with the piece of paper between my fingers. I began to wonder what form of strangeness I was destined for on Thursday night. The two Moms were all in favor of my attendance of whatever it was that I had been invited to. I was to report Friday morning with all the fascinating details.

Thursday finally rolled around and I set out for my next adventure. The address led me to a tiny storefront in Opa Locka. The windows had been painted black and the address itself was the only identifying sign outside. I cautiously opened the heavy glass door and peered around the room. "Welcome, welcome," chirped a gay lady who walked over to greet me. "Blessings Jeanne Marie, we're happy your here. I'll introduce you around shortly, but first sit down because we are almost ready to start."

I sat down as instructed, and looked around to see where the fates had sent me. It was nothing more than the remnants of an old bare walled store. It was filled with a couple of dozen folding chairs that loosely formed a circle. There was an old buffet table in the back with a coffee urn and some baked goods. And just as I began noticing the people who occupied the room with me, the lights dimmed and all eyes were on the center. There was Reverend Gilman, with her chubby hands folded on her lap and her faded blue eyes gazing into the unknown.

"Just set the trumpet down," she instructed the lady behind her. "We won't be need'n that tonight." Oh my God, I had seen movies about this stuff, floating trumpets, dancing spirits. It was too late to run and half of me was glad. The other half was gripping the cold metal of the bottom of my chair, cursing both of the Mom's who would get a good laugh about this in the morning.

I recognized the somber lady who had greeted us the other day at little stone house. She was the only one who remained standing in the circle. She nodded at the friendly lady who stood by the lights to let her know that it was dark enough. Then she began by asking everyone to join hands. I knew it. It always started this way in the movies. Joining hands was all right, but I would not close my eyes. My eyes were open for the duration. If anything was going to happen, I fully intended to see it.

The lady went on to lead a prayer. They referred to God as the Great Spirit, but the prayer was familiar enough. I was comfortable in knowing that we were all praying to the same God. She went on to ask for divine white light. She asked for shields of protection and blessings for the spirit guides who guarded the opening of the gates to the world beyond. "So be it," the circle responded and the hands were released. Everyone focused on the ancient blind woman in the center, waiting for the slightest move.

"Well good evening," she began in a voice that was hers, but a manor that was not. "Chief said I could come, to welcome you here, but I can't stay long." She sounded sing songy, lighthearted like a young girl, and went on to recite some amateur poetry. The poetry seemed to go on and on. She continued with the same subjects of peaceful gardens and loving spirits. Then just about the time I began wondering just how long this spirit intended to stay, her voice trailed off bidding fond farewells. There was silence for a moment, and then her feet began tapping like drums. A deep voice rumbled in her throat and the big Chief arrived.

"Me Chief, me happy to be here with you tonight." It was soon evident that chief was a man of few words and choppy sentences. He did welcome me, referring to me as "the little sparrow with a spirit of an eagle." Then he laughed heartily and said he'd be back later.

Everything became still again, and we watched Reverend Gilman as she began tweaking her ear. I wasn't sure what she was doing, then came a high pitched squeaking noise and she continued now turning her hand just above her ear as if it were an invisible radio knob. Now the other hand went up to adjust the invisible antenna. As outlandish as it was, by the third minute I was almost seeing the antennas.

Finally, he spoke in a slow odd pitched voice introducing himself as an entity from another galaxy. He proceeded to explain the importance of his visit, which entailed bringing a message of light, love and other equally admirable humanitarian qualities to the earth beings. This channeling secession lasted for a little more than two hours, and while I decided not to make any judgments, just in case, I couldn't quite grasp the purpose of this exercise. Nothing had been said that hadn't been said a thousand times before. They were basic truths, love light and brotherhood. It was a creative presentation, but the same information was readily available in a thousand other art forms. I did not understand why the messages necessitated this form of delivery, but Rev. Gilman did leave a lasting impression. I was never inspired to channel like she did, but I did appreciate her dedication, her unique style and her creative delivery. She had been right. I did take on "the work," and soon I found that there was, "so much that needed to be done."

My mother as always was on to other things. She had found a new game. I don't know what made her think of it, perhaps it was the spirits, but she was sure that it would work. And if I could do this she assured me, she could measure the results. She cut out a photograph from the newspaper of a young boy that had been found murdered. There were no clues as to what had happened to him. She had decided to put me in trance and ask me about the child. She had not told me what she was planning. She rarely did. She simply put me into a trance and handed me the picture. "Tell me," she asked. "Where is this boy now?"

"He is here," I said.

"Can you see him?"

"Yes." I answered. I did not know what she wanted me to notice.

"Where is he Jeanne Marie?" She questioned again. She was a little impatient now. I could feel her sitting beside me.

"He is dead." I answered matter of factly. I wasn't all too sure why she had asked. I looked again at the little boy. His eyes were completely hollow and before I could catch myself I was inside of his eyes looking out.

I must have shuttered. My mother noticed the change and asked another question.

"Where are you now?"

"I don't know." I began to cry, but I knew it wasn't me. It was him, but we were all mixed up. I was feeling his feelings. Within seconds, I began scream. "No, no please don't hurt me anymore." I saw the man, he lifted me up with his hands around my neck, and suddenly there was no more pain. The world was light and I inhaled a great breath and lay still.

"Jeanne Marie, Jeanne Marie." I heard my mother's anxious voice calling me. "You are to come out of trance now," she commanded and promptly snapped her fingers. "You will remember everything you have seen and felt when you awaken on the count of five. One...Two...Three...Four...Five, wake up now."

I woke up and looked at her. "What on earth are you doing now?" I asked.

"I'll explain in a minute," she said. "First answer the questions."

She looked visibly shaken, so I decided to cooperate without too many questions. My mother was not often shaken.

"First tell me about the child," she asked. "Where were you when this happened?"

"I was next to a canal," I told her. "I remember looking at a bank of the canal. I thought he was going to throw me in."

"What about the man?"

"His name was Carl." I answered still unsure of why she asked.

"How did you know that?" She was surprised.

"I knew him, he had big hands and he smelled like beer. The boy," I tried to clarify. "He knew the man. He was thinking about his truck a red one with the back smashed in a little. He had been playing on Carl's truck."

She wrote down what I said, word for word and placed it along with the little newspaper clipping. The boy had been strangled she told me. His body was found in a canal. The results only seemed to encourage her.

"Do you know what this means?" She asked.

"That I'm going to have to do it again?"

"Think about what this could mean," she said. "We can help to solve these crimes. Imagine what would happen if you could see them before they happened? The possibilities are endless!"

About that she had been right. It was endless, like death itself. My mother proceeded to collect cases from the newspapers. She was thrilled as each of the murders was solved. She could not get over the accuracy of the information we had gathered. My mother grilled me for months as I entered one tragedy after another. She could not possibly know what it was to be raped of life so many times. Each time I entered into their hollowed little eyes, I experienced an unspeakable trauma. I lived one death after another, while she perfected her technique.

I tried to find ways to cope with my emotions. There were so many lost children and some of them did not know yet that they would have to stay. Sadly they found that no one could hear them when they tried to tell them they were lost. No one could see them or help them find their way home. I tried to explain. Some of them wanted to come back with me. I tried to tell them they could not, but they did not understand.

It was always difficult to come back up from the hypnotic trance. As I was pulled back, it was as if I were being torn in half. Every time I crossed over, I knew I would have to leave another piece of myself behind and I would never be whole again. I could hear my mother's voice calling me back and I knew I would have to abandon the lost child I was supposed to be helping. How could I possibly be helping? These children did not care who hurt them. They did care how it was done. They only cared to be safe, to know where they were and how they could be found. I could not explain this to my mother. I could not explain this to anyone, but this is how "the work" began.

3

Through Other Eyes

L ife never seemed to stop with death. At least it did not for me. Sometimes I prayed it would slow down, but it never did. Children still needed to be fed, the house had to be cleaned and the bills needed to be paid. The business of life went on. Harmony, my daughter had just turned two. I was beginning to believe that everything they said about two year olds was true. Her brother Joel, now six, placed a handful of cereal in front of her. With both hands, she swept it off the table and onto the floor. Joel looked up at me shaking his head. "She did again," he said. "First she wants it, then she just throws it on the floor."

Harmony began to wail. I opened the door to the laundry room to get a broom. The clothes were piled higher than the machines. I closed it again. "I've got an idea," I said turning to both of them. "Let's all get dressed and go out."

Joel's eyes brightened, "Can we get McDonalds?"

"We'll go to McDonalds," I said raising my voice above my screaming daughter.

"Stop crying Harmony," he said taking her chubby little hands into his. "Were going to McDonalds!"

Hearing the excitement in his voice she stopped mid wail and looked at me. "That's right I said scooping her up in my arms. "We're all going out for the afternoon."

After McDonalds we drove to the shopping center. It was not the closest mall to our house. Maybe I just wanted to get a little farther away from reality that day, at any rate, we wound up at the Sears mall in Hollywood. I put Harmony into the stroller, took Joel by the hand and we proceeded to walk through the long corridors of the air-conditioned building. Before long I found myself looking through the dresses and every few seconds Joel peaked his head out from between them and said boo. Harmony squealed with delight and I day dreamed about some grand occasion that might come up where I could actually wear one of those beautiful sequin dresses.

Several minutes passed and I turned around to see where Joel was hiding. I called out to him, but he did not answer. I began shoving the dresses open on the rack to see if he was playing with me. I did not see him. A sales woman was in the aisle next to me. "Have you seen a little boy?" I asked her. "About this high," I said holding my hand to his approximate height. "Blond hair, he was right here a minute ago."

"No, I haven't seen him," she said without too much concern or interest.

I grabbed the stroller and began to search the aisles. Joel was always curious, constantly exploring, but he knew better than to disappear like this. He was young, cute and vulnerable, so terribly vulnerable. My heart began to pound. He was nowhere to be seen. I ran to a register with the stroller in tow. "My son, he's six. I've lost him in the store. Can you use the speaker to call him?"

The woman at the register picked up the phone to dial the speaker. "What is the boy's name?" she asked.

"Joel," I said quickly. "Tell him to go to a register, that his mother is looking for him."

I waited several minutes. There was no response. I asked her to repeat the message. He did not show up. Please I asked, call the mall security. I was scared. How many times had I seen children disappear? No, I never saw them disappear. I saw them after they were found or before they were found. I didn't even know, but I couldn't think about it anymore. This was my child and he was gone. I knew how important time was, how fleeting it could be. I was beginning to panic. "Please,

I'm going out to the parking lot, maybe he went to look for the car or something."

"M'am," the woman said respectfully, "Maybe you'd better wait until the security comes. They may want a description of the child. They'll need that from you."

"Of course," I replied. "I'm just a little scared. This has never happened before." At least not to me, I thought. God, please don't let this happen to me. I spotted the security guard as he came down the isle. I met him in the middle. "My son, his name is Joel," I began. "I was over there looking at the dresses and when I turned around, he was gone. He's six, about this high with blond hair and blue eyes. He's wearing a blue and white striped shirt, blue shorts and sneakers." Oh, God I hated this. I knew the whole spiel. I knew this scene. I had heard it a hundred times before. I felt faint. The guard called in the information on his radio. The woman at the register explained the announcements she had made on the speaker. The guard called again on his radio.

"Where did you park your car M'am?" he asked in a gentle voice.

"In the front lot, near the cafeteria. I'm sorry," I apologized I don't know what entrance that is."

"That's okay," the guard was an older gray haired man. He patted my hand to calm me.

"That would be the Southeast entrance," he called into his radio. "I think it might be better to come with me to the security office," he said. "They're checking the mall and the parking lot. It'll be easier for them to find us when they locate him."

I followed the man to the office holding Harmony in my arms and dragging the stroller behind. We sat down on the cold vinyl seat and waited. It seemed like forever, but I'm sure it was only minutes later. A stocky Latin guard came walking through the door with Joel in hand. I started to cry. I was sure I was over reacting. The whole ordeal had probably not lasted more than thirty minutes, but I cried anyway.

"Joel," I called to him. "Oh my God, you scared me. Where were you?"

"I went to get my toy out of the car. I was coming back Mom. You didn't have to worry." He looked up at the young guard for permission to let go of his hand. The guard released him and he ran into my arms. "The car was locked anyway," he said.

I looked up at the guard. "Thank you." I then turned to the older guard now seated at the desk. "Thank you so much for your help."

"That's what were here for. And you young man," he said standing up looking down at my son. "Next time you need something from the car, what are you going to do?"

"Ask my mom," he said sheepishly holding on to my legs.

"Okay," he said, "Don't forget that either."

Less than a week had passed when I saw the same parking lot on TV. A little boy, six years old was missing from the identical spot. I turned the sound up. They had a picture of the child on the screen. He was a dark haired boy dressed in little league outfit holding a baseball bat. He had been with his mother shopping the cameras panned out to the parking lot again. I reached for the phone. "Mom, turn on the TV," I said. "There's a little boy named Adam. Get the information because I don't want to watch it anymore. I'm afraid it might influence me. We have to help him!"

This was an unsolicited case. No one had asked for our help this time, not the police or his parents. I just felt needed to help in some way. All I could think was there, but for the grace of God go I.

My mother showed up with her notebooks and a small tape recorder. Joel jumped up to hug his grandmother and Harmony tagged along after him. After a short explanation about what we had to do, Grandma gave them each a treat and their father agreed to watch them while we retreated to the back room to work.

My mother looked for a plug for the recorder. "I know it might not record," she said. "But I thought it was worth a try. It's hard to write every word down as your talking."

"Yeah, I'm surprised you do it as well as you do," I said plugging the recorder in. "Your pretty fast with the pen."

"It's not so much keeping up with you, it's trying to watch you while I do. You know it's not so easy on this end either. Sometimes I watch you going through these things and just when I think I can't take it anymore, you blurt out all the answers. You know you're still my daughter and letting you go though all this so many times is pretty harsh on me."

"I guess we all gotta do what we gotta do," I said massaging her shoulders while she set up the recorder.

"Alright," she announced. "Are you ready?"

"As ready as I'm ever going to be," I said wedging myself comfortably between two large pillows on either side of me.

My mother began her hypnotic induction and before she finished I was long gone into some nether world. "Jeanne Marie," she called. "Can you hear me all right?"

It was difficult to speak sometimes. I could hear her just fine. I just couldn't get my mouth to cooperate so I gave answers using the fewest words possible. We were both aware of this difficulty, so we agreed to fill in the details after I woke up. "Yes," I managed to answer finally.

"Good. Jeanne Marie, I'm going to hand you a picture of a boy who is missing. I want you to feel this picture and tell me where he is. Tell me where Adam is," she repeated placing the photograph between tips of my fingers.

I held the photo, placing it firmly between both palms and then running my fingers over his face. Within a minute or so, I answered. "He is here."

"Where are you Jeanne Marie?"

I looked around to see. "It looks like... a house. I'm in a house." I tried to find something distinctive but it seemed dark. I couldn't see much.

"Look around you Jeanne Marie, do you know where you are?" She asked.

I suddenly felt like a child. "No," I felt like I was going to cry as I looked around. I was scared.

"Are you alone?" She asked.

I stopped feeling for a moment to look around once more. "No," I answered.

"Who is with you?"

I looked beside me. "A man."

"Do you know who he is?"

"No," I said in small child's voice.

"What does he look like?" My mother's voice was now condescending. She was talking to the child.

"Big."

"What else? Can you tell me what he's wearing?"

I stretched all the muscles in my throat and my mouth trying to answer her questions. "Hair; long, dark, uncombed, beard. Dirty, everything is dirty. Clothes, tee shirt, black jeans. Arms, big, dark hair, tattoo."

"Describe the tattoo, Jeanne Marie. Tell me what is looks like."

"Letters, A, H, wings."

"Can you see his face Jeanne Marie? Look carefully at his face. His eyes, try to focus on his eyes. Can you see his eyes? Very clearly now look into them."

I knew what she was doing. If the child could not tell us anything, we had to go through his abductor. "I see them," I said. Then like lightening I was suddenly looking through them. It was strange though, something was wrong in his mind. Things didn't appear right. They were distorted somehow. Drugs, the man was on drugs. He was between worlds somehow. Part of him was aware and part of him was not, but he knew something was in his head. He began yelling, 'Stop fucking around with my mind.' I didn't know if he was yelling out loud or only in his head. I didn't know what to do. So I continued to watch from within.

He walked outside. I heard his thoughts. He was crude, but he was not the one who grabbed the boy. He was only the one holding him. He thought about the west coast; California, pornography, drugs and money. The boy suddenly flashed into his mind. He was too hot, too hot now. He would have to sink him. I did not know what this meant. I saw pictures in his mind. He would head west. I knew the road. My God, I knew where they were!

I could hear my mother's voice in the background. I knew she was asking questions, but I could not hear them. She sounded far away. The man was yelling again and pounding his ear on one side. 'Get the fuck out of my mind.' Some part of him knew I was there. Another part only wanted more drugs. They must have been some kind of hallucinogens. Thursday, if they didn't deliver by Thursday he would have to sink the kid. All the plans had gone awry. Television, the boy's face was everywhere. The kid was too hot. I could feel the sweat on my forehead, panic. Then, I saw the final picture flash before my eyes. I let out a blood-curdling scream. "My head, my head, oh my God they've cut off my head."

"Jeanne Marie! Jeanne Marie!" My mother's frantic face was in front of me now. The children were pounding on the door to find out what was wrong with mommy. I could not stop screaming.

"His head, his head," I managed to verbalize. "Oh my God, they're going to cut his head off and sink him into the water. Oh God, they've cut off his head."

"Is he still alive?" My mother demanded.

"Yes, yes but not for long." I said. "Thursday, it will be too late! What is today?"

"Tuesday, today is only Tuesday," she said in a calming voice. "Jeanne Marie, the children are scared. I'm going to the door and tell them everything is all right. Just sit still for a minute and we'll figure it all out." She got up and went to the door. I heard her talk for a minute and close it again. "Now, let's start from the beginning. Are you okay now?"

"Yeah," I rocked myself back and forth, clutching the pillow in front of me. "I'm okay. I'm going to be okay, I promise. I'm sorry," I apologized. "I'm sorry. It was just so…" I buried my face into the pillow. "It was just so horrible. The whole thing, he was just a little boy, and the guy, it was weird, he knew. He kept yelling at me. Inside of his head, he just kept yelling." I wiped the tears from my face with the corner of the pillowcase.

"What do you mean he knew? What did he know?" She asked.

"He was on drugs, maybe LSD or something. I don't know, but he thought someone was messing with his head. I could see his thoughts. I knew what he was thinking. It was awful. I feel dirty. It was so awful. Mom, they're going to kill that little boy!"

"Maybe not, we've got enough information here to take to the police. You know where he is, don't you?" She looked up at me.

"Yeah, I think so." I took a deep breath.

"Do you think you can listen to the tape if I play it. Are you okay enough to fill me in? There are a lot of blanks on the tape. We need as much information as possible."

"I'm alright now. Go ahead and turn it on."

She pressed the rewind and the little cassette rattled until it could go no more. Then she pushed down on the play button and turned up the volume. Her voice was clear. My voice was low but audible. Then I heard it change, first into a child's voice and then back to my own again. We listened to her questions and my monosyllable answers. Then there was a long pause and a voice. It was not my voice or hers. We both looked at each other. It was a man's voice. We couldn't make out the words. It was eerie.

"Did you hear that when it was happening?" I asked her.

"No, that's not something I would have overlooked. Do you remember anything like that while you were under?"

"No, nothing like that, unless it was him, the guy who has the boy. I told you he was angry, crazy, he was on drugs. Do you think it could be him?"

"I don't know she said rewinding it again. "Listen, I'm going to play it again."

We both listened carefully this time. It was a man's voice, but the words were inaudible. It was almost a moaning, but angry somehow. "I don't know, Mom. That's just scary," I said. Just then the tape came to my screams and ended abruptly. "Are you going to play that to the police?"

"I took pretty good notes and you know the rest. I think we should make a copy of the tape in case they want to hear it," she said.

"Whatever you think. But that's really weird," I said.

"It doesn't sound like anything earthly to me, but we'll have to figure that out later. Right now, we have to get this to someone who can help Adam. You can fill in the details on the way."

We drove to the Broward County Sheriff's Department. A young officer was on duty that night. I sat back and let my mother explain things at the desk up front. She talked and every once in while the officer looked around my mother to sneak a peak at me. I couldn't begin to imagine what was going through his mind. But soon enough we were in the back room playing the tape for two young officers. When it ended they looked at one another.

"You said this was in West Broward," the first one turned to me. "If I showed you a map would you be able to show me where you think they are?"

"I think so," I said. He brought out a map and placed it in front of me. Right off this street," I said pointing to it. "And this road, right next to the canal. That's the one he'll take when it's over. He'll be going north."

"How do you know that?"

"I don't know, he knew. It's hard to explain, I just know."

"And the tattoo," he said. "Is it possible that it was H.A. not A.H."

"Entirely possible." I confirmed. "Actually, I was looking at it upside down so that makes sense."

"Have you ever seen a Hells Angels emblem?" The other officer piped in.

"No, I don't think so," I said. Then I thought for a minute. "Oh the wings, like angel wings. It's possible, maybe I have."

"Where the tape breaks off, what were you screaming?" He asked.

"My head," I shuttered trying not to remember. "The boy I mean. The man was going to cut off his head and sink him. I think he meant he was going to throw him into the water. And, it's going to be soon," I added.

"How do you know that?" he asked.

"I just know. He thought it. Someone was supposed to do something by Thursday or he was going to sink him. You have to get there before then."

He looked at the other officer. "Are you thinking what I'm thinking?" he asked him.

"Your guess is as good as mine. But I'm with you," he said.

The first officer turned to me. "We worked on a case a few years ago. I think I know the place your talking about. We found three bodies in a pond right next to an old house out there. Years ago it was a hangout for the Hells Angels. Their favorite execution was to "sink" their victims."

I sat still for a moment. "Then you'll check it out?"

"Yeah, we'll check it out. As a matter of fact," he said looking down at the map. "I know this is a lot to ask, but if my partner and I picked you up in the morning, do you think you could point out the house?"

"I'm pretty sure I can," I said. "But you have to get there in the morning. Tomorrow is Wednesday."

"Is eight o'clock too early?"

"No, I'll be ready." I sighed with relief. Hope was on the way. They would find him, save him from this dreadful fate. My mother drove me home.

"Do you want me to come with you in the morning?" She asked.

"No, actually I feel better now. I can handle it from here. Thanks, but you better get home and I'm going to try and get some sleep."

"Okay, but you let me know in the morning," she said stopping the car in the driveway.

"I will, I promise. Be careful driving home. I love you." With that I got out of the car and went into the house. The children were already asleep. I went to their rooms and just looked at them for a long time.

The next morning I was up early. I was dressed and ready to go by seven thirty. I dropped the children off at the day care center down the street, returned to the house and waited. By eight thirty I was getting nervous, the policemen had not shown up yet. I called my mother. "Do you think we should call them?" I asked.

"I think so," she said. "I have his name and number on a card. I think it's with my notes. I'll call from here and call you back."

She called back within minutes. "They're out of the office. I can't get any other information. Either no one knows about it or no one is talking. I don't understand, it seems like they would have called or something."

"Do you think something went wrong? What if the guy decided not to wait? He wasn't too stable," I added.

"It could be a thousand different things Jeanne Marie. I guess we'll just have to wait and see," she resigned.

The officers never showed that day. Thursday morning the news broke. The boy's head was found floating in a canal on the very same road that I had pointed to on the map. I wondered if it had been the same officers who had found it. This was something I would never know. How important was it anyway? I had failed again. Just once, I prayed, even one time would have made such a difference. It might have made it all worthwhile, just to know that it could be prevented somehow, that all these visions were not totally useless. But it never happened. Not once had the information ever made a difference in saving a life. Adam was dead, and I was left alone to somehow absolve myself of his memory.

For the next seven years my life and the work proceeded in this manner. I worked with my mother on case after case of missing children and unsolved murders. I spent my life peering through the eyes of the dead. I watched their last visions and listened to their last thoughts as I relived the violence and trauma of their experience. I worked with police, organizations, private detectives and the families of the victims. I could not or would not accept payment. I believed that it was a gift. A not so welcomed dark gift that demanded to be given. I had taken on the work.

It seemed somehow that I best served my purpose when I ceased to exist and nonexistence required no support. People heard me when I delivered messages from the lost children. They focused their attention with unbridled interest when my face contorted with pain or grimaced with fear. They watched for gestures and clues of their loved ones. They did not see me. I was invisible. I was only the medium.

I seemed destined to vacillate between these two worlds and neither one would allow me to stay too long. My own life was unstable at best. My marriage had failed miserably and I worked temporary jobs to support my two children. Sometimes I cleaned houses for people. It didn't pay too well but it didn't ask too much from me either. I barely kept a roof over our head and food on our table. It had been years since I had read a newspaper. I feared that even an accidental touch with the face of a victim could bring about a flood of unwanted knowing. I was tired of knowing, tired of feeling. I did not want to die anymore but it was the only life I knew.

The last case I worked on had affected me so deeply I knew I had to quit. I assured myself that I would face only one more death in my life, and it would be a final one. I hadn't known the victim. I had never even heard his name until after his death. He had worked closely with my youngest brother, in a photography studio. I had never heard him mentioned until he was killed.

He had been murdered leaving his friends and family in a state of shock. There were no clues and certainly no rational reasons for the atrocity. The owner of the studio had been a friend of my mothers for several years and was aware of our work with unsolved crimes. She called and asked if we would help. Arrangements were made for the following afternoon.

I was told only that the young man's name was Steven. It was Susan who had brought me the photograph. Susan had been his boss, friend and part time mother for the past few years. Susan was not the type to be prone to any psychic nonsense. She had been the official photographer for the Miami Dolphins for as long I had known her. I once heard Don Schula tell a story about her out running his quarterback while trying to photograph him. And, it was easy to imagine her running along the sidelines with her camera shooting her way to the goal post. She was dynamic, aggressive and quick witted, but not one I had ever expected to request or accept this form of information. Susan came in that afternoon with her good friend Virginia and a sixteen by thirty inch photograph of Steven. My mother explained the procedure to them first and then put me into trance.

I placed my hands onto the larger than life size photo, but the gates had opened too quickly. The pain came gushing into me. "Oh my God, they stabbed me in the face. Oh God help me." I knew I was screaming out loud. As I felt all the blood run out of body I began to shake uncontrollably. My teeth chattered so hard I could not speak, so hard I thought they would break. I began to pray inside that my mother would not hesitate too long to get me back. I was dying, very painfully. And I knew physically that I was close if not already going into shock. She quickly brought me out, but not soon enough. I couldn't warm myself, it was ninety degrees outside and they were wrapping me in wool blankets to get me warm.

It took a while to stop my teeth from chattering. I shoved the side of my finger into my mouth to keep them from breaking. I don't know how long it took, but I was finally able to speak. "Just give me a few minutes." I chattered. "I can't go back to that again." The vision painfully stabbed my memory again and again. It wasn't as though I could close my eyes and it would go away. It lived there now, somewhere behind my eyes, inside of my mind.

"Maybe if I try to look before it happened, maybe I would know what occurred, who did this to me, to Steven I mean. The trauma, it's just too strong and I can't just jump in like that." I wasn't really sure I could handle any of this, whether I would survive if it happened again, but I would remain under the blanket and try once more. I was put under again, this time with numerous hypnotic suggestions of warmth and comfort, as if a suggestion was any match for this event.

I was given his name and address. The only thing I knew was that he had been killed. I did not know how or where. It was early in the afternoon, a short time before his death. I could feel him. I had become some virtual part of him. I could see the visions of his world, peering through his eyes. I felt like an invisible visitor in his mind. I knew what he knew at that precise moment in time. All but one thing, I was aware of his fate, he was not. I knew what horror waited just in front of him, but I could not warn him. All I could do was watch through his eyes and listened to his thoughts as it happened. I had to remind myself, that it was the past, an event that could only be repeated, not prevented.

He sat lazily on his sofa contemplating the completion of his book. He was an artist, and his thoughts reflected his passion for his work. People had been there just a little while ago. They had been workmen. He felt safe and his mind filled with melancholy. There was a knock at the door. He was not in the mood for company, but he forced himself up to answer. A young man stood at the door. I knew his name was John, he was young, maybe eighteen or nineteen, his hair was sort of blondish and he wore dark mirrored glasses that hid his eyes. There was someone else with him that I did not know. I assumed he was a friend of John's. I did not know why they had come.

Steven hesitated, and they invited themselves in and sat down. A conversation began and John began goading him into an argument. The other man was quiet. He didn't talk at all. Steven had a sharp mind and a sarcastic mouth. He began responding verbally, fanning the flames of a senseless argument. I knew that was as close as he had ever come to fighting. He was sensitive, artistic and now temperamental. John started laughing and backed away, but the quiet man was becoming somehow aroused. He was a big man, with dark hair and eyes, he looked Latin, but there was something very peculiar about him. He was more animal than human. An ominous smile came to his face, and within seconds, he just began hurting him.

There were several blows to the stomach. Steven caught his breath and began cursing and yelling at both of them, but the big one just kept hitting. The yelling only seemed to stimulate him. Steven continued to fight the only way he knew how, frantically flailing and cursing at John. His face was bleeding and the animal went wild. Steven now feared for his life, his world was out of control. He remembered the scissors on the table next to him as he was going down and made a futile attempt to grab them. With keen instinct the animal spotted them. At first John just watched. Then, the stabbing began. The first blunt strike was directly into his left eye. They stabbed him again and again until he went from cursing to barely audible pleading for his life, his book, and his pictures. He could not die yet.

"Get me out! Get me out of here now! I can't do this anymore, please get me out, get me out." I screamed and began to sob uncontrollably. "I don't want to do this any more." I left Steven behind. Poor sweet Steven, he was hurting. He had never hurt anyone in his whole life. He had never even been hurt before and now he was dying, slowly and painfully being stabbed and beaten. He was being hurt to death.

I woke up frightened and sobbing, but I had awoken. I was alive. Steven would never wake up again. He would never finish his book. He would not see his parents anymore. He would never again share his gentle and loving nature with his friends. I was all he had, and I had run off and left him there. I had shared his last thoughts, felt his last pains and I could not even help him. I had just left him, and I couldn't stop crying. All the hypnotic suggestions in the world could not help me to stop feeling and I did not want to feel anymore.

My mother tried to comfort me. She spoke softly trying to calm me. Susan and Virginia just sat frozen in some shock of their own. I am sure they had no idea of what to expect, but then again, no one ever did, least of all me. I told them all I was fine. I lied. I told them I just needed a few minutes to collect myself. I held the blanket tightly around me and stared through watery eyes, afraid to close them, afraid to see any more pictures afraid to feel any more hurt.

They began confirming the evidence. I listened unmoved. He had been brutally beaten and stabbed to death. There had been workmen there earlier that day installing an alarm system. Steven was working on a book. He had been working on a photographical journal of Miami Beach. It was to be a historical documentary. For Steven, it was personal, an intimately artistic expression. He wanted to share his visions of the old city. The lens of his cameras, they had been his other eyes. It had been his life long dream to complete this work and he had been close.

Steven had always been sarcastic with his humor. He tended to mouth off easily. It was his defense, his only weapon. Everyone loved his gentleness. No one could ever imagine anyone hurting him. Nothing I had said brought them any information they did not already have, they had known him for a long time. And, with the exception of the first name and the description of the men who had done it, the police reports had contained the rest. It was not enough, but that was all that Steven knew. Consequently, it was all that I knew.

"There is one more thing we can try," my mother suggested. It was actually more of a question than a suggestion. I had rarely seen her waver. My mother always seemed so confident. I knew what she was going to say and I didn't want to do it. She knew if I could see the face of the offender clearly enough, I could somehow jump through his eyes. I could see from a different perspective. I could see through the eyes of the murderer. I knew none of them had any comprehension of what they wanted from me. They did not know what it was like being there, sharing intimately the warped visions of a homicidal maniac. I didn't care about any of them anymore. They did not know how much they asked. But there was Steven, poor Steven I had left him alone and hurting. I could not escape that pain inside of me. I knew I had to go back.

I prepared to go back one more time. This would be the last time. I promised myself. I would never do this for anyone else again. I was told to find John, to look from his eyes this time to know what he knew. This frightened me. If Steven's pain and suffering had become a part of me, wasn't it possible that some unspeakable part of John's murderous thoughts could also become a part of me? There was no one to ask, no one who knew. Before I could finish my thoughts, John was there. He was staring down at me. I was inside of Steven. I focused on John's face and tried to lock it in like a still frame on moving film. This time I would look through his eyes. I would be in his mind.

I was in the room again, watching Steven die. Listening to him plead. I knew the other man, only as a Marriel refugee who had recently come to Miami. He was an animal who loved to hurt people. John was there to let him rough up his prey. He would open the door to a sadistic cat and mouse game. He had not anticipated the murder. When it got out of hand he just watched. It was like a movie that played before him, except it took so long. He did not know why it took so long. When it was finally over he was afraid to leave, afraid of the animal and afraid of the bloody mess he had made.

Growing more and more frightened of the mutilated reality on the floor before him, he began telling the animal to cover it up. Impatiently, he picked up a chair and threw it on top of Steven's bloody remains. He continued yelling, now a little hysterically for the other one to cover it up. Together, they piled furniture on top of it. It was as if the word "it" might reduce a human being to a thing and a pile of furniture might hide what they had done.

When this was finished, they proceeded to clean themselves up, to wash away blood and sweat of the days' labor. They took a shower and changed clothes. Steven's clothes, they had put on Steven's clothes.

They finally left the apartment and John dropped the animal off on a corner on the beach not far from the apartment. John proceeded to go home. I watched carefully, remembering each street he drove. I mentally followed him as he drove up to his house. I saw the front of his house, the bushes that hid it from full view, the driveway and the last three numbers on the mailbox. I knew where he lived.

"The animal is gone. They will not find him in Miami. He is far away. John went home to that house, but they will not find him there. Look for him in jail, for some petty crime. You'll find him there." I didn't know where the last part had come from, but I was done and I wanted to come back now.

I felt cold now. It was no longer a lack of warmth. It was a kind of steely coldness that came from some unidentifiable source. The truth is I didn't really feel the cold at all. It was now as though I had become a part of it. It was no longer uncomfortable. I really didn't feel anything now and even if it was temporary, I was grateful.

They found John. He was sitting in jail, still wearing Steven's tee shirt. He had been arrested for burglary or some petty theft. The home address had been his parent's house. The other man had been a Marriel refugee, one of the criminally insane who had recently arrived in Castro's boatlift. He was picked up some months later in Texas. Steven's parents gave his equipment to another young photographer. I was told that he had agreed to work towards the completion of his book. They also began an organization to help support other parents of murdered children. I never met Steven's parents nor do I know to this day if they were even aware of me. It didn't seem important at the time and I did not want to bring them any more pain. It would not have served any purpose.

Steven stayed with me for a long time. I prayed for the completion of his work. I prayed for peace to conquer his anguish. In time I finally began to release his pain, but the experience was a shared one and as such, it would always remain within me. It had become a part of my memory, a part of my life.

The collective traumas had all been too much. I had too much pain of my own now and resolved that I would not open myself to anyone else's. I set out to make my way into the business world to support my children, but I was totally unprepared for this world and the harder I tried the more in debt I got. I wound up working two or three jobs at a time and this took its toll on my health. I worked as a temp in offices, waited on tables and cleaned houses. Whatever it took to support my children.

My health grew worse. I had lost too much weight and I began to feel as if one day I would simply fade away. It was as though my body might one day just disappear. I was beginning not to care. I thought I might be free then to join all the invisible others who tugged at my soul to join them. My life, to say the least was not going well.

I knew inside it was time to make changes and I had to make them quickly or I knew I could lose my life altogether. I was alone with two young children. I had no financial support. I did not have any health insurance and my body was giving out on me. I needed help. Counseling would take years. I would be dead or vagrant before I got an answer there. I had children to feed. I needed a solution and I needed it soon.

For the past few years through all my difficulties, my mother stood firm telling me that I was running away from my talents, that I was somehow refusing to face this "God given gift." All I knew for certain was that I had two kids and a house to take care of. I couldn't afford to be a mystic. I couldn't afford to be sick either, but I was. For two years now I had adamantly declined to respond to anything to do with psychic abilities, mine or anyone else's for that matter. My mother dropped her last subtle hint about "the work."

She suggested that there were many clairvoyants, psychics and spiritualists who supported themselves and found a place in society without giving up on their gifts. They formed churches or societies and accepted donations for their work. This was true, and I thought of the ones we had met in the past. They all had their little support groups who believed them to be prophets. Followers who trailed after them clinging to every word they said as if it were some divine revelation. People came to watch them perform their minor miracles. They came looking to them for answers to all their problems. I knew that they all had the ability to see from some other place, but I was not sure this made them prophets. I was not sure that this entitled one to become a religion. I was no prophet. Through some accident of nature, I had slipped through the cracks of the barrier that divided the worlds. It had given me a second sight. This allowed me to see many things, but it did not make me wise.

I was still not feeling well. I was out of work and beginning to feel desperate. What if my mother was right? What if I were to just cease to exist if I kept running away from the work? I did not want to continue living other people's deaths. I needed some other source of life. She kept telling me to go talk to some woman in Hollywood named Miss Eleanor. My mother had heard about her center where they were doing some sort of psychic research. "If nothing else," my mother suggested, "she might just be a good person to talk to. She's an old time spiritualist from England. I've heard she's very interesting and she has certainly been doing this for a long time. You never know, just try it, humor me and go talk to her."

I reluctantly agreed. The next day, I called Miss Eleanor. She spoke with a most delightful British accent and invited me to tea that afternoon. Miss Eleanor's institute was in the old section of Hollywood. It had been an old house, converted into an educational facility. The yard was filled with gardens complete with a little wooden bridge crossing over a lily pond forming the entrance way. I knocked on the door and Miss Eleanor came to open it. She was lovely. She had snow-white hair pinned up on top of her head and translucent white skin that covered her thin frame. She belonged to another time, but she was no stranger to this one. Her dress was long and she wore beads that hung below her waist. She moved with all the grace of a true British lady.

Miss Eleanor asked if I would like to tour her facility and I graciously accepted. We entered a large room filled with sunlight and white chairs. There was a podium in front of the picture window. It was beset with baskets of fresh flowers and green plants. Mirrors lined most of the other walls and everything was in white and shades of light green. It conveyed a wonderfully clean and fresh feeling. One room was a metaphysical library, filled with books that had been donated by former students. There were several small offices and a room that remained closed. I assumed that was her private living area. We walked through the great room again and on to the kitchen and breakfast room. Miss Eleanor proceeded to brew some tea and we sat down to talk.

I spoke to her as I would a kind and loving great aunt. I felt comfortable with her, as she was obviously dedicated to her profession and had mastered the bridge between two worlds. She had lived exactly as she believed and had gained my immediate respect. I tearfully poured out my dilemma. I told her about Steven, about my work in the past and how I had so abruptly quit. How this alleged gift had become a gift and a curse at the same time. That it had become a responsibility that had rendered me sick, broke and hopeless.

She had been listening attentively. Then she poured a fresh cup of tea. "Look around you my dear," she began. "This is my work, and this is my life. You cannot separate the two. Everything you see has been given in some way or another. One of the great laws of the universe is based on giving and receiving, one cannot give without receiving, nor can one receive without giving. If you are first to give, at least you are in a somewhat better position to know what you are destined to receive.

The fact is my dear, like it or not you have a special talent. It seems rather clear that you have two choices. You may keep it within yourself, and accept it as something received, or you may give it to others and accept it as something to be given. If you choose to receive this dear, you will have to give from else where, and you must always remember that you were given that choice. If you should decide to give it back to others, then you have opened yourself to receive. It's all a matter of checks and balances, and ultimately everything does balance. Accept every opportunity to give as an opportunity to also receive, and never be afraid to take payment for your services. Otherwise you leave someone else in debt. Take care not to create debts, lest you have to fill them later."

Her speech was a bit circular, and was not particularly profound. I summarized from it however, that I had better accept the fact that my "gift" was a skill and it was okay to support myself by using it. It was work. The only work I knew and I needed to get paid for it. This is the world of matter, and material things matter greatly here. I might only live in this world part time, but my children live here full time and they needed to be supported.

I cried as I drove home. I wasn't really sure why, but I did know it was for me this time. I did not want to end up like Steven. I did not want to die with unfinished work to be done. We had shared much more than pain and death. He had intimately touched my soul. I thought I had abandoned him in his last most tormented moments. Identifying his murderers had been such a hollow victory. It hadn't helped him at all. Vengeance had never been a part of him. He only longed for love, life, and artistic expression. He struggled so hard to complete his work. Perhaps that is what we truly shared. Perhaps it was not so much his death. Perhaps it was the recognition of that longing for life that I had been left with.

All this time, I thought it had been his pain and death that affected me and filled me with fear. I had died a thousand deaths, but surely I was not a coward. I was not afraid of death. No, death was not frightening. It was his life, the incompleteness of it that frightened me. It was the intensity of his vision of life that we shared. It was the illusion of the gift of second sight. It was a non-returnable gift of vision that would ask forever to be given. A powerful gift that required perpetual work, a work that had to be done. I feared all these things. I feared the pain of failure, the offense of incompletion. I feared the painful aloneness that came with this kind of work. This alleged gift of visions was a work so demanding, that it crossed the very boundaries of death.

Perhaps Steven had shared his visions. He had sheared them with me. He had shared them with everyone he had touched through his photographs. Surely he still saw through the mechanical lens of cameras he left behind. Truly he touched many thoughts through the minds and memories of the people he loved. My hopes were high that he would receive fulfillment from work that he had inspired to go on. That had to be it; nothing worthwhile ends with an individual. He had tried with all his heart and soul. What more could he do? What more could life ask from anyone? I only prayed that it was life that was doing the asking. If it was, I needed to know how to answer.

I called Miss Eleanor again the next day. I spoke with her for quite a while on the phone. I told her that I had made the decision to go back to the work. This time however, it would have to be in a different way. Perhaps now, I could work with the living. She suggested I begin by letting people know who I was, by letting them see and hear me speak about the cases I had worked on in the past. I accepted her invitation to give a lecture for the following month. She said she would be happy to help me get started by referring clients to me for readings. I would read for people who were not dead or dying. It was a whole new beginning.

This work wasn't so bad, reading for people who were still alive, people who participated in this world. The problems of the living were so different, so much lighter. I actually enjoyed it. Finances were still a problem, but it was a problem I found that most people shared. It was a problem of life and I was beginning to connect with it. I was beginning to live. I took a job on the weekends with the Psychic Fair. My strange ability was actually becoming an asset.

It was no accident that this Fair was listed in the entertainment section of the Sunday paper. We were a curious circus of sensitives with strange and unmeasured talents. We tickled your curiosity and tested your faith. We surprised you with insights of the past and thrilled you with predictions of things to come. We were all oddities sharing our unique predicament. We spewed words of wisdom we did not author and described visions that come not from our eyes. We were the prophets of our time, appropriately assuming the risks and ridicule befitting our ancient profession.

We all worked at J.C.'s fair, a bonafide Cassadega certified "Psychic Fair". There were no fortunetellers here. We were all ordained ministers at this fair. We all had our cards and J.C. had the legal papers to prove it so. J.C. called himself Doctor Jonathan C. Samuels, and he had the papers to prove that too. You would not see any Gypsies at J.C.'s fair. No soothsayers draped in kerchiefs and coins presided. No magicians and no cultist would be found in his books. And, despite the billing as a fair, there were no sideshows apart from the occasional "free" mini lectures describing the mysteries and marvels of psychic phenomenon.

I was actually having fun. I worked for Mary, one of J.C.'s crew managers. She was affectionately referred to as 'Mother Mary' by all but one gentleman astrologer named Tom. He continued to call her Em, as he had for the duration of their forty some year marriage. Every weekend, for fifteen years, Tom loaded and unloaded the books, trinkets and tarots while Mother Mary poured her home brewed coffee for the crew.

"Tom, I'm making your coffee first, you work so hard, you sit down and the girls will finish. You don't mind finishing up do you girls?"

"Of course not," Cassie, my co-worker winked to me, as if there were a choice. "You know we all love Tom, where would we be without the Sun and the Moon, or without Jupiter and Mercury for that matter."

I smiled back and we continued sorting the books for display onto the seven long buffet tables that lined the entranceway of the room. This weekend we were at the Holiday Inn in Ft. Lauderdale. Hotel meeting rooms were all pretty much the same. A long empty room with multi color carpet, textured wallpaper and ice-cold air vents. The hotels provided skirted buffet tables, chairs and white cloths for the five card tables we used to read on.

Cassie and I had put most of the books out when Philip, another crewmember walked into the room and gave us each a warm welcoming hug.

"We saved the jewelry for you," I chided. Sorting the jewelry was always saved for last. It was the one chore we all tried to avoid.

"That'll teach you to be late," Cassie added with a smile. "But I guess we'll excuse you since Mercury went retrograde this morning. This should be a fun day," she concluded sarcastically. "I'm ready for coffee."

"I've got it all ready. Here's your sugar the cream is already in. You did a wonderful job girls," Mary commended handing us our coffee. It was the only time I ever drank coffee. She made it with such love, and rewards always tasted so sweet.

"So, Phil," Cassie began. "What's the latest on the war zone? Is our fearless leader still making progress?"

"From what I hear, he has certainly crossed the Mason Dixon line. He bought the old town center." Philip continued delicately unwrapping the trinkets. "All he's got to do now is sit and wait for the old gentility to die off."

"Well," Mary chirped in. "Progress is inevitable, and we are all sharing in the benefits."

"That's true," I added as I sipped my coffee. "It also wouldn't be happening without our contributions." This was a dilemma that we all shared, and it was the topic of numerous debates among the psychics at J.C.'s fairs. Cassadega was a lovely little town in central Florida. I believe it was founded sometime in the early thirties by a group of devout spiritualist from up state New York. Originally, the town was used as a winter resort but as time went on, the people retired there and continued to practice their spiritual religion as well as their psychic arts. In time, the town gained quite a reputation as seekers from all over the country began making spiritual pilgrimages, hoping to receive a message or two from the world beyond. J.C., being above all an astute businessman began purchasing the land surrounding the tiny psychic haven. The elderly founders held off the commercialization of Main Street as long as they could, but J.C. already owned one side of the street. The money we raised at the fairs went directly to the purchase of the town. The town would soon become no more than neon psychic parlor for the tourist. It was a sad, but inevitable truth.

"I don't know what's happened to Opal," Mary announced, interrupting our conversation with a pained voice. She put her hands together in a prayerful expression and released a sigh. "She's late again. I hope nothing's happened to her. She has such problems poor thing."

Opal was the fifth member of our working crew. Philip and Cassie rolled their eyes up, like elder siblings in reaction to Mother's predictable response. We all knew Opal would be in as soon as the morning work was done. She would enter with breakfast from McDonald's and a tale of weekly woes that would cause Mother Mary to clutch her heart in empathy for the injustices done to this poor unfortunate child. My pity had been replaced long ago by utter amazement at the series of events that occurred in poor Opal's weekly sagas.

"It's 9:00 o'clock. We're just going to have to start without her. We can't start late, if it ever got back to J.C. that we started late... why what in heaven's name would J.C. say?" Mary was always worried about what J.C. would say.

"Well Mother," Philip began in his most patronizing tone, "I suppose he would say, let's get the show on the road."

"Philip's right." Mary reluctantly conceded. "Come on Tom," she motioned. "We'll just have to start without her. It's time for the circle."

We all grasped hands and gathered round for the prayer. Mary asked Philip to lead. A request Philip quite naturally accepted. He paused as he thoughtfully closed his eyes, but before the first word could be delivered, this tranquil scene was interrupted.

Opal made her entrance. The only thing coordinated about Opal was her clothes. She dropped her briefcase with a thud as she attempted to juggle her McDonald's bag o'breakfast, her oversized purse and a bulky white sweater. The purse was the first to fall. Then assorted toiletries, bits of paper receipts and cards, cigarettes, wallet and loose change spilled over the top of the table and across the floor. Poor Opal, she looked up and shrugged her shoulders. "Oops," was her only comment. She hesitated for a moment, waiting no doubt to see if anyone was going to come to her rescue.

"Oh, this is just perfect." She went on picking up a few personal articles. "I lost my other job, of course I only had it three days, but this has just been a terrible week. And now I'm on my way to work again and my car broke down. Something must be trying to tell me something. I wish I knew what it was. It's probably trying to tell me to stay home. Come to think of it, I don't even have a home right now, so it can't be that. Anyway I had to leave the car down the street. I had no money, so some man helped me get it to a station but I don't know what to do. Oh, I'm sorry." She apologized, just becoming aware that we were all suspended in the circle. Dropping the makeup she had just picked up back onto the table, and leaving the rest of her scattered effects on the floor, she walked up to join the group.

Philip was not partial to being upstaged by such nonsense, but, being the gentleman he was, he put away his mental daggers and continued despite the lost momentum. Cassie tapped her foot impatiently, Tom shook his head silently smiling and Mary grimaced with pain. Prayers being said, thanks being given, the circle ended and the day began.

"They're all good psychics." Mary began her Mercurial speech to the first customer. "I can't tell you which one to pick. Each one uses a different tool. Some use cards, some use psychometry, touching objects, but they're all equally good. You just pick the one you feel comfortable with. There is a book on the table." She opened it up and began her description of each of the psychics. "Come on in," she welcomed two women who were walking through the door. "The first one is Philip. Philip reads with tarot and numerology. He is also a well known teacher and lecturer. That's him in the back, in the purple shirt and black jacket. Next we have Cassie. Cassie also reads with tarot. She's well versed in astrology and is a fine lecturer. That's Cassie," she pointed. "With the dark hair wearing the white dress. Then we have Opal. Opal reads with tarot and also with regular playing cards. That's Opal in the blond hair wearing the pretty blue outfit. And we have Jeanne Marie," she pointed to me with her chin. "She's the little petite one with dark hair sitting at Philip's table. Jeanne Marie is a psychometrist, she reads from objects like watches, jewelry or photographs. Jeanne Marie is well known for her work with missing persons. She also uses little Austrian crystals. And, last but certainly not least, we have Tom, our resident Astrologer. He's been written about many times in the newspaper. This is a picture of him." She pointed to the book containing a yellowed news clip of her husband. "You're welcome to take your time and look through the book. You'll find a little biography of each of the psychics there." She continued, quoting the various prices averaging about a dollar a minute as the women began leafing through the book. "How many minutes would like sir?" She asked the first gentleman who walked in.

He was a nice looking young man in his late thirties. He was dressed very causally, but wearing an expensive watch. He put his sunglasses in his top pocket and reaching into his pants pocket he leaned over to Mary, "If you were getting a reading, who would you pick?"

"I couldn't tell you that sir, the one who would be best for me might not be the best one for you. Each one is talented in a different way. They each have a different style," she declined. "I don't have any psychic abilities, I leave that to the readers." He considered her advice and chose the astrologer. "Good choice," Mary reassured him, handing him a ticket. "You take this ticket over to him, and enjoy your reading. Now ladies, what can I do for you?" She asked.

"I don't know," the first one replied. "I've never gone to a psychic before. What do people usually come here for?"

"It's hard to say," Mary answered thoughtfully. "Some of the people that come in here have such problems," she sighed. "Others are just curious, but we are always here for the ones who need us and we help. These readers are really very dedicated."

The second woman now joined in. "Oh, I see psychics all the time," she assured her friend. "Some of them are very accurate, go see Philip, I've seen him before, and I'm going to see Cassie," she turned to Mary as she opened her wallet to pay.

"How many minutes would you like with the readers ladies?" Mary asked.

"We'll take the thirty minute one," she replied handing Mary the money.

I was spared from an early start. I stood up and smiled as Philip's first reading approached. Heading back to my own table, I sat in my usual spot in the back of the room. My black velvet pad was laid out on the table before me, but the tiny crystals were still safe in their little black pouch. I hesitated to pour them out of the bag. For some reason I was in no hurry to begin this morning, but work was inevitable, and that's what I was there to do. I opened the pouch and poured the sparkling stones into the light. I picked up one of the stones and felt it between my fingers. By themselves, they were nothing more than cubic zirconias, lab grown crystals. They were created as nothing more than inexpensive substitutes for diamonds. Each stone was unnaturally perfect, gem cut in all the traditional geometrical jewel shapes and sizes. Alone, each was nothing more than the translucent part of a pretty decoration. Together, the colorful little pile of stones became a reflection of destiny.

The tranquil moment soon ended. It was disrupted by the presence of a disturbing new energy that seemed to fill the room. I knew it was not benign. As I looked up, I saw two women talking to Mary. I could not hear what they were saying; I could only feel the surging sense of urgency they both conveyed. The petite girl turned around and looked straight at me. Her face was not that of a girl. It was the face of a very distraught woman. I could feel each step as she approached, fortified with purpose and determination.

"Here," she said, pulling a child's stuffed animal from her bag. "This is all I have, my little girl... she's gone. I need to know where she is... please..."

Her sentence broke off. I knew it was all she could say. I reached out my hand and accepted the stuffed unicorn. It was no longer white, and looked well warn from a child's expressed love. I looked at the face before me, swollen from too many tears and lined with a fear that only mothers know. I took a deep breath and closed my eyes. Soon I descended into the familiar darkness. I felt a cold wave sweep the blood right through me, and before I could release the child's toy from my hands, the flood of visions had already begun. "No, no, Jenn," I whispered, I knew the sounds were probably barely audible, because it was so difficult to speak. As I struggled back to conciseness, I spoke softly, trying not to alarm her. "This isn't the time or place to do this." I said, "I need some help. Can you to come to my house tonight. The child's father is near, is he traveling?"

"Yes," she answered, with hope beginning to stir. "He is on his way back from Texas, I'm meeting him at the airport this afternoon." She paused for a moment and looked into my eyes. "Her name is Jennifer, I call her Jenn."

I took one of my cards and began writing my address on the back. "Come about seven, my phone number is on the front. If you have a photograph of her, bring it. I'll do everything I can."

She gratefully took the card. "I'll be there," her voice had lifted. She stood up and we both looked down at the toy. She picked it up and returned it safely back into her bag. "Thank you."

Philip had just finished his reading and instinctively came walking up behind me. He placed both hands on my shoulders. "Good God," he exclaimed. "What on earth did you touch into? You're white as a sheet. Breath," he commanded, as he continued to rub my shoulders. "Are you okay?"

"Not at the moment, but your a psychic." I smiled faintly. "And you already know that." Philip left his hands resting on my shoulders, and I was thankful for that.

Mary was already on her way to my table. "What happened? The lady bought an extended reading, what did you say to her, she left already?"

"It's alright," I reassured her. "I told her I couldn't do something like that here. It's not something I could do in a light trance, and I can't do it alone. I'm going to do it at home tonight."

"You do what ever you think is best to help her, that poor woman. It's a good thing J.C. isn't here. You know J.C.; he would have a fit if he knew. But you do whatever you have to do to find that little girl. And you keep the ticket too." She lowered her voice, "I know you need the money."

I thanked Mary for the ticket and her support. As the reality of the situation began to register all I could think of was how much I did not want to do this again. I liked being here. I had peers. I belonged. We dealt with people, with faith, perspectives and the whole of array of human intercourse. This was life, and life could be shared. I didn't want to go back. I didn't want to be alone. I didn't want to die any-more.

4

Of White Bones & Sailing Ships

I called my mother to help. If the little girl was dead, I did not want to look for her alone. I thought of my own children. I hoped they would never have to know of these things.

My mother arrived first that night. No matter how she tried to hide it, I knew that somewhere inside she liked the excitement of the thing. It was not the tragedy, but the mystery and the involvement of it all. Perhaps I would too if I were somewhere else, but I knew all too well where I would be.

The mother arrived with the child's father. They were no longer married. He was in the military and had just flown in from somewhere out west. They were of course both pale and worried. I opened the front door and she began. "I will give you anything, I have a house, it's all I have but I will sign it over to you. Just help me, please help me find my little girl."

My heart was breaking and I hadn't even started. "I don't charge anything. I already told you I would help you however I can. This is my mother. She will explain how we work. Sit down and make yourself comfortable. It might take a little while."

So many people came in like that. You can understand why it was so difficult to accept anything from them. Unfortunately there were too many who did accept their offers. Charlatans and self-professed psychics who would take everything these families had. My mother proceeded to warn the woman, in her own motherly way about this very thing.

"I'm going to tell you something right now young lady," she said. "And you need to listen. Don't ever do that again. I know you're scared and your hurting but giving away your house and everything you own will not help your daughter. And anyone who tells you different is not there to help you. They're only there to steal from you. Do you understand?"

The girl sniffled and hugged my mother. "Thank you," was all she could manage to stammer out. "Thank you both."

I motioned to my mother to get started. I could not afford to get any further involved with emotions. We all sat down and my mother repeated the hypnotic procedure, as we had so many times before. It was not long before I was handed the photograph and through my closed eyes, I watched the little girl's fate.

There were flashes of her bike the man and the pickup truck. He had strangled her. I saw all these things. They had already taken place. The most horrible thing was, the little girl knew what had happened. She was bright and articulate. She knew I was there with her. "It's broken," she said sadly.

"My body, it's broken and naked. He took my clothes off. I'm cold. Please," she begged me. "Don't let them look at me. I don't have any clothes on. I don't want them to find me."

I tried to tell her that they would cover her, when they found her. She cried and begged me to make them stop looking. "Just tell them to wait, until there are only bones. If they wait," she assured me. "They will turn white from the sun. Then they would be clean again. Then it would all be okay. I won't mind so much then."

I was torn. I knew her parents needed to find her but I knew too exactly how she felt and I did not want to betray her. The truth was I only knew that she was in a field, somewhere in west Broward. My heart ached for her. She was only a little girl. I had only spoken out loud about the bike, the man and the pickup truck. I could not speak the rest in front of her parents. I told them only that we needed to search in a field in West Broward. It was a large county. I wasn't sure exactly where to begin. The mother thought she knew the man with the pickup truck I had described. They rushed out to contact others. They had leads to follow. It was enough to begin a search.

I told my mother after they left what had happened. That I knew she was dead and that her little girl did not want to be found. I cried and could not be consoled. I had my mother, she did not and she was only a little girl.

The next night we received a call. The mother thought she might know the field I had spoken about the night before. She asked if I would go there. There was a search party organized to help. I agreed to go. I hoped that at least I could see that she would be covered when she was found.

A female detective walked over and asked me what I felt. "She has been asphyxiated," I said. "She was dumped in a field. She's cold and wants to be covered." Tears began to well. I tried to remember that there were others, still searching; still hoping and I prayed that somehow I could be wrong.

The detective's face was filled with concern and she clenched her teeth. "It's just so damn frustrating," she blurted out. "It never gets any easier."

It was nearing three a.m. Hope dwindled with each passing hour. Another compassionate police officer asked me to follow him. As we walked he warned me again to watch out for water moccasins, with each progressive step we sank deeper into the mud. "I know you must be exhausted," he said gently. "I thought the quiet might help you get a direction."

"I'm sorry." I apologized. I wanted to cry again, but I was just too tired. No one understood how it worked. Everyone waited for some divine inspiration to come spewing from my mouth, and there was none. I did not have the heart to tell them that there just wasn't anything to tell them. That out here I didn't know any more than they did. I only saw visions. I did not know any more than that. Then I tried in vain to tell them, "I just can't feel her anymore. I only saw what happened. I don't know where she is."

My mother walked up and put her hand on my shoulders. She guided me silently back to the dirt road. As I lifted my head I saw the girl's mother walking towards me. She approached like a stoic soldier, mounting her courage, leading the vigil. I was sure the woman could move mountains with sheer determination.

"I know you won't lie to me." She began, with careful deliberate words, "but I have to know…she's gone isn't she?"

I nodded "yes." We embraced and the sobs were no longer silent.

The little girl's body was found two weeks later in a vacant field in west Broward. My heart fell when I heard. It had not been long enough. Her body was discovered naked and exposed. I knew she was no longer cold, but there were photographs, television reporters and gawking spectators. I cried for her and with her. I will always remember her, sadly, as the little girl who wanted nothing more than to be clean white bones when she was found.

Newspapers called, and television reporters tried to reach me. I unplugged the phones, and essentially hid from the world. I could not speak. No one knew why. I did not want to work anymore, but I knew I could not hide for too long. You cannot hide from life anymore than you can hide from death, sooner or later they would find me. Sooner or later, they would find us all.

I went back to work at the fair. It was a strange lot, but it had become my extended family and I felt a sense of belonging. They were all understanding and supportive to me. Not that my own family wasn't, but most of my friends still greeted me to the tune of twilight zone and all four of my beloved brothers were relentless with their witticisms. I had always been the strange one in the family, but at least now it was sort of an open issue. There was something nice about that. I might have been part of the sideshow in the circus of psychics, but it was filled with colorful people. It was happy, alive and I liked what I did for the most part. I was comfortable and I was able now to laugh with them. I was not so alone.

It was during this time that I met Dash. We met at a chamber of commerce luncheon. A friend had invited me to join her there. Everyone was dressed in suits and ties but Dash stood up in a red golf shirt to claim the door prize he had won. After grandstanding a humorous and lengthy acceptance speech, my friend decided to introduce us. "That's Dash Abram. He's one of Ft. Lauderdale's most eligible bachelors," she whispered. "Everyone knows him. Come on you'll meet him. Just be careful, he's a real womanizer."

She was right. On our first date, he took me to a black tie charity dinner at some socialite's mansion on Los Olas. In attendance were businessmen, celebrities, and local politicians, none of whom I recognized or even knew of before that night, but Dash introduced me to them all. Dash had been an architect in New York. Then he became an attorney, a judge and finally a businessman in Florida. He was charming, brilliant and even at twenty years my senior, I found him irresistibly sexy.

That night, he took me to his penthouse overlooking the ocean. As we stepped through the front door, a huge glass wall adjacent to us framed a magnificent view of a luminous full moon rising from the dark sea. "Look," he said gently kissing my fingertips. "I had that painted there just for you." Then he took off my wrap and dropped it to the floor. "Beautiful, bella bella lunna." With both hands he cupped my face and began kissing my lips. Then he bent down and removed my shoes, kissing each foot as he did. As he moved me gently towards his bedroom I was so mesmerized by him I hardly noticed that he was undressing me along the way. Articles of clothing were dropping to the floor, strewn along a moonlit path to his room. By the time we reached the edge of his immense bed, I was completely naked and surrendering to his every caressing touch.

Sex with this man was a religious experience. I was in love, instantly. What else could it be? "You're young, beautiful and absolutely delicious," he said covering my white breast with the dark linen sheets. "But I've got to be honest sweetheart. I don't want to hurt you. I'm not the kind of man you should be with."

"Why not?" I asked playing with the covers between us.

"I have a reputation," he said very seriously. "It's not a good one. And trust me, it's all true."

"I know. I don't care."

"Don't say that Jeanne Marie. Some women should be married and they should be taken care of. I'm just not that kind of guy. I don't marry. I'm not the right man for you."

"You think I need a man to take care of me. That I'm a nice girl?"

"Exactly. And I'm not a nice guy."

"Dash I've been married. I don't want to get married again, probably ever again. Besides, how nice can I be? Look who I'm in bed with."

"I don't know sweetheart, you felt awfully nice to me," he said smiling. "But Jeanne Marie, there's more to it than that. I'm the shallowest person I've ever known, and trust me I've known a lot of them. I introduced you to half of them tonight."

"You did!" I smiled. "And it was great. I loved it."

"You're different sweetheart."

"What do you mean different?"

"I don't know how to explain it, but there's more to you. You have depth."

"You mean my work. I'm spiritual Dash, a clairvoyant not a nun!"

"Jeanne Marie, you're the angelic type. My type is more... Well, you met Sheila tonight. Our illustrious hostess, you know the blond in the flashy gold gown who almost spilled her drink on you."

"Sheila is your type? Dan's wife?"

"Before she was Dan's wife."

"Oh God, how could you?" I said covering my face with the sheet.

"I told you. I'm completely shallow," he said kissing my neck again.

Dash was the kind of man every mother warned her daughter to stay away from. I would never have to worry about marriage with him, he was one hundred percent safe and I loved him completely. Dash flew me to Vegas and Reno. He gambled at the crap tables and I meditated at the foot of the desert's mountains. These get aways were always at a moments notice. They were short lived but filled with excitement. We dressed up in fancy clothes and attended all the major events in town. It was perfect. While Dash procured his business and social contacts, I had the perfect opportunity to observe all the frivolous and interesting people he introduced me to. With Dash I was always noticed but never seen. When I was with Dash, I was his girlfriend and nothing more. With him there were always compliments, without any questions and continuous romance, without responsibilities.

Dash and I agreed early on that we would never interfere in each other's personal lives. Anything deeper than last week's gossip was simply not discussed. It was an honest relationship, and sex and fantasy were the substance of our union. For me it was a divine diversion to an otherwise all too serious mystical life. We never lived together. When I went home, I dedicated myself to my spiritual work and my children. Dash was never idle. He had plenty of business to take care of and he was always scheduling social functions for us to attend. He was the perfect compliment to my life.

Then came Monday morning. I woke up like Cinderella to the many dark cinders that obscured my fantasy. I cleaned the house and dropped the children off at school. John, my younger brother had been in a motorcycle accident. I thought I'd stop by to see how he was doing. He was still home recuperating. Two of my brothers and a few of their friends had also stopped by to visit. It was not even noon, but they were all sitting around drinking beer and talking trash. I walked in on the tail end of their conversation.

"Have you seen his new place, it's a dammed fortress," Raymond said taking a swig of the beer in his hands.

"Seen it!" Jason said, waving his lit cigarette like a flag. "I watched em build it. You should see fucking alarms he put in that place. Every single inch of it is electronically monitored. I saw em install it, a whole little room of TV screens. He's got the best system money can buy, guaranteed impenetrable. Hey why not, he's making some serious bucks. I'd like to be doing half of what he is, I'd be fucking rich too."

"What's the guy doing showing you all that shit Jason?" One of his friends asked. "He must not know you too well."

"He knows me plenty," Jason answered.

"Yeah, it must be nice. Big house on the beach, boats parked out back, drugs whenever you want em, and all that money. How many boats does Gary have now anyway?" Raymond asked.

"Oh lets see now, counting his latest formula one Cigarette with twin three fifties and his fifty foot Hatteris, I'd say about five." Jason answered.

"Beats the hell out of working for a living. Except for an occasional pick up and delivery of course," Raymond lit his cigarette and took a draw and blew it out again watching the smoke curl in front of him. "But I could sure learn to live with that. Damn I'd love to be in his shoes right now."

Gary was someone we had all known since we came to Miami. He had grown wealthy from the drug trade. Everyone present knew as well as I did that Raymond had a serious drug problem, but they all went on and on making a hero of Gary. Suddenly something began to brew inside of me, like hot stew boiling up in a cooking pot, ready to spill over the sides. I had never experienced this feeling before. Then, without warning, it was as if some powerful being had just pushed me aside and took over my body.

I made a great sweeping motion as I spun around. Then I pointed my finger directly at my eldest brother. Whatever it was inside of me began to speak, with my mouth. "Mark my words," I droned. "It may be two weeks, two months or two years. Gary may possess all the wealth in this world, but he will lose everything including his life. Be very careful who you choose to follow or you'll wind up in the very same boat."

The room was suddenly still, no one moved, and now I was afraid. I didn't know where those words came from but they frightened me terribly. Whatever the presence had been, it was gone, and only I was left standing there. I did not really know what to do at that point. They all just sat there stunned with their mouths opened. I did not wait for their response. They all thought I was weird enough as it was. I could only imagine what they thought after that. I just turned around and ran out the door.

Two weeks later I watched the evening news as they showed the bodies of Gary and his young pregnant wife carried out of their plush fortress on the beach. Someone had walked in, and shot them down with machine guns. Colombian drug lords it was assumed. They had passed through the security gates, the guard dogs and the impenetrable alarm system. They still wore their gold Rolexes when their bullet-riddled bodies were found near the pool. They still had cash in their pockets and none of their possessions had been touched. I sat in front of the TV, stunned. Gary had lost everything, including his life. I was frightened. What would happen to Raymond? No one had ever mentioned the eerie incident since it happened. They all knew. Raymond knew, but would he remember?

I thought of Gary. He had not always been involved with drugs. Once he had saved my life. Gary loved boats and he loved the water. At one time I think he had even trained for the Olympics as a swimmer. Before that, he had been a lifeguard. He had been tall with Nordic features, always tan and very handsome. One summer my family and I were out on his boat. I wanted to stay home and study, but my parents had insisted I go.

I sat on the bow rocking with the waves as they hit the side of the boat. Jason and his friend had gone diving for grouper while we waited above. "How deep is it?" I called out.

"It's only about fifteen feet," Gary answered.

The sun was beating down and it was hot. "Is it okay if I dive in?"

"Sure, go ahead."

I dived, and as I did the bottom of my bikini caught on the ornament on the bow of the boat. When I surfaced I looked up. There it was, the bottom half of my bathing suit hanging on the bow of the boat. Raymond ran over and grabbed it. "Looking for these?" He taunted.

By then everyone on the boat was laughing. "Just throw them to me," I yelled back.

"You're going to have to ask nicer than that," he said twirling the bottom to my suit in the air.

"Raymond, I'm not kidding. Just throw me the damned thing."

"Why? Is it cold in there?"

"This is not funny," I yelled. "Will you just throw me my suit, you idiot."

"Idiot, I don't think you're in much of a position to be calling me and idiot," he said. "Just for that I think you aught to come up here and get them yourself."

Finally my mother stepped in. "That's enough Raymond, throw her the bathing suit."

"Awe, come on. I was just having a little fun," he protested.

He finally threw them down. I slipped them on and began swimming, as far away from the boat as I could get. Someone yelled out to me. I think they were trying to tell me not to go too far, but I didn't care. I just kept swimming. I wasn't too far away when the temperature suddenly changed. I felt a stream of cold water, and before I could stop, it had become a river. I knew I was in a current. I tried to swim to the side, but I couldn't. I couldn't get anywhere, and I couldn't feel anything but the cold rushing water carrying me even further out to sea. It was Gary who dove in and pulled me out of that dangerous current. It was Gary who had saved my life, and now he was dead. Gary, his wife and his unborn child, a whole family was dead. The warning, I thought, that terrible warning. Did I somehow cause it to happen? Maybe I should have warned him too. I hadn't even tried. If I had, would it have helped?

All I knew was that for me, life would go on. For the next couple of years I continued to struggle financially, but I provided for my children and lived vicariously through the fairytale moments I spent with Dash. Then something happened, and I began asking those questions all over again.

It had been almost two years since Gary had been killed. I was working in Coral Gables, at the hotel where the weekly psychic fair was being held. I had come in late that morning, so I silently walked in, sat down at my table and poured my tiny crystals onto the black velvet pad. I nodded my head to Mary, signaling I was ready to work. It was during the fourth or fifth session when a note was slid under my pad, as I read for the person before me. When I finished, I opened the curious note. The scrap of paper read simply, call your mother. It's about your brother. I called the number on the paper.

I was told that Raymond was dying. He was in a coma and would not regain consciousness. I was to meet my family at the V.A. hospital that was somewhere near Jackson Memorial. I had a vague recollection of where Jackson Memorial was, but not a clue as to the location of the V.A. Hospital. The sun was setting and darkness was quickly moving in. I drove towards the hospital. It was a huge complex. Somehow I drove right to the entrance. I parked the car and walked straight to the intensive care unit. I don't remember following any signs, and to this day I do not know how I found my way there, but I walked in, right into the arms of my frantic parents. "This can't happen. God won't let this happen. There has to be something we can do."

They tried to assure me that there was nothing anyone could do. That it was in God's hands now, but I refused to believe this. I knew he was in the room next to us and I wanted to see him. My mother took me by the hand and tried to prepare me for what I was about to see. I assured her I was okay, but it was everything I could do to fight the faint feeling in the pit of my soul. I saw him immediately as we walked through the glass doors of the I.C.U.

"Stand on the other side of him!" I was frantic I could see a gray fog rising from his body. He was trying to leave and I could not let him. I would not let him. "Grab his arm, and push all the energy you have into him." I held onto his right arm while my mother held his left. "Whatever you do don't let go!" I stood firm. I grounded myself, growing invisible roots through the floor, through the ground and into the very core of the earth. I became a living battery and within a few minutes his hand began to move.

My mother and I held tight. I knew she did not understand exactly what was happening, but she did not move and she did not let go. Then it began to happen. He began to wake. We acknowledged the slight movement of his eyelids to one another with our own eyes. Neither of us could speak, but we both knew. It had worked. His eyes slowly opened. He recognized my mother. Tears welled up in my eyes as I heard him try to speak to her. He was back. A miracle had taken place and he had come back. He was alive. I was sure he would recover. He had a choice. Who would not choose to live?

By the following week he began a miraculous recovery, or so it seemed. He spoke to each member of the family. "Jeanne Marie," he told me. "You're the strong one." He looked into my face but not my eyes. "You always were. You'll survive. No matter what happens, Jeanne Marie, you'll survive."

I was angry. I didn't even know why, but I was angry. Within days, he was in a white metal bed, in a sterile room. The gray fog had somehow consumed him. His proportions paled in comparison to the size he had always been. He had always been my big brother, but now he looked so small, so frail. His entire aura had been nearly depleted and I knew he would soon die.

The last time my brother spoke to me, he looked into my eyes. The life was all but extinguished in his own. "Jeanne Marie, would you go to the store and get me some rock candy…please?" I looked at him incredulously. After all these years, he had asked me to buy him rock candy. My throat swelled shut. I could not question nor could I answer. I just left. I went to get him the candy. Somehow he knew. Somehow we both knew. Raymond died before I returned.

I didn't speak to anyone for a long while. I did not understand what the gray blanket of fog had been. I only knew that it did not belong to this world. A few days later my mother asked me to write the eulogy for my brother, who had requested he be buried at sea. Jason, my younger brother would read it, as he was now the eldest son. I first wrote in long hand and then felt it should be typed, and so I typed:

To my brother: Raymond Born February 4, 1950. Buried at sea January 12, 1986. We have all come here today Raymond, mostly just to let you know that we love you. As a brother, we have never known not loving you or not knowing you. Being the first-born was no easy task. You paved the way for us all. We all got the benefits of your experiences as well as your mistakes.

No one has ever questioned the love we share in this family, and it's grown larger and stronger because of you. Loving and sharing was always synonymous with home to you. The first time we came to Florida you met a friend who not only became your life long friend, but in the years to come became a part of our family. You brought Jimmy, and so the rest of us followed, the family grew. Then you went to the other side of the world, to Korea. We all shared in your anticipation and desire to bring a part of that world home. You gave us Kim, your wife, and as the world became a little smaller, the family became a little larger. Later we all got to experience being expectant aunts and uncles, grandmothers and grandfathers, with the adoption of your two beautiful children from so far away.

Our home and family has always had a policy of open doors to friends and family members alike. If one loved you, you were destined to become a part of us all. There was only one catch at our house. The only thing you ever had to watch out for was your room. Rooms were always at a premium. Every time one of us moved out there was someone standing in the hallway ready to move in. You had to put your name on a waiting list and hope you didn't need it before the next wedding. We all came back once or twice, excluding Richard, our youngest brother, who waited a long time for his own room and is taking no chances on losing it.

We all shared some of the best times of our lives on or in the water. We have bathed together, swam together and traveled together, always sharing the common waters. We have all shared a lot of happiness and love in these waters and now we all hope you will take some of that happiness and a lot of our love with you. You are the captain of your soul, and no matter where you choose to be, we will always be your family. There will always be a little room in each of our hearts for you to come home

The sentence was never completed, the typewriter suddenly stopped, the paper was automatically dispensed from the machine and white smoke began to pour out of the top of it. I pushed my chair back and stared in horror. I was so stunned it took several minutes to think rationally enough to pull the plug out of the wall socket. The white smoke poured out of the machine, rising in great curls that filled the room. The smoke just lingered. It didn't spell out any cryptic messages or outline any ghostly faces. It just lingered, filling the room with a pure white fog. As I allowed my fear to subside, I felt strangely peaceful, the fog was white, it was clean and I knew my brother was free from whatever painful thing had tormented him in this world.

I later took the machine to have it fixed, for it had not typed another word since the fog filled evening. The repairman told me that it had simply short-circuited. The entire circuit board had fused together for some unknown reason. There was no explanation. The last word had been home, one of my brother's favorite words. Having no other choice, I left it at that. The sentence like the sentiment would simply never end.

We buried my eldest brother at sea. We all went through the motions as if it were a play that would soon be ended. The ocean was rough and it began to rain. It was a miserable day. I walked up to the cabin where the captain solemnly steered the boat. The captain was an old family friend. We both stood in silence. I looked out over the water hoping to gain a new perspective when the captain began to speak. "It's a funny thing." He said, not taking his eyes off the water. "Standing here on Gary's boat, burying your brother like this. Gary was killed two years ago today. We buried him at sea in the same boat."

No, it couldn't be! How was it possible that they both wound up in the same boat on the very same day? Raymond and Gary, they had both saved me from being carried out to sea. Now they would both live there, forever at the bottom. The horrible warning, why did it come if it could not help? I swallowed lead. Everything in me sank to my feet. I no longer felt the boat rocking. I was too numb to cry and too drained to sort my thoughts. I would think about it later. My brother's life had ended, and with it, I knew, something in my own had ended too.

5

Through Marion's Eyes

Several years had passed. Christmases and birthdays had come and gone, and everyone grew a few years older. Everyone but Raymond, but suddenly that all seemed such a long time ago. I dipped my brush into the paint can. I was painting my bedroom, a beautiful shade of periwinkle blue. I was almost finished with the last of the trim when the phone rang. It was a call from a man I did not know, a call that would set the wheels of destiny spinning into high gear.

"I was given your name by one of your clients," he began. "I was told you have some special talents, that you might be able to help me locate someone." I did not respond to this. He went on, "I don't mean to sound desperate, but I am trying to help someone find their daughter. She's been missing for some time now and she may be in grave danger. I was told you have a gift. It would mean a great deal to her family if you could help. There are a number of extenuating circumstances that I cannot go into right now but time is.... running out."

My mind filled with dread. It was not something I had not heard a hundred times before. I wanted to hang up, tell him he had the wrong number, the wrong person, but I knew I could not say no. I never could. I also knew something was wrong here, something that had nothing to do with the missing girl. Good judgment however, requires one's eyes to be open and my work required them to be closed. So I gave him directions, told him to bring a photograph of the girl and made an appointment for the following day.

He arrived promptly. He was a young man in his early thirties, casual but conservatively dressed and he had a large manila envelope in his hands. The man was visibly uneasy. I led him upstairs to the small office I worked in at home. "Please sit down, make yourself comfortable because this may take some time. It is important that you understand..." I paused. "There are no guarantees. I do not know if I can help you. And, what ever I can see here today is what I can give you. Nothing more. Do you understand?"

"Yes, yes I understand." He answered a little too quickly. Something didn't feel right. I didn't really trust the man but I felt committed somehow to help him. "I brought several photographs, of her and the family members." He volunteered.

"Take them out of the envelope and place them face down in front of me. When I ask you, place the photograph of the girl who is missing in my hands. Movements distract me, so don't make any sudden moves or anything." I smiled trying to make things a little more comfortable, but he remained very serious about the whole business. "The only other thing is please don't ask questions until I finish. You can respond if I ask you a question, providing I am able to speak at that moment. Sometimes it's very difficult to see and talk at the same time. Do you understand?"

"I guess so, you need me to be still and keep quiet until your done. I think I can manage that. Do you mind if I take notes while your talking?" He seemed a little more genuine now.

"No, I don't mind at all. There is a pad to your left, help yourself and feel free to write down any questions you might have as well. So, I guess we are ready. I'll need a minute or two to meditate. Remember place the photo in my hand when I ask for it." I closed my eyes and within a moment I was on my way to the other side of vision. "Give me the picture." He placed a driver's license in my hands and my fingers searched for the face of the girl. "Tell me her name. What is her name?"

He gave me a name. "No, that's not her real name. You know this is not her name don't you?"

"Yes, I do but this is the name she goes by." He sounded truthful.

"Her name is Marion." I began stroking the right side of my face, "Oh, God what have they done to her face." I could feel the hair swept to one side to cover the left side of her face. I knew I was physically taking on her gestures. "She doesn't look like this picture anymore, but you know this."

"It's badly scared. Her face, someone hurt her and she tries to cover it with her hair. She was very beautiful." He said.

I ignored his comments. "She doesn't want to be found. She's working as a prostitute." I began and suddenly, without warning I was overcome with a feeling that was completely unfamiliar to me. "I donn…" My mouth was suddenly not cooperating, the words trailed off into little more than a slur and my whole body was going completely limp. I began to slide down my chair. I was practically under the desk when I was finally able to drop the photo. As I began to regain some motor control, I realized what had happened. "She's on some kind of very heavy drugs. I don't know how I am going to communicate with her. She's not exactly… coherent." I looked at the man in front of me. He was not a member of her family. "Why are you looking for her?" I was actually bluffing. He thought I knew who he was at this point, but I didn't. I didn't know anything about him and I didn't like it. All I knew was Marion did not want anyone to find her and he was not her friend. He probably gathered by now that I was not going any further until he answered my question, honestly.

"I am a DEA agent. Well, at least I was one until this case began. And your right, she doesn't want to be found. I have never even met her. And, I am not sure how to put this or why this has happened, but I have become…" He paused, "involved with her family. She has a mother in Pompano, and a two-year old child she left behind. You are also right about the drugs. We know she has been addicted for some time now. She was very self-conscious about her looks. She had been a model and just before all this happened and she was on her way to a very successful acting career…then her face was slashed."

I knew this was not why she left, but I said nothing. I just waited for him to continue.

"She was a witness," he began. "She saw a murder take place, it was between two DEA agents. She was frightened and she ran because she didn't know which one to trust so she trusted neither. For that matter she probably hasn't trusted anyone since. The police are looking for her and she doesn't want to be found. The problem is she's destroying her own life in the process of running. It's not unlikely that she is working as a prostitute, but none of this was her fault. She was just in the wrong place at the wrong time. I need to help her. I need to find her before it's too late. Her child deserves a mother and her mother should not be grieving for her daughter. It's just wrong." He paused, silently tapping his fingers on the desk.

"I left the department several months ago. I just couldn't let it go. I couldn't just write it off and forget it happened. I couldn't let her become another anonymous case number. She was a person. You see so much in this line of work, so many casualties of some undefined, invisible war. I just needed to do one good thing before I quit. I needed to do something that helped someone. There were just too many people hurt, too many people dead. I saw the pictures of her when the investigation began. She was so beautiful. She looked so innocent. It's like, if I could help her, what we had to do would have been somehow worth while. I learned everything I could about her. I keep in touch with her mother and her son. I know it all sounds pretty crazy. A lot of people think I've lost it, but that's really the point. I did lose something, and it was the bad thing that I lost. Now I'm trying to replace it with the good one. I know it's emotional, and I realize that it's not professional. That's why I left. But you must understand, I only want to help her."

It was a propelling story and I knew everything he said was true, but I also knew that much of it was omitted. It did sound crazy, but who was I to judge. What I did sounded pretty insane to most people. Truth is if I weren't the one having to do it all the time I would think it was crazy too, but I never had that choice. I decided it was not my job to judge. Looking back, this may not have been a very good judgment call. But it was precisely this lack of good judgment that usually gave me my most valuable lessons. Besides, his motives may have been a bit unbalanced but they seemed to be genuine enough. He had no intent of hurting her and there was always the hope it would somehow help both of them. God knows. They both needed some help.

"All right, I'll try it another way. At least I am prepared for the drugs this time." I took a few deep breaths and closed my eyes once more. The descent was almost a relief for a moment anyway. "Okay hand me the picture." I held the photo and ran my fingers over the face. Suddenly I zoomed into her head at some sonic speed. It had happened too quickly and I did not know why. I tried to stay clear of her thoughts, and focus solely upon seeing through her eyes. If she were looking at another person, I knew I could gather the information we needed through them.

Within seconds she opened her eyes. As I peered through them, at that precise second she called a name "Tiburon." It was lightening fast. I never saw his face. Only his eyes looking back at me, not at her, at me! Not once in all the years I had been doing this had any living soul ever seen me through someone else's eyes. I did not know how he did this, but I knew he had seen me through her eyes. Somehow he knew I had been inside of her. Even worse, he knew that I had seen him. He knew now that I knew his name. I was not sure what to do. I simply snapped back involuntarily. Now I sat with this man at my desk and I did not want to speak. I just wanted to un-see everything. I wanted this ex-agent to leave. I would tell him what I saw, and as always I would wish that when he left he could somehow take the memory of this event with him.

"There is a man, he knows some kind of voodoo from the Islands." I could not think of any other word to describe what he had. The only thing I really knew was that it was some sort of strange power and it came from the Caribbean. He was from the Islands, somewhere in the Caribbean. "She called him *Tiburon*. He is in a bar called Woody's in

Key Largo. The girl is with him now, but he knows you will be coming and she will be gone by the time you arrive. He will be waiting. He sent her to some other Island on a white boat." I did not hear things as I usually did, so I was not sure how I knew them. I opened my eyes and looked at the man in front of me. He did not seem surprised. I was not sure why this was so.

He stared down at the notes in front of him for a long moment. "Do you know anything about white slavery?" He exhaled as he asked.

"I know what the word means," I answered. "Nothing beyond that."

"The man she is with is a white slaver. He has girls working for him on yachts in the Caribbean. He keeps them on drugs until he wears them out. When they are no longer of use to him, no longer profitable, he feeds them to the sharks. A convenient disposal." He pressed his lips together in silent anger. "I know who he is and I know the place." He thanked me for my help and assured me that I had been of great help to him. I did not feel good about any of this and I was glad he was leaving. His lack of reactions in all this was weird. Then, just as he was ready to walk out of the room, he removed a photograph of the girl and laid it down on the top of my desk. "Just in case anything else should come to you, I want you keep this."

I tried to hand it back to him. I tried to tell him that I never got second thoughts about these things. I made it a policy never to work twice on the same case, but he was so insistent about it that I chose not to argue with him. I was relieved when he left and decided to forget the whole thing. I was very successful at that until about eleven that evening.

A few friends had come over that night. I had gone upstairs to the bathroom when something out of the corner of my eye caught my attention. For a fraction of second, I thought I saw something. It was not even a thing exactly. It was more of a movement, a shadow of a movement. I turned and looked directly into the mirror, where I thought it had originated.

Suddenly a great black ethereal ocean formed in the glass right before my eyes. It swelled up and like some enormous dark wave and came crashing through the mirror. I must have passed out; because that was the last thing I could remember. My body landed with a thud on floor, which gratefully alarmed my friends downstairs that something had occurred. When I woke up I realized I was lying on the floor in a pool of blood. Someone was lifting my head and asking too many questions. I couldn't seem to answer them quickly enough. A young man who must have been a paramedic was trying to explain that I had hit the back of my head on the tiles. I would need stitches. They would take me to the hospital to make sure there was no concussion.

My daughter Harmony was thirteen, going on thirty. She had called, first for the ambulance, then for my mother. The next morning my mother brought me home from the hospital. I sat down at the table in the kitchen while she filled the kettle for tea. I tried to explain about the dark looming waves in the mirror, about Marion and the mysterious man who had seen me through her eyes.

"And you think there's some connection?" she said.

"I know there is Mom. I don't know what or how," I said emphatically. "But I know there is."

"But you've done this so many times before. I've been there with you. Did you do or say anything different this time?"

"No, it wasn't me. That's the point. It was someone else. Someone else was aware of what I was doing. They knew I was there, and that's weird. That's too scary even for me."

The phone rang and I looked at it before reaching for the receiver. "Do you want me to get it?" My mother offered.

"No, it's okay. Other than a little head ache, I'm fine."

It was the ex-DEA agent. I recognized his voice. "I thought I'd let you know. Right after I left last night, I sent two of my old partners down to the bar in Key Largo. They were already down south so I figured they could get there a lot quicker than I could. I was hoping they could get to her, but like you said, she was already gone. The guy you saw, Tiburon he was there…waiting for us." He hesitated waiting for my response. When none was given, he continued. "I hate to ask you this, but I need you to look again. We need some more information."

"No, I'm sorry," I said widening my eyes and pointing to the receiver trying to gesture the identity of the caller to my mother. "I'm not feeling very well. Besides, I don't think there's anything else I can tell you."

"I thought if you could just, try once more…" he pleaded.

"No, I told you before. I never see anything afterwards." I hung up the phone and my mother sat down.

"The DEA agent?" She asked.

"Didn't I tell you. This whole thing is weird. He wasn't even surprised. They found the guy I told them about sitting in the bar waiting for them. Mom, I called the guy by name for God's sake! And this agent, he isn't even curious, he just wants more information?"

"That's definitely odd. Especially for a detective, a policeman or whatever he is. I've watched those visions turn into evidence for years now, and no matter how many times it happens, I'm amazed. And I've never seen a detective that wasn't amazed."

"Me too," I agreed.

Two days later I was in the kitchen cooking. The water was boiling in a corning ware pot. Just at the moment I was ready to drop the pasta in, the glass pot exploded into a thousand tiny pieces. The water came up like some surreal animation and covered my body all the way from the waist down to my knees. I screamed, anticipating the pain, but none came. I felt the front of my jeans to see if the water had really hit. They were drenched with hot water but I was not burned. Glass was all over the kitchen. I just sat down in total disbelief. Something was happening, but I had no idea what it was. I couldn't even identify it. How was I suppose to protect myself from it?"

A few days later, the ex-agent called again. This time I assured him I could do nothing else for him. I would not look again. I knew he did not really accept this as a final answer but I would not think to touch anything regarding this matter again.

That afternoon there was a knock at the door and I ran downstairs and peeked through the peephole to see who it was. "It's just me Jeanne Marie," my mother called out.

"What are doing in Lauderdale today? Sorry" I said opening the door and straightening out the crumpled rug in front of it. "I was just moving the furniture back into my room upstairs. Wait till you see it, the wallpaper came out great!"

She followed me upstairs and surveyed my work. "Oh, it did come out nice, and what a pretty blue. It sure softens the furniture. I never wanted to say anything, but it looked kind of dark in here before."

"I guess it did, but I really like it now. It feels good. What do you think about the arrangement?"

"It looks good. You might want to move that little table over here next to the door," she said pointing to the spot.

"Well, set your stuff down and give me a hand."

"Oh, I almost forgot what I came here for. Here, this is for you."

"A present?" I smiled opening the bag.

"Well, it's not really a present. It's just something that needed to come to you."

"I know what it is," I said tearing off the tissue paper to expose the beautiful rosewood crucifix. "Didn't this belong to grandma?"

"Yes, it did, and I just knew I had to bring it to you today. Jeanne Marie you know it's been hanging in your old room for years now. I went in there this morning to get some thread, you know I have all my sewing stuff in there, and it fell off the wall."

"It just fell?"

"I swear it just fell," she said. "I was on the other side of the room. It wasn't like anything could have moved it. And I was the only one home. I just knew I needed to bring it to you for some reason."

"I think it's exactly what I need right now. Thank you," I said hugging her. "In fact I think it should go right here over this little antique table. Have you had lunch?"

"No, but I can't stay long. I told your brother I'd watch Stephie this afternoon. I just wanted to give this to you first."

"I guess it's a little late for lunch anyway. I didn't realize what time it was. Harmony will be coming home from school soon. Come on I'll walk you downstairs. I need to find a hammer and a nail to hang this up."

I hung the little wooden heirloom next to the door and went downstairs to get a white candle and some matches. I thought it would be a nice gesture, a sort of dedication. Setting the candle on top I began to say a little prayer as I proceeded to strike the match. My daughter who had just come home spotted this little ritual from the hallway walked into the room.

"Oh, mom that's so sweet. Where did that come from?" She asked directing her attention to the cross.

"Grandma brought it to me. I thought it was such a nice thing."

She smiled warmly and stepped closer to join me in my little blessing. But just as she leaned over to put her arm around me, I leaned forward to touch the match's flame to the wick of the candle. From nowhere a great silver flash exploded behind me. Harmony jumped back against the wall screaming in terror. I was on fire. I could see the flashes of light behind me. I grabbed the bottom of the long sweater I had on, pulled it over my head trying to extinguish the flames. Harmony was still screaming.

"It's okay, it's okay. The fire's gone." I put my arms around my child. "Everything is going to be all right now," I assured her, but she was not able to stop screaming.

My hair was singed and the sweater looked as if it had been burned with some strange hot iron. The actual marks on the sweater were in some sort of pattern. From the bottom center it came up in a straight line almost to the shoulders and then split in half. These marks continued over each shoulder. It was perfectly symmetrical in the shape of the letter "Y". I tried to console my daughter who could do nothing but hysterically repeat that I looked like a big sparkler.

"The flames, they were silver, silver like a big sparkler. You looked like a big sparkler." She could not calm herself and I could not help, no matter how hard I tried. I just held her close to me and stroking her hair and rocking her. When she finally did calm down a bit, she would not speak to me.

"But I'm alright. Look at me I'm fine. My hair is a little frizzy." I lifted the ends of my singed hair to show her. The whole thing suddenly struck me as funny. I couldn't control the urge to laugh. Harmony looked at me incredulously.

"This is not funny mom. You almost burned to death right in front of me. What am I suppose to tell people? Oh, my mother, she just went up in flames one day."

"Spontaneous combustion?"

"Yeah, I come home from school one day, and my mom's not there. She's just a little burned spot on the floor. I guess she decided to just spontaneously combust today. Mom, this is not funny."

"Oh come on, by now you have to know I don't do these things on purpose. Harmony, I swear I would never do anything to frighten you like this. I know it's terrible for you, but I don't know what else to do."

"Mom, why can't you just be like other mothers? You know work in a bank or something."

"I don't know, sweet heart. I don't know why I have to do what I do. I guess everybody is born with something they have to do, like singers and poets… or painters."

"Then write or paint Mom. Just do something else, anything else. Can't you see how dangerous this is? You help everyone else, they're all sad. All those poor families, and the poor little kids. I don't mean I don't feel sorry for them. I do, but what about us? We're your kids and we have to live here too, can you imagine what that's like?"

I knew after that day that I could no longer pretend. I had two children to think about and I could not keep telling myself that maybe something might be wrong here. I knew in no uncertain terms that something was very wrong. Something I knew nothing about. Something that prior to this, I did not even acknowledge existed. I did not believe in 'evil powers'. I knew a lot of psychics and mediums, but no one I could think of who might have knowledge of this. I knew I had to find someone who did.

It's not like you can just look up, unknown but powerful Caribbean witchcraft, in the yellow pages. I really wasn't sure where to begin, or even where in the Caribbean these magic isles could be. Haiti, Trinidad, Cuba. The Caribbean was filled with islands and Miami was brimming with island people. Then I remembered Anna. Of course, she was a medium, and she was Cuban. Anna had given me an amulet once. I'm not sure what it was made of but it was covered with red and white beads, with a single shell like a tiny mouth in the center.

We were at a friend's house. "My guide told me to give you this. He said that you will be needing it for protection."

"What is it?" I asked her.

"You'll know when the time comes what it is for." Then she placed the unusual little talisman in the palm of my hand. Yes, Anna would know who I needed to talk to. She would know who could help me understand what was happening. Hopefully, it would be someone who could teach me to prevent it from happening again. Anna sent me to a woman in Hialeah named Maria. "She is a priest, Anna assured me, "a Santera."

Maria lived in a small cinder blockhouse in one of the older sections of Hialeah. From the outside there was nothing unusual save a large rusting chain bolted beneath the threshold of the doorway. A pretty dark haired girl, who looked to be about sixteen, greeted me at the door.

"Come on in," she said in perfect English. My mother is with some-one, but she will not be too much longer. Go ahead and sit down," she pointed to the living room and then disappeared into the kitchen.

I thanked her as I sat down and began looking around the room. There were five huge clay jars carefully placed on homemade wooden shelves. They were all draped in large colorful beaded necklaces. Each necklace was woven with what appeared to be dozens of strands of dec-orative glass beads and they appeared to be made for giants. In front of the jars, two candles in tall glass jars were burning. Between these large urns were numerous statues of the saints.

A magnificent statue, of a woman dressed in red and white flowing robes was the largest. She was nearly three feet tall. In one hand she held a sword and the other a challis. At her side was a tower, like the ones found in medieval castles, and at her feet was an array of fruits and flowers in various stages of decay. All of the sudden it registered, in one instant flash of recognition, I knew. This was Saint Barbara! She had been ornately draped with all sorts of trinkets and wore a gold crown on her head, but she was undeniably Saint Barbara. This recog-nition was oddly comforting and disconcerting at the same time. It was good to know there was something familiar in the room, but why of all the saints did it have to be her?

I nervously continued to survey the room. In the far corner was a large three legged black iron pot containing all sorts of metal imple-ments. It looked rusted, dark and grungy with feathers stuck to the contents. Then I saw what might have been dried blood splattered inside the pot. There was a large butcher knife plunged into the center. It looked positively ominous.

Behind the door was a clay saucer, the ones made to set terra cotta flowerpots into. In the center of the dish was a small cement mound with a face made of seashells. It had a feather and some other unidenti-fiable things sticking out the top of it. The dish was filled with candies, little plastic toys and a half smoked cigar. In front of the display was a small cup of Cuban coffee along with bowl of decaying fruit. I figured I must be in the right place for Caribbean witchcraft, but was I in the right place if I wasn't Caribbean or a witch?

Two women finally surfaced from the back room. An elderly red headed woman was crying and seemed to be profusely thanking the other in Spanish. The other woman called to the young girl as she walked the lamenting woman to the door. The teen came begrudgingly out of the other room. A few loud words were exchanged and the girl turned to me. "My mother doesn't speak much English, I will come in to translate for you. My name is Kari, and this is my mother Maria," she said.

I smiled to her mother. "Thank you Kari. I'm sorry to impose on you like this, but I really appreciate your help."

"I don't really mind," she said. "It's just that I have a lot of home-work and this house is always busy, too many people. My mother gets tired but she never stops working. But she'll never listen."

Maria sat down at a large wooden desk. Behind her was a picture of an old black man with a straw hat and bare feet. He held a walking stick in one hand and a red cloth sack in the other. There was a table draped in white lace to her left with a dozen or so stemmed glasses in various sizes filled with water. A white candle and a vase of flowers completed the curious adornment.

Kari pulled up a chair and sat down beside me. Maria looked at me for a long moment. She was a small woman, probably about fifty but she looked much older. She seemed overly warn down by time and hard work. Her hair was black but graying. There were dark circles under her eyes, but this did not diminish their sharpness. Maria seemed hesitant to begin. Her face was expressionless. She simply stared at me. Then, without moving her eyes she dipped her fingers into a hollowed gourd filled with water and sprinkled it onto the floor. She began to speak, but not in Spanish. The language was not familiar but I assumed she was saying some magic words. Then she spoke, very sternly and pointed to me with her chin.

"She wants me to tell you she is sorry, but she will not read for you today," Kari said.

I looked at the mother, and then spoke to the daughter. "Can she tell me why?" I asked.

Kari spoke to her mother. Maria seemed upset, but I had no idea what she was saying. Finally Kari looked at me. "She says you see from the eyes of the dead. And what you see has followed you. She says it is very dangerous and she doesn't know if she is strong enough right now to help you."

I looked into the mother's eyes. "Is there anything I can do? Is there someone else who can help me?"

Her eyes softened a bit and she waited for Kari to translate. Then she stood up and left the room. I looked to Kari for some clue. "She will find out," she said. You have to wait. She will be right back."

Kari left also. Part of me wanted to leave as well. I felt terrible. I knew what a toll this must take on both of them. I had never been on the other side of the desk before. I thought of my daughter. How she worried about my health. How she felt about the people who came to see me. There was a never-ending stream of seekers, always needing help. Help, it seemed that no one else could give.

It seemed like a long time later, but they both returned. Maria spoke to her daughter and then waited. "She says she can help you, but she will need some help. It will take, *cuanto Santeros?*" she asked her mother.

Maria replied, "siete."

"Seven, you will need seven Santeros, priests to do this cleansing. For this you will need some things, but she says you must do it right away. She says you have opened your eyes to something that could hurt you. She said you would understand." The girl paused. "Sometimes it is better not to see. I am glad she is the only one in our house who does. I have to learn all this because of her, but I don't understand that much. It doesn't bother me a bit either."

Maria slipped a paper into her daughter's hand. Kari began to read and pointed to a word for clarification. "You must come back on Thursday. Bring with you a change of clothes, all white. Everything, even your underwear must be white. Wear old clothes that you have worn a lot when you come. And, be prepared to spend the day. Come in the morning," she checked once more with her mother. "About eight."

I looked into her mothers' eyes. She was tired and I thanked her for her help. I reached over to shake her hand but she pulled back like I was contagious. I nodded, letting her know I understood, even though I did not really understand very much.

The next day I bought an inexpensive white cotton dress and some new white sandals for the occasion. I had no idea what to expect. I imagined Santeros might show up in tribal costumes, a lot of feathers and beads. Maybe even masks. I hoped it wouldn't be too scary, or too dangerous. No one knew where I was going. What if I didn't come back? After all, I heard they did sacrifices in these religions.

Thursday morning I pulled up to Maria's house just before eight. There was a police car out front. I wasn't sure what to do. What if they were arresting her for doing sacrifices or something? I did not get out of the car. Another car pulled up behind me. I was trapped. I couldn't get out now if I wanted to. A man and his wife got out of the car. She had on an old-fashioned peasant outfit. He was dressed in white. Other than that, they looked like a normal Latin couple. They knocked on the door and Kari opened it with a big smile. They all hugged and greeted one another. It looked safe enough. I followed their lead and knocked nervously on the door. Kari opened the door. "Come in," she said with a smile. "Everyone is just now arriving. Would you like some Cuban coffee? There is food on the table. I am sorry, but I don't remember your name."

"Jeanne Marie," I said. "Yes, I would like some coffee." The house was bustling and conversations were loud and jovial. Several women worked in the kitchen preparing coffee and whatever else was needed.

They wore gingham aprons, beaded necklaces and kerchiefs. They looked like old-fashioned countrywomen. An image I hadn't seen in a long time. I did not see Maria. No one seemed to speak English. I waited quietly sipping the sweet syrupy coffee.

Kari was busy chasing a little boy through the house. The child must have been about two, with a chubby face and boisterous laugh. He squealed as Kari caught him and swooped him off the ground. "This," she said a little out of breath, "is my cousin. He is my work today."

"Is there anything I'm suppose to do?" I asked.

"No, just wait," she said trying to hold on to the squirming child. "They have a lot of preparations to do. But they will come and get you when they are ready for you."

By now, the curiosity was getting the best of me and I couldn't think of a subtle way of asking. "Kari, I saw a police car out front. Who's is it?"

"Oh, that is my uncle. Most Santera's have a policeman in their house. He is a Santero. They park their car out front to let the others know not to bother the house. People get crazy about things they don't understand, mostly the sacrifices." She lowered the boy to the floor and he took off with Kari close behind.

About an hour passed when Kari came into the room with another woman wearing multiple strands of beads, which hung down to her waist. "You brought the clothes?" Kari asked.

"Yes, they're right here in the bag." I said lifting it up.

"Carmen, will take them for you," she said. "It will not be too much longer." The woman took the bag and they both disappeared.

It was about ten before someone finally came to let me know they were ready. An older heavyset woman dressed in blue and white gingham took me by the hand and led me outside. "My English is not so good," she said.

"I am sure my Spanish is worse," I replied. The woman led me through a patio to a small shed in the back yard. We passed through the group of people I assumed were the Santeros. The men were all in white, but I was shuffled by too quickly to see what they were doing.

"Here," the woman placed her hands on my shoulders and firmly planted me in place. "Do not turn around. You understand?"

"I understand," I assured her. The woman left and I stood still, mostly from fear. I was standing just inside the doorway of the little metal shed facing the outside. There was a lot of large green leafed foliage that blocked all visibility from the neighboring houses. It had to be at least ninety degrees outside and the sun was baking the small tin roof creating an oven inside. I began to pray that I wouldn't faint or anything. I was losing my nerve and contemplating an escape when a little black dog showed up. He was just a puppy and he looked at me curiously and wagged his tail. Then it struck me, what if they were going to sacrifice the dog. Not the puppy, my heart sank. If I could get out of here, I thought, the puppy was going with me. Just then someone called him away. It was too late to do anything. They were all walking towards me!

The blue gingham woman put her hands over my eyes and walked me further into the little tin house. "You must keep your eyes closed," she said. "Do not open them. No matter what, do not open them."

I closed my eyes, and again from fear I did not move. I was frozen. First there was what sounded like prayers in some unidentifiable but vaguely familiar language. Then there was singing and chanting and the heavy scent of tobacco, cigars. Someone was circling me, blowing the smoke at me. I did not move. Suddenly someone grabbed my shoulders and began to turn me. As I spun slowly around, I could see the floor from the tiny slits at the bottom of my eyelids. A man held a white chicken and a large black snake. There was a large black pot like the one in the house, the grungy one with all the iron things inside. Someone began thrashing me with leaves, sweeping my body with what must have been a bundle of herbs. After numerous turns, they began to spit mouthfuls of rum all over me. I was covered in the sticky alcohol, dizzy from the twirling motion, the heat and the smoke. It was all very disorienting.

Once again they turned me around. This time I felt the warm feathers of a live chicken sweeping over me from head to toe. There was more chanting. I could not tell what was going on. I was fairly certain when I heard the chop of a machete that the snake was no longer a threat. Then just as I was beginning to think I might survive, flames burst out from behind me. I heard the screams emanating from the women. My eyes popped opened and I saw the bloody heads of the chicken and the snake on top of the black iron pot. The flames had surprised everyone. It was obvious they had not been a part of the ceremony. I wondered now it had actually been flames that were behind me. Again I was not burned. Could it have been another flash of silvery light? Not that there was much of a chance of ever finding out, but I wondered all the same.

There was some commotion after the flames. Then someone began ripping my clothes from the back. Now I was really paralyzed. I couldn't help wondering if the flames had pissed them off. But there was no way out and nothing I could do but trust. God only knew what was going to happen next.

Before long, I was standing there naked with all my clothes in shreds at my feet. My eyes were glued shut at this point. I had completely surrendered to my foolish fate. Once more I was smoked, thrashed and sprayed. Then a final herbal rinse was poured over me from a large plastic bucket. At this point my eyes flew open again. Maria stood in front of me and the blue gingham woman beside her was holding my new white clothes. "Dry a little bit," she said. "With your hands, you cannot use a towel."

I wiped the herbs off my body, grateful that at least some of the stickiness was gone. I put on my panties and two other women helped me into my dress. My shoes were placed in front of me and I slipped them on. I was then guided back into the house, through the yard where the little boy was playing with the black puppy. I smiled at my own ignorance. I was led to Maria's office. Kari popped her head through the door. "You are almost finished. As soon as they are done out there, my mother will tell you what you need to do next."

I waited. And, once I stopped shaking, I felt strangely peaceful. It was if some heavy problem had been lifted from the top of my head. A while later, Maria came in with Kari behind her. She looked relieved but still a little leery of me. "Now," Kari said. "She will try again to read for you."

Maria dipped her fingers into the gourd of water. As she sprinkled the drops to the floor she said the words for her blessing. Then she picked up a handful of seashells and touched them to my forehead, the back of my neck and the palms of my hands. With more mumbled words she dropped the shells onto the cloth on top of her desk. She looked down at them carefully, scooped them up and repeated the ritual. She studied them for a moment and then began speaking.

Kari translated, "The shells say you are an *Omo Chango*, a daughter of Chango. He is your saint, the one who protects you in your work. You are a very great *espiritus*, a medium. You see through the eyes of the living dead. She says someday you will become a Santera, and because of this the purpose of your life will be filled. She says when the time comes, do not come to her for this because you must find another *Omo Chango* to be your *padrino*, your godfather. She says to be careful of the deep waters and the sharks. Do not swim with the sharks."

I must have looked puzzled. I had no idea what she was talking about. Kari shrugged her shoulders. "I am only telling you what she says. She is saying that someday you will be initiated into this religion, but not by her. Meanwhile, stay out of the ocean." She looked once more to her mother for instructions. "That's all she can tell you."

"Please tell her thank you for everything she did for me today. And, thank you Kari for all your help," I added.

"No problem, you will be fine now. Oh, I almost forgot," she asked her mother something else in Spanish. "This is very important. You have to take something to the cemetery when you leave. Come on, I explain what you have to do."

Kari led me to the back patio where the others were now gathered. Two men were filling large buckets with water and carrying them to the shed. Kari walked over and began speaking to one of them. He went into the shed and a few minutes later surfaced with a cardboard box and handed it to me. The blue gingham woman walked over and placed some pennies into the box. "For Oya, she guards the gates of the cemetery. It is an offering," she said. The woman with all the necklaces came up beside her and began to speak to Kari. "Carmen says you have to go to the cemetery and place this box in the first trash can you come to. When you are finished, walk out of the cemetery and do not look back. You understand?" Kari asked.

"Any particular cemetery?" I asked. "I mean is there one around here I should go to."

Kari turned and asked Carmen the question. "No, she said it's not important which one. But if you don't know the area, I can give you directions to one that is not too far away."

"It's okay," I assured her. I knew of one that was on the way home. I would stop and make my delivery there. Everyone hugged me when I left, including Maria. I never saw her or her daughter again, but there were no more fires or other terrifying events in my house after the cleansing. I did not know how it worked, or what powerful and dangerous thing I had tapped into. The only thing I knew for certain was how little I really knew of this world.

6

Meeting the Saints

The cleansing, it seemed, got rid of many things. Things that I had not bargained for, and things I was not prepared to lose. Within three weeks, my fifteen year-old son moved out to live with his father. I had not heard from Vic since our son was born. For all those years it was as if he had never existed. Then just as suddenly as he had gone, he reappeared one day. As a mother I tried to understand the necessity of my son's decision. I tried to tell myself that a boy needed a father. I could be his mother, but I could never be his father. I knew there was nothing I could do but accept it. Next my nine-year relationship with Dash ended abruptly and irretrievably. It was all a terrible blow. It took all the strength I had to pull myself out of the ocean of self-pity I found myself drowning in. But I knew I had to, even if I did not know why.

I thought of the statue of Saint Barbara in Maria's house. I had no idea how she fit into this whole thing, but I knew somehow that she did. She had been standing there, right in the middle of everything. I wondered if she was punishing me, if perhaps she had never forgiven me at all. Surely, I thought, I have paid my dues by now.

I remembered how it ended with Vic, the birth, the pain and all the blood that followed. Vic had just come home. "I called the doctor," I told him. "There's too much blood. I think I'm hemorrhaging. The doctor said to get to the hospital. You have to get the baby Vic. We have go."

"Why did you call a doctor? We can't afford another fucking doctor bill."

"Vic it's serious," I was too weak to argue. I had lost too much blood already. "Please, you have to get me to the hospital."

But Vic only became all the more enraged. He smashed his fist through a large aquarium in the living room. Gallons of water poured out onto the floor, along with the tiny fish. The little fish gasped for air, the baby began to cry. I tried to scream, but I did not even do that very well. I was paralyzed with the fear of his rage. He cursed and ranted. Then he smashed a few more things and finally he left. I made it to the phone. My parents were there in the hospital when I woke up and the nightmare was over.

I should have known better the second time, but Steve had been so patient when we met. The first time Steve took me out, my son spilled a large cup of coke in his lap. It was all over him and his new car. I kept trying to apologize, but he just smiled. I thought he was so incredibly patient. He had never even raised his voice. I wanted to marry him. I wanted to be what my parents wanted me to be, a wife and a mother. I promised to bear his children, and take care of his home. But the harder I tried the more it seemed he despised me for it.

"Of course you didn't do anything wrong. You never do anything wrong. Jeanne Marie is a damn saint. She's perfect," he would scream in my face. "Everything she does is perfect, look at the kitchen, it's perfect." He picked up the garbage can and dumped it across the top of the counter. "And dinner, I'm sure that's perfect too." He knocked the casserole dish to the floor. Steam rose up from the hot food and I backed up growing more frightened by the second. I kept backing up, until I was standing against the wall with no place to run.

"Please," I begged him. "Don't hurt me. Stop doing this, I don't know why you're doing this." The terror was always worse than the pain, but I think he knew that. He would always smile while it was happening. I was not brave. I cowered in fear and I was too ashamed to tell anyone that I had failed again.

Finally, I thought, I understood. It was me. It had been me all along. It was not the men I married, and it was not what I did that caused these terrible things to happen. It was simply who I was. I had not figured out exactly why, or how it worked. But I knew that some women brought out the best in the men they married. For some unknown reason, I brought out the worst. I brought up the shadows. I made their dark side appear. My very presence it seemed unleashed a violent anger that hid within them. It must live I thought, in every man. Somehow I was like a lightning rod, and I attracted their shadows. Perhaps this is what Saint Barbara had tried in vain to warn me.

This was true, with every man but Dash, my romantic cavalier knight in shinning armor. Wonderful frivolous Dash who made the world come alive for me. I was sure it was because I did not marry him. I loved him, but I knew I could not marry him. For the first time I thought, perhaps I had acted with some courage. Or, had I only feared the consequences of another marriage? I was not sure, but we had the perfect relationship. I had been happy, content. Then came Maria, the cleansing, and everything began to change.

Dash and I did not discuss religion, or spiritual things, psychic or otherwise. He knew what I did. He knew I was a clairvoyant and he chose not to know any more about it. "I don't want to know." He would tell me. I wasn't really sure if he was a little afraid of it or he just wasn't interested. We simply did not discuss it. Oddly enough, he was the one who first brought up the subject of religion.

"There's a dinner at the Mayor's house tonight. There will be a group of people from the church there. We're invited."

"The same mayor we ran into in Palm Beach?" I smiled. "You know the one who was not with Mrs. Mayor at the hotel."

"No," he turned a little red in the face. "That was a different mayor. This one is from the First Christian Church."

"Is this a religious thing?"

"Sort of, it's just a get together and they all belong to the same church. We need to bring a covered dish."

"A covered dish? You want me to cook?" I laughed at the thought of such a domestic request from Dash of all people. "Who are you scheming to meet now?"

"No one. I was just thinking it might be time to start going to church."

"You're kidding right? Somehow I just can't see you there, I mean Dash you're not exactly…"

"What a good Christian?"

"Well it's not that you're not good," I said seductively, rubbing his leg with mine. "It's just that they may not recognize the best part of you."

"You know I think Eve said something like that to Adam, and look what happened to him," he said.

"I was just kidding Dash. I'll go with you. I'll even make a covered dish."

We went to the party, and I may as well have been the consort of the devil himself. As we walked in, the males and females separated immediately into segregated prayer groups. Dash had abandoned me to the women's group. When they began to summarily descend upon me, I tried to explain that I was actually very spiritual. I tried to explain that I too worked with the holy spirit. That with God's help I was able to help others, children and families, but that only seemed to confirm their worst fears. My efforts only sealed their certainty that I was not only a consort, but directly employed by Satan himself to do my unholy work. They offered to save me from the flames of eternal damnation if I vowed to give up my work.

I was angry, and on the ride home I let Dash know it. "I don't like being judged by people who don't know me Dash. And, I'm sure they meant well, but I don't need to be saved and reformed either. God made me very spiritual in my own way."

"Don't you think maybe it would be good for you?"

"Don't I think what would be good for me? Becoming a Christian? Do you think that because I am clairvoyant I am not a Christian?"

"No, I just thought it might be good if you decided to be a real Christian."

"A real Christian? I can't believe you're that naive? All these years, you're pat answer to any hint of a spiritual conversation was, 'that's not a topic I wish to discuss.' Now, suddenly you want to enroll me into a real Christian life!"

"What if we got married? Where would we have the wedding?"

"Married? We can't get married. It would ruin everything."

"What do you mean it would ruin everything? We've been together a long time. I...you know the L word. Love, I love you."

"I can't believe you're doing this. I love you too, but that has nothing to do with it. Dash don't you see. Marriage would ruin everything. Just the thought of it is causing problems already. Why does it have to be different?"

Dash didn't see it at all, and there was no way I could explain to him what I did not even understand myself. Dash joined the church. Three months later he married a woman he met there. And, as Dash began to fill his spiritual void I found myself engulfed in another kind of emptiness. He had been my physical world. Without him I was out of touch with the entire earthly experience. I was devastated.

I had several torrid sexual affairs trying to fill the terrible void. It was then that I began to realize, that sex was its own entity, a power in and of itself. It had little to do with the man involved, and there was a certain satisfaction in that. That powerful internal electrical charge came not from the man, but from the divine action itself. The only problem was, that the power was fleeting. It was a temporary surge, and it eventually became nothing more than a futile attempt to plug into an existence that I could never fully connect with.

I kept the little red and white beaded talisman that Anna had given me on the table next to my bed. I believed it was somehow protecting me. I still did not know what it was, or even exactly what it was protecting me from. I wondered if the small charm, like the cleansing was affecting some part of my life that I was yet unaware of. I held it in the palm of my hand, but it did not speak. I did not know who made it or where it was from. Finally I decided it was time to ask Anna these questions.

I went to Anna's house. She had recently married and moved into a brand new house in West Hialeah. It was a small Mediterranean townhouse. I drove down the street looking for the numbers on doors. There were rows and rows of identical little houses with red barrel tile roofs stacked neatly together as far as the eye could see. I followed the addresses until I finally found hers. Anna opened the door before I knocked. "So, you found me," she said smiling.

"It wasn't really that hard," I assured her.

"Come on in. Do you drink Cuban coffee?" She asked.

"Not usually, but I'll try it." Anna's house was immaculate. There was not much furniture, a black vinyl sofa, small wall unit with a TV and glass and chrome coffee table. A bright white ceramic floor lit the way into the small kitchen.

"We haven't been here long," she said spooning the dark coffee into the bottom of the tiny pot. "Two months now. But we like it."

"It's nice. And, it's always fun to decorate a new house."

"It would be if we could afford it after the closing," she said. "But it's a blessing to own a house in the first place."

"That's true." I was looking at a statue of a saint in a red dress on her counter. It was Saint Barbara, the same one I had seen at Maria's house only smaller. She too had placed a dish of fruit in front of her. "Anna why do you keep food in front of the saint?"

"The offering to Santa Barbara? Oh, I forgot you don't know about Santos do you?"

"Santos?" I asked.

"The saints. We pray to the saints and ask them to do things for us. In return, we must do something for them. Sometimes they ask us for nothing more than a little offering of fruits."

"Saint Barbara, what does she do for you?"

"Oh," she smiled. "Santa Barbara is a great protector. You see the sword in her hand? A warrior, actually, she is really a he but that's a long story. All you need to remember is that when you need protection, she is the one who will protect you."

"What do you mean she is really a he?"

"How do I explain? Ah, do you remember the little round beaded thing I gave to you?"

"Yes, that's what I came to ask you about."

"Okay. That is a *como*," Anna snapped her fingers searching for the right word. "A charm. It was red and white. Those colors are for Chango. Chango, who is in our religion Santa Barbara."

"I don't understand. How can Chango and Saint Barbara be the same?"

"I told you it was a long story. You know, in Cuba this religion was brought by the slaves, hundreds of years ago. At that time they did not let them practice it. The church was very powerful. So, for convenience, maybe more for survival, they put their charms behind the saints and prayed to them. Everyone was happy."

"How did they pick Santa Barbara to be Chango?"

"Sometimes the stories of the saints and the orishas were close, like hers. After they killed Santa Barbara, her enemies were struck down and killed by lightning. Chango is the guardian of lightning. You see?"

"Sort of," I said. My mind was reeling. Saint Barbara was the one Maria had been talking about all along. If she was the Chango she spoke of, I knew I had to find out more. "Anna, remember when you sent me to Maria?"

"Yes, she did a cleansing. It worked, no?"

"Yes, it worked. I don't know how, but it worked."

"It is not necessary to know how. It is enough that it works, no?"

"No, it's not enough. I mean I need to know how it works."

"You will have to know a lot of things to know that. That's not something I can help you with Jeanne Marie. I know a few things, but I don't know that."

"How did you learn them?"

"From my *madrina*," she shrugged. "My godmother."

"Well if you didn't have a godmother Anna, how would you find one?"

"You have to remember I grew up with these things, it's in our culture, in our blood. These are things that must be learned from the older ones, like Maria. It's not like you can read it in a book."

"Anna, do you remember when you gave me that charm? You told me it was for protection, that when the time came I would find out what it meant. You said it was a message from your guide. Who is your guide?"

"Santa Barbara, Chango."

"Maria told me this too. I don't know why, but it's time now, and I need to know what it all means."

"Then you need to go back and see Maria," she said handing me a miniature cup of coffee.

"No, Maria said not to come back to her. She said I had to find another Chango."

"Well I am afraid I am not the one, because I have never been initiated. I practice the religion, but I am not a Santera, maybe someday, but not now." Anna jumped up setting her empty cup down. "I can give you something though. I do have one book from the botanica. In English! It has stories about the religion, the mythology. You can borrow it if you like."

I read the book, twice. It was filled with colorful stories of earthy African gods and goddesses. It was not unlike Greek or Roman mythology. Except that it was older, a little more primal and still alive! Somewhere, hidden in the very city I lived in, it was being practiced. Somewhere among those practitioners was the Chango who was destined to teach me protection.

Inside of the book Anna had written a phone number and beneath it a note, 'Santeria books'. I copied down the number before returning the book to Anna. The phone number had a Miami area code. I decided to call perhaps there were other books on the subject. I called the number hoping it was the store, the botanica Anna had mentioned. A man with a Spanish accent answered the phone.

"I am looking for a book, about Santeria," I began nervously. "A friend loaned me a book on the mythology, but I would like to have a copy of my own. I thought you might be able to help me find it."

"Yes, I have the book you are looking for. Are you in Miami?" he asked.

"I am not too far from Miami. Where are you located?"

"South Miami," he said. Then he proceeded to give me the address.

"Perfect," I said. "I'll be there in about an hour."

I didn't mind the drive, but I hoped I would not get lost. This was not a section of town I knew. When I found the address, I was surprised because I had expected it to be a store, or a business of some sort. It was a house. Very plain, impeccably clean and manicured, but a house never the less. I rang the doorbell and an attractive man with piercing blue eyes and blond hair answered the door. "Oba?" I asked.

"Yes," he smiled. "You are the one who called about the book."

"Yes, I'm sorry," I said a little embarrassed. "I didn't realize this was your home. I mean I thought I was calling a store."

"No, this is my home," he looked at me and paused. "I am the writer. Would you like to come in?"

"Well, I hope I am not imposing on you," I stammered. "My name is Jeanne Marie, and I just wanted to buy your book."

"You can do that," he said and opening the door for me to enter. "Come, I like to sit outside." He led me through his modest home to a patio facing the back yard. "Please sit down," he said. "I'll get the book for you."

The yard was small but beautifully landscaped. The trees were filled with large spikes of purple and white orchids. All sorts of large broad-leafed tropical plants lined the perimeter and bright red ginger lilies filled the open spaces. It was obviously tended to with a lot of painstaking care, but it retained some primitive natural quality. It was a kind of orchestrated jungle. Man made, but made to convey the wild. Oba returned with the book and sat it down on the table.

"I was just admiring your yard. I can certainly understand why you prefer to sit outside," I said.

"Yes, I much prefer nature to being inside," he said breathing in the fresh air. "So, what is it that brings your interest to this subject?"

"It's a long story," I said. "But the truth is something has drawn me to find out about this religion, so here I am."

"Ah, so you think it is curiosity that leads you. I have found through my experience in this religion that this is rarely the case."

"What do you mean?" I asked.

"We are usually led to things because we need them, or because they need us. It is important to know 'who' leads you, otherwise you are following blindly."

"Are you saying curiosity is a who?" I asked.

"In this religion, everything that is alive is a who. Since everything you feel; curiosity, love, anger, sadness, is alive, they are each part of a who."

"You mean our emotions," I asked.

"How many decisions have you made in your life from fear, loyalty, love, jealousy, anger?" He asked.

"Most of them, I suppose." I answered.

"Yes, because you live from your heart. This is where they live." He said patting his chest and lowering his eyes. "They guide your life one way or another, and you do not even know 'who' they are?" He looked now and questioned me with his eyes.

"So 'who' do you think brought me here?"

He looked into my eyes for a moment. "That is something you should find out," he said.

"How do I do that?"

"Perhaps Elegua can tell you," he said enjoying the little intrigue. "If you would like, I can ask him."

"Yes, I would like that. When do you think you might be speaking to him?" I asked.

"Well, he is in my office right there." He said pointing to the room next to us. "If you would like, we could ask him right now."

I smiled, not knowing what he was really talking about but I liked him and I really wanted to know. "Yes, I would like that. Let's ask him," I said.

He got up and I followed him into his office. He looked down beside the door. "Elegua," He said very politely. "I would like you to meet my friend Jean Marie."

I looked down at the white tiled floor. There was a lump of cement with seashell eyes much like the one I had seen at Maria's. I looked up at Oba. "Elegua, I presume?"

"Yes," he said smiling.

I looked down again. "It's very nice to meet you Elegua," I said looking to Oba for an answer.

"Oh, he doesn't speak like you and I," he said. "These are his mouths," he said holding up a little red cloth bag. "Sit down and I will show you."

We both sat down and Oba spread a little grass mat onto the table. He then placed a small hollowed gourd next to him. Dipping his fingers into water he repeated words similar to the ones Maria had used. "This is a blessing," he said. "We say it in Yoruban, African because it is the language of *Orishas*."

"*Orishas*," I repeated. "Who are they?"

"They are nature. They are the forces of nature like fire, the wind and the water. You will hear the *Orishas* called gods, saints and guardian angels. They are all attempts at translating the word. It does not translate easily. *Orishas* are the forces that make us move. They are the life forces that effect our lives and they are sacred as such."

"I see," I said. "Everything living is a who."

"Yes, and like people, some are more powerful than others. So we begin." Oba picked up the shells in his left hand and touched my forehead and the back of my neck. "Hold out your hands together." I held them out and he poured the little shells into my hands. "Now," he said. "Ask Elegua what it is you want to know."

I looked down at the handful of shells. "Elegua," I said looking up at Oba.

"No, this is between you and Elegua," he said. "I don't need to hear the question, just whisper it to him."

I whispered my question into the shells and he placed his hands under mine waiting for me to release them. "Now we see what they have to say," he said releasing them onto the mat. Quickly he swooped them up and threw them again. In one fluid motion he gathered the shells in one hand and picked up something else in the other. He motioned for me to open my hands once more. "Take these and separate them very quickly. Hold one in each hand and do not open them until I ask for the right or the left." Again he threw the shells. "Right hand," he said flipping his hand over to receive the object. It was a small white ball that looked like chalk. "*Ire*," he said. "That is good, it means positive." He repeated the procedure several times. Then he sat for a moment formulating his words.

"In this sign," he began. "*Chango* says you are his legitimate daughter. *Chango* is thunder and lightening. You have been hit once by lightening?" He looked into my eyes for a confirmation.

"Yes, yes I was hit by lightning. It was amazing. It came right through the window and knocked me clear across the room!"

He nodded in acknowledgement. "In this way he reveals himself to you. *Chango* is very flamboyant, he likes to be seen and heard. When he shows up, listen, because he does not like to repeat himself.

In your work, you see many things, but you do nothing. By this I mean you have been powerless. What you see affects you. But, what do you do with these effects? Do they make you angry, sad, what?" He looked to me for an answer.

"Sad, sometimes afraid," I resigned.

"*Chango* does not like sad and he does not tolerate fear. Sadness belongs to someone else. He would much prefer laughter, or even anger. Those are things that stir action. *Chango* is very active. You have retreated, and you do not allow him to guide your life. Without his guidance, without him, you live a life of sadness, an empty life. You cannot find happiness looking through empty eyes, walking with the dead. *Chango* says you are alive. You are his child and you have been lost for a long time."

All these things were true. I had retreated. I lived in an invisible world, a world I viewed from the eyes of the dead. It was time to reclaim my life here on earth. "How?" I asked. "How do I find *Chango*?"

"Well. You have found him. I am *Chango*," he said.

"You are *Chango*?" I looked at him in amazement.

"Yes," he said. "There are many *Changos* and I am one."

"And what about the nature of *Chango*? You know the thunder and lightning, the life force." I said. "How do you get to know him?"

"Ahh, you want to know that *Chango*. Well that is not so easy, but it can be done."

"Well, that's the one I need to know," I said confidently. I knew then, in no uncertain terms, that he was the one who would introduce me to *Chango*. He was the *Omo Chango* Maria had spoken of. The one I was destined to meet and choose to become my Godfather in this religion.

"If you are certain," he said. "Then you will need to receive your warriors. This is the first step. It will open the way for what is to come."

"And, how do I do that?"

"Next week, Monday, come to my house. Wear white clothes. You must wear a dress or a skirt. Come early, before seven thirty. These are the expenses of the ceremony." He wrote down a figure on the piece of paper.

There was a price to be paid, and I knew I was prepared now to pay it. "Is there anything else I need to know? To prepare for the ceremony I mean."

"The book. You will need to know the names and histories of the Orishas. Learn them."

7

Blood of the Earth

I returned the following week to undergo my first ceremony. I arrived in the morning, wearing my white clothes as Oba had instructed. His house was very peaceful. It was at the end of a quiet street in a well-kept blue-collar neighborhood. Inside, the house was nicely decorated with black and white ceramic floor tiles, clean lines and simple furnishings. "Would you like some Cuban coffee before we begin?" he asked.

"Yes, thank you," I said entering the small dinning room area.

"I couldn't help noticing the paintings," I said. "They're really beautiful. I see they are all done by the same artist, do you know him?"

"Yes," Oba now stepped out of the small kitchen where he had been preparing the coffee. "He is a very good painter and a very good friend."

The colors were vibrant. They were all of women, stylized females in chick poses. One particular painting simply captivated my attention. I couldn't take my eyes off it. The picture portrayed three women sitting at a table in a sidewalk café overlooking the ocean. On the left was a doorway, and from that doorway, an ominous gray shadow was cast across the table directly onto the first woman. The shadow loomed over her. Her hair was light yellow, her face pale and frightened as she pointed to the source of the shadow. The woman to the left was in black. She had dark hair seductively combed to one side. Her face was luminous, like a half moon. She raised one hand to her lips and casually whispered her secrets to the woman on her right. This woman was dressed completely in red with hair the color of flames. In one hand she

165

held a glass of red wine, and as she leaned over to listen to the secrets, she covered the handle of a knife with her other hand.

"Destiny," he said interrupting my daze.

"Destiny?"

"The name of the painting. Actually it is 'The Table of Destiny'."

"Oh," I sighed a little relieved. "Yes, they do look like the three fates sitting there."

"Do you know what this means, the table of destiny?"

"No," I said still studying the painting.

"The Table of Destiny is *Ita*. In our religion it is where all destiny is revealed. All the predictions in life take place on the Table of *Ifa*. The story is that Chango first owned this table, but Chango preferred to dance. He did not have much use of the table because Chango was clairvoyant by birth, so he traded it to his brother Orula for the dance."

"The artist, is he also a Santero?" I asked.

"No, he respects the religion, but he is not initiated. Not everyone is meant to be a priest." Oba motioned for me to follow him out of the room, while he continued speaking. "So you have not changed your mind, you are ready to begin the way of the saints?"

"The way of the saints?" I asked.

"Yes, this is what Santeria means. You are taking on the ways of the saints, the ways of the Orisha. You will become one with them, this is what it means to make the saint. You must learn their ways so they can live through you, so they can speak through you. In this way they come down to earth to help the people who live here," he explained.

"Like a medium?" I asked.

He thought for a moment. "Yes and no, in time you will see. Their ways will become your ways and you will know."

"Oba," I said. "You will have to start from the beginning. I know nothing about the *Orishas*, none of them. I read the stories in your book, about the mythology. I am a little familiar with their names and their histories. They are a lot like the Greek and Roman pantheons. Many of the characters described are like the ancient Gods and Goddesses, so I can relate a little. I'm assuming that Elegua is a lot like the God Mercury. He is the Orisha for communications. The trickster, right?"

"Yes, this is true. But the Yoruban pantheon is much older than the Greek one. It came into the world before it was polluted by politics and egos. It is more primal, and purer because it was kept alive."

"What do you mean it was kept alive?" I asked.

"With this," his hands motioned pulling words from his mouth.

"You mean by word of mouth?"

"This is one of the most sacred things in our religion. The religion is alive because it comes from the breath. From the mouth of one priest to another for thousands of years it has been passed on in this way. Like a flame it is shared from one house to another and it remains alive today. In order to learn, you must watch," he pointed to his eyes. "And, listen very carefully."

We finished our coffee and I followed him out back to the patio. "Before we begin we must do what is called a rogation. Sit here, I have everything prepared. I will be back in a moment."

I waited patiently and when he came back he was carrying two white plates. He set them down on the table behind me and began. "First you must take your shoes off and place your feet flat here on the mat. Hold your hands open on your knees," he placed the hem of my skirt just above my knees and turned my hands up in a position to receive. Then he sprinkled some water from a hollow gourd and began a wordy prayer or petition of some sort in what I now recognized as Yoruban. When he finished he threw four pieces of coconut to the floor. He looked at them carefully before scooping them up and placing them back onto the plate.

I sat still as he proceeded to put some white sticky substance on my throat, the back of my neck, on my knees, in my hands, and on the tops of my feet. Finally the majority of the substance was placed with both hands on top of my head. He said some words as he pressed down on the top of my head. Some of the liquid trickled down the back of my neck. Each respective area was quickly covered with white cotton and my head was covered in a white scarf, wrapped and tied securely to hold the substance in place. "We do this to feed your head," he explained.

Could a head get hungry? I wondered. Perhaps that's why our minds wondered. Could they be looking for food? My head was beginning to feel more focused somehow. Like all my scattered thoughts were coming back to sit at the same table. Something was happening, from the outside in!

The coconuts were consulted once again and a white candle was placed in each hand. He proceeded to clean the substance from my neck, knees and feet. It was carefully removed with the cotton covering and placed back onto the plate. All the while he continued his melodical chants and finally he lit the candles. Then suddenly he pulled me up by the hands from my seat.

"Lift them up high so you can call on them with light. Now," he said sternly. "Blow the candles out and sit back down in the chair. Rub your hands together over the plate, letting go of the pieces of cotton and the candles a little at a time. As you do this, you ask for what it is you come here for, and what it is you need in your life."

I thought for a moment before I began. I wanted to make sure I asked for the right things. What did I need? I needed protection for my children and myself, definitely, but what else? I was being given the perfect opportunity to ask for anything I wanted. Stability, I am not sure what made me ask for it. Perhaps it was because I had never had it. Somehow I thought a stable life was what I needed most. So I silently asked for protection and stability from my guardian Orisha, Chango.

"Sit quietly now and contemplate the things you are about to receive," he told me.

I sat facing the quiet gardens taking in the morning sun. Then it was as if an immense invisible hand was placed firmly on the top of my head, imparting some indefinable serene strength that was beginning to flow through my entire body. I took a deep breath inhaling soul of the moment. Someone or something was present, standing behind me, holding the crown of my head in his hand. Could it be my guardian? Was this the energy of Chango?

It suddenly all felt right, coming to this house, preparing for the initiation. I wished that I knew a little more about the religion, exactly what an initiation entailed. But my eyes had never been opened for any of my other explorations, why should it be any different now? Someday, I thought, I will learn, and I will understand what brought me to this place. Until then, I place my faith in God, in whatever plan he has for my life.

Oba finally returned. I was so completely relaxed he startled me with his approach. He led me into the room he called his office. On the floor before me was a fresh cement statue I now recognized as Elegua. The crude statue with tiny seashell eyes was sitting in an empty terra cotta clay dish. Next to the dish was a black three-legged iron pot filled with what appeared to be tools. Beside the pot was a small silver rooster with bells hanging from the sides of what looked like a chalice.

I began think of my Christian roots, about commandments and idols. 'Thou shalt not have any other gods before me.' Was I putting them before him? No, they all worked for God, I thought. The orishas worked with him like his angels, and the saints. They were simply different parts of the earth, forces of nature that God himself created. No, they all came after God, not before him.

What about idols and graven images? Had I really thought this through? I looked at the strange collection on the floor in front of me. They were not likenesses of God. No attempt had been made to duplicate his omnipotence. I looked at the black pot. These were symbols, tangible images of the powers of nature, teaching tools. Yes, somewhere inside of each of those symbols was hidden the pattern of its nature. No wonder they had been forbidden throughout the ages. They contained a powerful knowledge, vital information for priest, but dangerous knowledge for the masses.

Oba began abruptly. "So, now we begin as we begin everything, with Elegua. Before you begin this path, you must have some help. That is why today you receive your *Guerreros*, your warriors. You will experience many obstacles, many dangers and many enemies along the way. You have chosen the path of the spiritual warrior and in this world you will always need the help of the *Orishas*. I present you first with the *Elekes*, the necklace of Elegua. He held a long strand of red and black beads on my head, first lengthwise and then sideways making the sign of the cross. "Put out your hands to receive them," he told me."

I did as he asked. Then he dropped them to the floor. "Pick them up." Once more I did as he instructed. "Should you ever fall from his grace, may Elegua pick you up again also."

This is your Elegua." he picked up the little gray mound in the dish and held it over my hands. "Elegua is small but powerful. He is the bridge to all the other powers. Without his blessings, no doors will be opened. None of the Orishas will know what you ask for because they will not hear what you say. Elegua is communication, the link between you and God, between you and all that is divine. Always feed him first; and always honor him first because without him, you are without God. And if you are without God, you are truly alone in this world."

Next he picked up the black pot. He placed it into my hands still holding the weight of it in his own. For a split second I started to pull back. Something in the cold touch of that black iron pot made me uncomfortable.

"This is Oggun. He is the brother of Elegua. Oggun is the energy of all the metals in this world, but particularly iron, the metal of labor and hard work. Inside the pot you will see his tools. These are tools that till the soil, a rake, a shovel and a hoe. He also has a small machete and a knife and an anvil. These too belong to him; everything made of metal is a tool of Oggun. He will help to keep you fed, as his tools are the ones that feed the world. He will also protect you from your enemies, as he is a great warrior. He has the strength of weapons in his realm.

Swords, knives and guns also belong to Oggun. Be careful how you call on him to fight for you, because inside of this pot, which is also, his house lives another Orisha. His name is Ochosi.

The crossbow symbolizes Ochosi. He is a great hunter, and a straight shooter. He is the Orisha for justice. When you come to ask for the help of Oggun, remember justice resides there also. Ask only for what is right and be very sure that you know what is right and just before you ask for it. When Oggun acts, it will always be in line with the arrows of divine justice. Ochosi will make sure of this. So, be very careful, sometimes what we mistake for justice on this earth, is nothing more than anger or revenge. And, this can be a very dangerous thing."

"And this," he picked up the little rooster with the bells, "is Osun. Osun is also Elegua's brother and one of the four warriors. He has only one job. His job is to warn you." He tipped the silver rooster over and the little bells jingled as he laid him on his side. "If Osun should ever fall down of his own accord. He is telling you that you are in grave danger. For this reason, you must place him where he will not accidentally be knocked down. Do you understand?"

"Yes, I understand," I said. I suddenly remembered the crucifix. 'It just fell off the wall,' my mother said. Yes, God had a way of letting us know these things, but what were we suppose to do after the warning?

Oba noticing the expression on my face tried to assure me. "Don't worry. In time, you will come to know all of these things. Now, do you have any questions?"

I looked down, into the little seashell face of the cement mound. It was like bringing a newborn child home. There was no question that he belonged to you. The child was after all born from you. Still, he was stranger, a new little person with his very own soul coming home to live with you. But, this little cement head was no warm and cuddly child, how was I supposed to care for him? Were they supposed to speak to me? How on earth were these 'things' supposed to protect me? "What do I do with them?" I blurted out.

"Take them home," he said simply.

I looked to him for the rest of the answer, but it was obvious that none would be given today. "Okay, and what about the initiation? What do I need to do?"

"Come to my house one week from Friday, about three. Bring with you white clothes. Everything must be white. Of course your warriors must come back with you. Bring three white towels, two white sheets, five white scarves for your head. And, plan to stay here for seven days," he said casually.

"Seven days, are you kidding?"

"No, I am not," he said wrapping my new Elegua in newspaper and packing him into a box for the ride home.

This was pretty much the extent of my preparation for the priesthood. I drove home recounting the only story I knew of the four warriors. It was the story of how the warriors came to work for the world.

Obatala was the husband of Yemaya and the father of all the Oriashas. As it was the duty of Obatala to check over the earth and make sure that everything was in order, he left every morning to make his rounds. Because Oggun was the eldest child living in the house, Obatala left him in charge during his absence. Oggun was very strong, but he was also very selfish, and soon he began to abuse his power.

He did as he pleased in the house, spending most of the day making fun of his father and disrespecting his mother. And, because he also controlled the food in the house he used it to his advantage to bribe his brothers Ochosi and Osun. In time, the abuses escalated, until he began the unthinkable. Oggun, who had no respect for any woman, began on a daily basis to rape and defile his own mother, Yemaya.

His poor mother was torn. She loved her husband, but she was deeply ashamed, and she feared what might happen if Obaltala found out. So, the abuse continued, and Oggun continued to bribe his brothers with food, which they greedily accepted. The only one left to contend with was Elegua, the youngest, who refused to be bribed by Oggun. Oggun was furious, so he withheld his food, but Elegua refused to give in. Finally Oggun grew so enraged that he threw his little brother out of the house.

When Obatala returned he inquired about Elegua. Where upon Oggun lied and said he did not know what happened to him. Ochosi and Osun said nothing. Elegua did not return for three days. On the third day, he was waiting for his father where the roads crossed. Elegua, who knew the paths of his father came there to tell him what was happening in his home. Brave little Elegua told him everything. Obatala fluctuated between anger and disbelief. It was the young Elegua who wisely advised his father to wait until the next morning. When he could see for himself what had been happening when he was not at home.

The next morning Obatala left as he usually did and Oggun began his tyranny as he usually did. But on this day Obatala returned early. When he entered his house and saw with his own eyes what atrocities Oggun had committed. He nearly went mad with anger. His eyes grew steely and he lifted his hand to curse his son. But before he could even open his mouth and utter the first word, a now terrified Oggun jumped in with his own. "Father do not curse me, for what I have done I will curse myself. I will work, from this day forward, day and night. I will work from this day on for all the Orishas and all the world." And so it was that Oggun began working tirelessly day and night providing his services for all the inhabitants of the earth. Oggun became the knife, the hammer, the till and all of tools and functional metal objects.

Obatala turned next to Ochosi. "Ochosi, because you gave in to the bribes of food instead of doing what was right, you will never again be tempted by intimidation or coercion. From now on, you will be the dispenser of justice and enforcer of laws. Also you will take on the job as the hunter, providing food for the hungry." Ochosi became the crossbow.

Then he looked at Osun. "Osun because of your greed, you chose to accept food in exchange for your silence. From now on you will remain silent. You will have one job on this earth, and that is to warn us of impending dangers. You are to stand up over the doorway, and you will come to the ground only to warn us when danger or death is near." Osun became a silent effigy.

Finally he spoke to Elegua. "Elegua, because you were the only one who did the right thing, you will from now on, always be fed first. The crossroads will belong to you. You will be in charge of opening and closing all the paths and opportunities in life. You will be in charge of communications, and it will be your business to know everything that goes on." And so it was that the four warriors came to work for the world.

I thought of Oggun, what a terrible role he had played. What a frightening energy he was. But there was something genuine about the story, something necessary about the whole terrible ordeal. But why was he such a brute, and why rape? It was only a metaphor I reminded myself, something to explain the use and misuse of the tools that tilled and ravaged the earth. I looked down at the black pot filled with miniature tools. I knew there was more, but I was tired, and I did not want to think anymore. I would go home and get some rest. The next day, I would make arrangements for the events that would follow.

It was late Friday afternoon when I arrived to make my final leap of faith into the religion. A plump grandmotherly woman greeted me at the door. She was dressed in a white peasant blouse and a full skirt made of strips of blue gingham and white lace. A white kerchief trimmed in lace and tied at the nape of her neck covered her hair. She smiled but did not speak as she took the bag from my hands motioning for me to come in. The old woman lifted the suitcase and plopped it down on the dinning room table. She proceeded to unzip my orderly but over packed bag and began riffling through it.

"It's okay," my Godfather said as he walked in through the kitchen doorway. "She will be your *Yubona*, your Godmother. She needs to get your things ready. "She is an *Omo Yemaya*, a child of *Yemaya*. From this time on she will do everything for you. From this moment on, you are a child and if there is anything you need, you must ask for her permission."

"But how will I ask? I don't know Spanish."

"Don't worry. She will understand," he said.

The plump woman pulled out the small bag of toiletries and some other personal items and set them aside, along with my makeup pouch, hairbrush and blow dryer. She smiled as she made a comment in Spanish to a woman who was making coffee in the kitchen. The woman in the kitchen laughed out loud as she replied to her, also in Spanish.

"They want to know," my Godfather said smiling. "If you thought you were going on a cruise."

"A Cruise?" I asked, looking rather perplexed. The humor completely eluded me.

"You will understand when the time comes. Until then, you begin with this," he said handing me a small black notebook. "This is to be your *libreta*. In it you will keep a record of everything you learn in your new life, your life in *Osha*, which begins today. All the things you will need to remember will be recorded in your *libretta* from this day on. Keep it with you always. It is sacred to your life. Now, sit down at the table over there," he pointed to the dining room, "and begin by writing what it is you came here for. Write what it is you came to my house to find."

My own libretta, I thought of the word. It sounded like libretto, something written for the opera. I envisioned a little book filled with the music and poetry that would open my path to the saints. Here in these pages I would begin my new life. Here somewhere in the southern portion of Miami's sub terrain, I sit in the house of my soon to be godfather, preparing to learn what ever it is I need to know. Why did I come? What am I hoping to find here?

I tried to think of all the things that led me to this place, all the strange things in my life that brought me to this particular space, here and now. I am sure that it is more than one specific event. It is more likely a compilation of a lifetime of events that led me to this one. But,

I suppose if there were one event, a single incident responsible for my being here today, it would be the one that began with the ex-DEA agent.

As I wrote, there was a knock at the door. I heard the commotion and turned to see who it was. A very tall, very muscular woman with her arms and legs covered in tattoos entered the room. "Jeanne Marie," Oba said walking her to the table. "This is Roxanne. She has come to be initiated also. She has come to receive Oggun. In *Osha,* in this religion she will be your brother, the brother of Chango is Oggun."

I would have easily mistaken her for a man had she not been wearing a dress. She was huge with short dark hair and a ruddy face. "It's nice to meet you," I said hoping the uneasiness in my voice was not too detectible.

"Same here," she held out her large hand for me to shake.

I shook her hand. Her grasp was firm like a man. What had I gotten myself into? Chango and Oggun were brothers, but they were also mortal enemies. They fought all the time. Why would my Godfather choose to initiate us together? Oba gave her the same instructions he had given me earlier and then left the two of us alone in the room.

"Chango? She asked in a mocking tone.

"Yes Chango," I said resolutely.

She shrugged one shoulder and opened her notebook. "So you live in Miami?"

"Yes, well actually I live in Davie, it's west of Ft. Lauderdale. What about you? Do you live in Miami?"

"New York. I just came down for this."

"Have you known Oba for a long time?" I asked.

"Nope, just since yesterday," she said not looking up from her writing.

"Yesterday! Oh, you must know your Yubona then."

"Nope, haven't even met her yet."

I waited a minute, trying to think of a better way to ask the questions when she began to volunteer the information. "I've been talking to him on the phone. A santero in New York sent me here for the initiation. Most people there come to Miami for this."

"Do you know much about it? The religion I mean."

"Not too much. I go to a santero back home. He told me it had to be done. So, I took a leave of absence and here I am."

"What kind of work do you do?"

"I'm a guard at the prison."

"An appropriate place for Oggun," I said.

"Yeah. What do you do?"

"I'm a counselor, a spiritual counselor, a clairvoyant."

"Touché, good job for Chango."

"Yeah," I agreed. "Chango is supposed to be the clairvoyant of the group. I guess we're off to a good start."

"I hope so. They told me if anything went wrong with this ceremony, I could lose my life, my freedom or both."

It sounded serious. Suddenly I did not want to know anymore. The mood had subtly changed. The newness and the excitement had somehow dissipated. In its place an uneasy heaviness now permeated the room. In this woman's very presence was an energy I was not prepared for, and if Roxanne was Oggun, what would happen when they intensified that energy? Oggun was no gentle spirit to begin with. I could only wait and see.

The first ceremony began at sunset; it was the ceremony of the river. Not knowing what this was, it was explained to me in this way: "Today you are brought to the river, today you will learn her name as I present you now to *Ochun*. Look into the water. Remember always that much lies beneath the reflections on top of the water and do not be fooled by what you see. In time you will learn her ways. In time will know *Ochun*. She is like the honey we offer her. She is all the sweetness of this life. She is love. But, you must be aware; she can also bring with her the bitter lessons of deception and heartbreak. Life and love are bitter sweet, and this will always be so. In this ceremony, which is the first of every initiation, we come to pay respect to her because she is the guardian of childbirth. We must ask for her blessings, for a safe passage and a healthy birth into your new life. Birth can be a perilous journey and *Ochun* can be a powerful guardian."

This introduction was followed by many words now spoken melodically in African, the language of the ancestors. The language it was said, that the guardians preferred. His voice flowed with the rhythm of the waters. And while I could not understand the words, I knew innately these prayers were sung in such a way as to charm her into listening to our request.

I was accompanied by three priests; my godfather, my godmother and a female priest of *Ochun*. We stood on a secluded bank of the river somewhere deep in the everglades of South Miami. I was not sure exactly where I was. I had never seen this part of the glades before. I had never known of the existence of this river before.

First an offering of *chin chin* was presented. It looked to be a mixture of sautéed greens and shrimp in a bowl made of a hollowed gourd. I was told that this was one of *Ochun's* favorite foods. This mixture was fed to the river, followed by a generous amount of honey poured over the water as prayers were sung in her honor. Next, a clay jar was filled with the river water and set aside for later use. I was directed to step down onto the rocks at the river's edge.

They all began to sing, with my godfather's voice leading the chorus. His words came closer together as the rhythm gathered momentum. Voices spiraled and my godfather suddenly spun around on his heels. With his back to us now, his eyes were no longer upon us. Within an instant the women began tearing the clothes from my body. I stood still, allowing them to drop like a broken strand of pearls at my feet. I knew this was the first step to shedding my old life. It was shocking never the less. I remained frozen in position, my naked body spawning goose bumps from the chill. I instinctively tried to cover myself with my hands. My Yubona brushed them down and motioned for me to leave them by my side and stand still. I obeyed.

As I stood there, in total stillness looking across the river, I became increasingly aware of my surroundings. We were somewhere in the midst of the everglades, a swampy jungle that appeared exactly the same on this day as it had some million years prior. The overgrown vegetation, the steamy water, it was all exciting, wild and intensely primal. Then I noticed for the first time two large alligators swimming freely through the water on the other side.

They were large prehistoric creatures moving with an eerie gracefulness across the water. The creatures were born with massive jaws, filled with sharp teeth and their bodies were covered with an armor of scales. These animals were made to hunt. They were natural predators. I did not take my eyes off of them. Those huge reptiles lived here. And, in the everglades where the predators swam free, I was nothing more than an easy meal. I was naked and empty handed. My heart was pounding. I wanted to run. I tried to take a single step back when my godmother abruptly planted her hands firmly on my shoulders. She pressed them down to let me know I should not move.

Then she placed her hands over my eyes to close them. From this darkness, I was suddenly jolted into another awareness as a bucket of icy cold river water was poured over my head. I shivered and shook from the cold. It was everything I could do to just catch my breath. They proceeded to bathe me in the cold water from the river and even as I shivered I hoped that they too were aware of the large reptiles that swam freely in these waters. They worked quickly however, and before I knew it they were patting me dry with the white towel and dressing me as though I were a child.

The clay jar used for the water was filled with river water, wrapped in a red cloth and handed to me to carry back to the house. I had survived the baptism. I began to relax a little. I belonged here now. Ochun had welcomed me. Just as she welcomed the plants that grew by her side, the fish, and the birds, even the alligators that lived in her home. The river is alive, and this is the power and the beauty of Ochun.

The alligators had gratefully climbed out of the water and onto the grassy shore across from us. The sun was setting in glorious shades of pinks and mauves over the moss-covered palms. And, the waters of the river reflected a perfect image of the earth and the sky. Oba led a beautiful chorus of songs offered to the river in gratitude and as I stood on the waters edge refreshed and warmed in clean white clothes. I began for the first time to comprehend the Orisha Ochun. Ochun I prayed silently, this moment will be forever etched in my heart. Thank you for everything you have given me today.

When we returned to the house Roxanne was pacing on the back porch. I could only assume she had completed the same ritual at the river. She was wearing a new set of clothes. The white skirt against her tattooed legs looked almost comical on her. I was led to the other side of the yard. They seemed to be making a concerted effort to keep us separated.

There were several preparatory rituals that had to be performed. I was told great pains had to be taken to prepare the crown of my head for my impending birth. This preparatory ritual was referred to as the Lavatory. Another rogation was done, this time I was presented with a white pigeon. My *Yubonna*, my godmother dipped the feet of the bird into a bucket of fresh water and cleaned him. I was instructed to turn around as she swept my body with the feathers of a live bird. Another woman held the pigeon while my *Yubonna* completed the ritual with the sticky white stuff. After the gooey substance was placed on top of my head I felt a warm liquid running down my neck and forehead. I wiped the liquid from my forehead before it ran into my eyes. It was then that I realized it was blood. The thought of it sent a shiver up my spine.

The beautiful white bird was placed on a white plate in front of me. The head had been torn from its body and the white feathers were stained now with red blood. I could still feel its warmth as they tied the scarf tightly in place. I had now participated in a blood sacrifice. A life had been taken on my behalf. I am not sure how to think of it. How do

I justify it? Where do I put it in my mind? I thought of the alligator in the river. If he had eaten me, would he have been evil? Or would he have been surviving, doing what alligators do for sustenance? If my head was hungry, didn't it have to be fed? All these questions swam freely through my mind. Somewhere inside, I know I am a part of this, and I am here for the duration.

Oba walked towards me with a small bag I knew contained his shells. He proceeded to recite a long litany of prayers and finally he cast the shells onto the floor. My yubona reached down to pick the shells up and he stopped her. He made it clear that she should not touch them. Then he reached down and gathered them up himself. Once more he threw the little shells to the floor and picked them up again. Then he motioned with his chin for my yubona to leave.

"Because of this sign," he said. "She cannot be your yubona."

"Why? Is there something wrong?"

"In this sign, someone else will have to be your yubona," he said quickly walking away from me and into the house.

Something felt wrong, but I knew I could not ask again what it might be. So I waited. An hour or so later he came out with another woman. She was a stately woman with sculptured white hair, impeccable makeup and a fresh manicure. She looked out of place, carrying her white kerchief in hand. She was not like the others. She was no peasant woman. "This is Helena, she will be your yubona," Oba said. "You will address her as *Iya*, godmother. She is an *omo Obatala*, a child of *Obatala*. *Obatala* is the head, the head of all things. He is father and king of all the Orishas. The woman smiled and nodded gracefully. I smiled. There was something about this regal woman I liked.

So many things had taken place already. The house had somehow transformed itself. This was not the same house I had visited only a week ago. It was filled with strange faces and foreign customs. I was in America, but this was Miami. I was aware that I was in some subterranean place deep within the heart of Miami, and that this, was yet another world within that city. It operated in its own time and space, in accordance to its own natural laws. I was fully aware that I was the foreigner here.

When I arrived only a day before, it had been the twentieth century. But as I stepped through the threshold of this house it had become some primal time. Long before history thought it necessary to record itself. I did not know the language. I could not speak or understand one word of Spanish or Yoruban, the African language of this religion. My godfather was the only one present who spoke English to me, and this he had precious little time to do with so many preparations at hand. I had placed my trust, and literally my life in his hands, yet I barely knew this man.

This was to be, they told me, the day of my birth. The day I would be born into the religion, into my new life as a Santera, a priest. I did not yet know what this meant. I laid there in the darkness on a thin straw mat. There was a bare tile floor beneath the mat and it was as cold as ice. I was literally chilled to the bone. The small candles on top of the white plates had long since burned out and I knew it was morning but the sun had not yet made its appearance. My body was stiff from the cold and I laid still like a corpse waiting to come back to life. I wondered if I would ever feel warm again.

Roxanne was on a matt on the other side of the room. She appears to be sleeping. We were both instructed not to speak without permission. It was very late when everyone finally settled down to sleep for the night. Oba had lost his temper several times that day with Roxanne.

"Listen!" He yelled at her. "You are not here to ask questions. You are here to listen, with respect to your elders." Roxanne shut up, but she glared at him like she wished him dead.

Gratefully, the long night had ended. The sun was beginning to rise and I hesitated to turn my head and peek through the window beside me. I tried to write in my little book by the light of the candles. Time seemed strangely displaced. The night seemed to last forever. It had been still and sleepless, but soon the light broke through the darkness and the room was once again filled with light, movement and warmth, precious warmth.

My head was covered with a white cloth. It was loose, but still tied in the back. I thought of all the things that lay beneath that covering, the layers of herbs, the sticky white stuff and the dried blood of a white pigeon. I thought again of the sacrifice. I could still feel the warm blood, the life force of that beautiful creature pouring out of him and onto the top of my head. His bloodless carcass still remained only partially covered between the white plates on the floor above my head.

In the house, people were beginning to rise. They moved quickly, and within minutes the house was stirring, the kitchen was lit and coffee was brewing. I waited for my Godmother to give me permission to get up from my place on the floor. From the doorway of the kitchen she motioned for me to roll up my straw mat and offered me a cup of *café con leche*. I only wanted its warmth, but the hot sweet liquid was filled with an unexpected, extraordinary flavor.

I was stiff, but moving. They led me quickly out of the room, to a quiet corner of the back patio. I was motioned to sit in a chair with my back to the rest of the house. People were beginning to arrive. I could hear their greetings, talking and laughter. I simply couldn't understand anything they talked or laughed about. Everything was foreign. I assumed I was to relax, meditate and write something profound in my little book. It was obvious that I had been set apart from the social interaction. I would continue writing in my libretta. I assumed it was to be my diary.

I wish I could say that I had some deep spiritual contemplations, but the truth was, I was more than a little anxious about what was to come. I was told nothing. I was still cold. I had not been allowed to brush my teeth or wash my face. The same white towel stained with the blood of the white pigeon from the night before was the only thing I was allowed to wrap over my shoulders.

My *Yubona*, my godmother handed me a cup of some green herbal liquid and motioned for me to drink it. I had no idea what it was or what affects it might have on me. I only knew I must drink it. I was given a plate with bread, cheese and ham but I was not hungry. I was far too apprehensive. I was instructed to eat and wait in silence. I did not know how long the wait would be.

As I sat there, I closed my eyes, only for a few seconds. That's when it happened. I recognized it immediately. It was a scent. The strong unmistakable sent of Joseph. My eyes popped open. It was as if he had just walked by, invisibly, but right in front of me. Why Joseph? Why here of all places?

The last time I had seen him was at a shopping mall in Miami. I had named my son Joseph, and my child was in my arms when he approached me. "You named him Joseph?" He asked peeking into his tiny face.

"I named him for his grandmother, her name was Josephine."

"But you thought of me," he pleaded. "Just a little."

"Maybe a little, but very little. So, how is your wife?"

"We are divorced. The marriage didn't last long. I tried to call you, your mother told me you were married."

"And I have a son," I added. I could not tell him I was no longer married. I did not have the power to resist him and I did not have the courage to pursue him.

"He's beautiful, like his mother."

"Thank you," I replied turning around to leave. But he grabbed my hand and pulled me towards him. My heart pounded as I anticipated being too near him. Then he gently lifted my son's tiny hand and kissed it.

"Thank you," he said. "For remembering me."

I knew he believed that I had named my son for him, and that was the last time I saw Joseph, alive. It was several years later, when he came to me in a vision. I was lying down on the sofa. I hadn't been feeling too well that morning. I closed my eyes to meditate and there it was, his scent. It was unmistakably Joseph. My eyes remained closed and I could hear his voice calling to me. He laughed as he spoke. "I'm dead Jeanne Marie, I'm dead." Then I saw his face smiling at me. "It's true, I'm really dead."

It was a mocking tone and I didn't like the joke. "Stop it, stop saying that. You're scaring me," I yelled out loud. Then I saw the picture, right where his face had been in my mind. A blue van, crashed into a chain-linked fence and a man slumped over the steering wheel. I knew it was him. I knew instantly it was Joseph.

I jumped up and ran to the phone. I dialed information trying to get his phone number. His business was no longer listed. He had probably changed the name and the location. It had been a long time. I gave the operator his name. It was listed as a private number. "Please, I begged the operator. "This is an emergency. It could be life and death. I need his number." She did not have it. She would put me through to a supervisor. The supervisor finally agreed to take my number. She offered to call him and give him my number. But I knew, by then I was sure that it was futile. I could not reach him.

An hour later the phone rang. My heart jumped as I grabbed the receiver. I thought it might be the operator, but it was my mother's voice. "Jeanne Marie. Oh I'm so glad you answered."

"What's wrong Mom? You don't sound right."

"You haven't had the TV on have you?"

"No, I was just laying down. I wasn't feeling too good. Why?"

"You better sit down Jeanne Marie."

"Why? Has something happened? I know something's happened. It's Joseph isn't it?" Panic was beginning to overcome me. I did not wait for her to speak. "I tried to warn him. I tried to Mom. They wouldn't give me his number. He wouldn't stop laughing. I tried…I knew…" I began to sob uncontrollably.

"Honey calm down. I didn't think you knew. I just didn't want you to see it on TV. The pictures they're showing…I didn't want you to find out that way."

"The pictures?" I stopped crying in a moment of confusion.

"It's all over the news. He was driving home and someone just shot him. They don't know who or why, but he's dead."

"A van, a blue van? I asked.

"Yes, but I thought you didn't see it," she said.

"I saw it Mom. Just not on TV."

"Honey I know this is a terrible thing for you. I know how you felt about him. These things just happen sometimes."

"Yeah," I was suddenly calm. It had all been inevitable, it always was. "Yeah, things just happen sometimes."

"So Joseph, why here, why now? Was that what you meant when you said you would make time stand still for me someday? No, I have not forgotten you Joseph. I still remember you. "I still remember everything." I whispered, inhaling once more in hopes of recapturing one last trace of his fading fragrance.

I'm sure I was teary eyed, and still deep in thought when someone suddenly came up from behind and threw a sheet over my head. I was pulled to my feet and blindly being led to where, I did not know. I was only aware that the initiation had officially begun, and pure adrenalin had begun pumping through my veins.

With the sheet still covering me, I was guided to a place outside, then told to run straight ahead very quickly. As I ran I was thrashed with small whips made from tree branches. Then I was captured by familiar hands and led to yet another place. I was instructed at this point to knock three times on the door. My hand was lifted to the place and I was told from this time forward my eyes were to be closed at all times. I knocked. A voice answered the knock.

"Who is it?" I immediately feel calmer as I recognize the voice. It is the voice of my Godfather, and it is in English. I am prompted by the answer, as I do not know what to say. The word *Yawo* is whispered into my ear.

"*Yawo*." I answered.

"And what do you want?" He called back.

Again I am prompted with the answer.

"*Orisha.*"

"What *Orisha* do you want?"

"*Elegua.*" I answer in this manner, repeating the same procedure for each Orisha. I name each of the guardians I am to receive until; at last I knock three times and give the name of my own guardian, *Chango.*

"And to whose house do you come to receive these Orisha?"

"The house of my godfather." I answer. "*Oba.*"

"Well, then you may enter."

With this reply I am aware of a warm syrupy liquid being poured over my bare feet. I am led through the doorway. The sheet is lifted from my head and I am once more warned not to open my eyes. I hear talking and scurrying feet, the sound of water in a hollow metal pan. Suddenly my clothes were being torn from me once again. Whatever modesty I had left was completely overridden by shear terror.

Next two women were lifting me up and I knew my feet had now landed inside of the metal pan. From nowhere a bucket of cold water was poured over my head and before I could catch my breath my body was being bombarded with hands rubbing soap and herbs over every part of me. I dared not move or utter a sound. I think I was paralyzed anyway. I was surprised again as the rinse came from another bucket of cold water. By this time I was beyond the shock of the experience, I was just cold, wet and scared.

Again I was lifted, this time out of the pan with some sort of blessing. I was being patted dry with a sheet. I heard the women's voices as I was being dressed. My hands were pushed down as I tried to help in this process. This was no gentle spiritual cleansing. It was a practical bathing with stern hands and evidently a clear timetable. Every thing seemed to be happening at an accelerated speed. Every motion was quick and deliberate. There was no time for thinking or observing. It was all rather disorienting.

I do not know many hours were spent from one remembered moment to the next, but I cannot account for this. I was aware at some point that my head and shoulders were covered with some kind of cotton fabric. There may have been more than one layer. I am not really certain if I felt it or saw it, but I knew, the interior was red, a crimson fiery red. The air beneath this scarlet shroud was thick and heated. I could feel the crimson cover growing hotter by the moment, intensifying by the second until I was completely consumed by this veil of fire.

Suddenly, there was a voice, a magnificent voice, singing me to him. I could hear drums in the distance and I sighed with relief as tranquility entered my being. My head swayed to some irresistible primal rhythmic calling. The drums began to get louder, the voice got stronger and I could feel something other than myself rising to their rhythm. The pace hastened. I tried to stop this, but the thunderous sounds of this insatiable music would not stop. I could no longer control even my arms that were now being raised without my permission. I was not sure if I was actually growing to some hideous height or if I was floating upwards. I was rising however, and just as I thought I would touch the top of the ceiling, two strong hands grabbed me from behind and pulled me back down again. The music ended abruptly and the silence in the room was deafening. I had no idea what had just taken place.

I was lead and positioned into the center of the room. The red veil that covered my head and face was removed and someone placed their hands over my eyes. "Now." I heard the heavily accented voice of an older gentleman. "See for the first time *Yawo*, this is your new home."

I opened my eyes to the throne in front of me. It was beautiful. From ceiling to floor the entire corner of the room had been draped in rich satins of deep crimson red alternating with shimmering silver white laces. It was so luxurious, such a stark contrast to all the primitiveness of the day. The tile floor was covered with the same mat I had attempted to sleep on the night before and in the center sat an ornately carved wooden pillar. On either side of the straw mat were large enamel bowls filled with what appeared to be dark stones, beads and other metal artifacts. All of the bowls were covered in some liquid green herbal mixture. I was led beneath this canopy and positioned in the center facing the room full of priests who had assisted in bringing me into this world.

One by one, beginning with my godparents, they prostrated themselves in front of me, each with their own respective salute. My godmother hugged me, kissed me on each side of my cheeks and said, "God Bless you my child," in perfect English.

I looked at her in amazement. "You speak English?"

She smiled and backed away making room for the next Santero in line. I reciprocated every salute, and as each Santero touched the mat they gave me, the new *Yawo* their blessings. This was the time when in turn they each had the opportunity to make their own special request. The *ache*, the energy was fresh following the birth of a new *Yawo*. The initiation process itself is more commonly referred to as 'making the Saint'. Everyone in attendance had provided a bit of their own *ache*. They had pooled their collective powers to make this possible, to open the passage for my birth.

I found myself somewhere between elation and exhaustion. Many things I cannot recount about this day because for the most part, I understood very little and saw even less. I do not know if this is how it should be, but it is the way it was. My arms and legs ached. Each salute was like a push up and I was not used to so much exercise. The muscles in my arms were sore. The top of my head felt strange, as if the skull had been actually pried opened. I reach up to touch my head. It was then that I realized that all my hair had been cut off. My head had been shaved, painted and covered again in layers of sticky herbs and cotton. I was grateful they covered the mirror in the bathroom, glad not to know what I must have looked like. I was not sure why this was done, but I was too tired to really care.

I was told I could sit down on the wooden pillar referred to as the *pilon*, the throne of *Chango*. For a moment I was comfortable and I breathed a sigh of relief that the process had finally ended. I was now a *Yawo*. Everyone but my godmother had left the room. It was quiet for a moment. "I'm glad we have a moment alone." I said. "I'm glad it was you who was chosen to be my godmother."

"Well, to tell you truth I did not expect this at all, but I am glad too. Your godfather called me and said I needed to do this. So, here I am. You are my first goddaughter. Ah, but we will have plenty of time to talk later. For now you must rest."

A few minutes later Roxanne was brought in. Her head had been shaved and painted. She wore burlap pants and a skirt made of palm fronds and had a large machete that hung down her side. She looked more than ever like a man, a fierce one at that. Her face was reddened, from tears and or anger. When they uncovered her eyes, a Santero pulled down the sheet that had been covering the corner adjacent to mine. It had been decorated for Oggun. It was in such stark contrast to the rich satins and lace for Chango. Oggun's décor was done in metal mesh, which had been woven with large green leafy plants. It was made to look like a forest.

Her godmother sternly reached up and placed her hand on the shoulder of Oggun. With the other hand she motioned for Roxanne to lie down on the matt so the process of saluting could begin. No one in her party looked very happy. I wondered what had taken place outside, if her initiation was very different from mine. It was after all a very different energy.

One of the older women motioned to me to get off my little stool, the pilon, and sit down on the mat. A plate of food was placed on the floor in front of me. "Eat." She said. "You will need your strength for the next part." I winced, realizing then that the ceremony had not yet ended.

It was the quantity I believe, that at first was so shocking, but I was not so sure of anything anymore. I felt sick, faint and prayed that my knees would not buckle as I swooned in place. I only hoped that I could remain standing long enough to finish. It seemed an eternity. Realistically, it lasted several hours. I was completely unprepared for the number of sacrifices, the amounts of blood. Blood ran everywhere, including down my own thighs. In addition to all the events of the day, my menstrual cycle had begun. It was not the right time for it. I was not sure why, but I could feel the warm sensation of blood trickling down legs. Perhaps it was a cleansing. Maybe it had come purely from empathy. A stream of dark menstrual blood was flowing from me, dripping onto my feet, mixing with the splashes of vital fluid from animals being killed.

Blood poured from everywhere, all around me red liquid was splattering on white tile. Everywhere I looked there were splashes of the sanguine fluid. Crimson on the white clothing, it was on the hands and feet of every person in the room. The smell of fowl, animals and fresh blood mingled together in some faintly familiar primal perfume. The familiarity itself was eerie. Even if it was from some ancient genetic origin, it was repulsive to me that it could possibly be recognizable. But inhaling it, was a mixed sensation, somewhere inside I knew it was one of the oldest scents on earth. It was the scent of the essence of the earth itself.

There were so many lives being offered for mine. Each one was offered to nourish and strengthen some part of me. It was a humbling experience. I was beginning to understand that one of the purposes of this sacrifice is to imbue the initiate with a sense of responsibility for those sacrifices. I know that lives had been taken, offered on my behalf. I had knowingly accepted their life force and I was now responsible for the direction, growth and survival of that force. It was something that would be forever after, unconscionable to waste. All that red blood, it was the very fluid of life. It was warm to the touch and I felt the very motion of the flow of life. I had smelled its pungent aroma and I now saw that there was so much more to flesh and blood than I had ever realized. I felt such a tremendous respect for that earthy part of life that had up to now been little more than an imposing vision to me.

"Tomorrow." My godfather told me, as the day began to unwind. "All the animals that have been sacrificed will be eaten at the celebration. Today they feed the soul; tomorrow they will nourish the body.

Tomorrow is the feast day. It will be your coming out, your presentation to the world."

Regrettably, I childishly expressed some mild distaste about eating the very animals I had just watched die. He suddenly grew very somber. Then he told me in these words: "You are American, and you may believe that in life, all the little animals of the wild are sitting on the forest floor, laughing and singing together, having a party. They are not. This is not Disney World. Animals live by hunting, killing and eating one another, because this is the way of nature in this world. Do not ever forget this."

This was my first day as an initiate. Looking back it all seems like yesterday, but I think too that maybe that will always be so. There is something wonderful about the feeling of being born yesterday. It is no doubt naïve, but it is also open, open to life, its lessons and all the adventures that life brings. Everything is perpetually new and waiting to be explored. In so many ways I think this is beautiful, and at the same time, quite dangerous.

The physical dangers for an infant are much the same for every species on earth, starvation, illness, exposure and predators. For a spiritual infant, they are much the same, but these ethereal hazards are not visible to everyone. This is the job of the godparents for those first years. They must protect their offspring until they are strong enough and wise enough to protect themselves. In order to do this, they must know these dangers, and intimately understand them.

That night the godmothers dressed each of us like children and prepared us for bed. We were told to remain under the cover of our thrones. The canapés above us were there for more than décor. It was explained that this was also done to provide our heads, which were now sacred with protection. To leave this place, even for a moment was dangerous.

I lay down on my little straw mat. I was so tired. I was sure I could sleep. I looked up at the canapé of red satin. Everything was as it should be, I assured myself, and I felt safe in my protective little corner.

Then Oggun began to speak, "You look awfully content over there in your little house."

"Well, it's a lot better than last night," I said. "At least the worst of it is over."

"You can say that again. I almost left before it was over."

I sat up now. There was no way out of the conversation. "I saw you looked pretty upset when you came in."

"You're lucky, they like you," she said. "Oba and I do not get along."

"You have to remember, he's from the old school. You know, they think you should learn by experience, and experience takes time. According to them, you don't give the answers away. They think you should earn them."

"Yeah well, I didn't come here to get jerked around," she said running her fingers down the edge of the machete. "Do you know why I'm here?"

"Just what you told me before," I said wishing she would put the big knife away.

"I almost killed someone." She gritted her teeth as she spoke. "The woman I was in love with."

All this, I thought, and a big tattooed lesbian is going to hack me to death with a machete tonight. Why didn't I get a weapon? I looked into the bowl containing the implements of Chango. Inside were his weapons; miniature replicas of hatchets, swords and knives, but they were all made of wood. How were they supposed to help me?

"We'd been together for over three years," she continued. "I know I have a bad temper. But she knew it too! Anyway, we were coming home one night, walking over the train tracks, and she started with me. I don't even remember exactly what she said. But it was just irritating. What more did she want from me? I took good care of her. I worked hard, everyday. Then it just happened." She lifted the machete, gripping the handle tightly in her hands. "I just started hitting her. I was blind with rage. The next thing I knew, I was sitting on the tracks with her head in my hands and they were full of blood. I almost killed her." Her voice trailed off as she tried to focus through her tears.

"Roxanne, I can understand why you're here." I tried to reassure her. "The spirit of Oggun is very powerful inside of you. It must be the right time to begin focusing him into a positive path. This is a whole new life, it's the perfect opportunity for you."

"It's not that easy Jeanne Marie. You have Chango. He's a happy guy. Everybody loves him. I am Oggun. Do you know the history of Oggun?"

"Just what I've read so far," I said. "But even that should let you know, he's a vital energy in this world."

"Then you read the story about him. He raped his own mother," she glared at me.

"I don't think they meant that to be taken literally," I tried to explain. "Think about what it represents. Oggun is metal, tools, and he is also industry. Yemaya is his mother, and she is the earth. What they say is true. Industry has raped the earth. Look what's happening in our world. And every time a shovel is inserted into the ground, in its own way it's raping the earth. But where would we be without the shovel, and the tools for farming? Where would we be without industry? Think about it."

"That makes a lot of sense. I guess there are a lot of good things about Oggun," she agreed.

"I think so. Oggun is a hard worker. He's the one who clears the forests and feeds the world. And look at all the things he provides for us. Without him we wouldn't have any transportation, all of our vehicles are metal; cars trains, even airplanes. And tools, not just farm tools, tools for everything we do, they are all metal. Even in medicine, surgery's done with knives. Just imagine the world without metal."

"Yeah, those are all good things to think about. But you know he has a dark side, a dark violent side. Car accidents, wars, shootings, knifings and jails, they all belong to him too." She looked at me for some consolation.

"The truth is Roxanne, I haven't even figured Chango out yet. But I do know they all have a positive and negative side to them. I think it's up to us to keep them in line within ourselves."

"I'm tired now," she said finally lying down on her mat. "See you in the morning."

I thought about Oggun as I lay there in the dark. I thought of the story of the rape of Yemaya. Maybe it was not Saint Barbara who was angry. Maybe it had been Oggun all along, but why? I never did anything to Oggun, how could he be angry? Then I remembered asking Steve the same question. I could still hear his voice in my head. "No, you don't do anything wrong Jeanne Marie, how can a saint do anything wrong. No you don't do anything at all." The hatred was for who I was, not what I had done. Was it simply the nature of Chango to attract the wrath of Oggun?

Even when I was young it had happened. Raymond, he had always bullied me around when our parents were not home. There had even been four brothers around me, just like the four warriors. I smiled. Then I remembered the rape. The black car, the fiery furnace, it all was Oggun. All his tools had been there, the black shovels and iron pokers. It had always been Oggun. Even with Joseph he had been present. Joseph had chosen to make love to me in a dark factory, filled with rows of machines. He had been killed violently by a gun in a van, Oggun's signature death, but why?

I looked over at the giant female Oggun sleeping beside me. Somewhere hidden in the contents of these Orishas were the answers. I wanted desperately to ask about the tools of Chango. Why were they only made of wood? Would Oggun not allow him a sword made of metal? Saint Barbara carried a sword, or was she just displaying the same sword her father used to cut off her head? There was no one to ask, and it was getting late. Perhaps tomorrow, maybe then I would find out more.

The second day was a sort of coming out party. It was the first presentation of the new Chango to the world. My godmother and another woman dressed me in the traditional outfit. I could not seem to control myself. I laughed as they dressed me in red satin breeches and waistcoat trimmed in elaborate silver piping. My head was washed and repainted with circles of bright colors. A crown made of the same crimson satin decorated with cowry shells and bright feathers was finally placed on top of my hairless painted head.

Roxanne's godmother had taken her outside and only my god-mother and I remained in the room. I looked at her and smiled. She was in fresh white clothes and a clean white kerchief. Some of the polish was chipped from her nails. "Iya," I asked did you sleep here last night?

"Oh yes, at least I tried. Being a yubona is not so easy I am finding out. But that is my lesson. How are you feeling this morning?"

"Actually, I feel pretty good. I finally got some sleep."

"You know I was worried about you last night. How did you fare alone with this Oggun?" She raised her eyebrows letting me know she understood.

"I have to tell you, at first she scared me to death. I thought she was going to kill me with that machete. Iya, why did Oba do that to me? Why would he initiate Chango with Oggun?"

"I wondered the same thing. In fact I asked him last night, but all he said was that it was necessary for you. In time, I suppose he is right, you will know."

I thought about the tools. "Iya I have a lot of questions. Am I going to be able to ask them? How am I going to learn?"

"I can only tell you this. You will have a great deal of time to learn about your Orishas. Do not question your Godfather too much. What you need to know, ask of your Orishas, ask Chango your father. In time dear, you will know everything you need to know. But, for now, we must get you ready. Today many people will come to pay their respects to the new Yawos. This is a very happy day."

It was a celebration and a blessing for people to pay their respects to the new santeras. Not all of them were initiates. On this day, it was an open house and a big feast. All the sacrificed animals would be expertly prepared and cooked. They would now serve to nurture the whole community. Everyone who attended would partake in the abundance of breads, meats and fruits, all the earth's blessings.

I saluted all the santeros who had been there the day before and many of their husbands, wives and children who came on this day. I was not allowed to leave my throne. So I remained under its protective canopy throughout the day. I was newly born, and my head had to stay under cover for the first few days. Everyone laughed and partied outside while Roxanne and I received guests and blessings in our respective corners throughout the day. We ate on our mats on the floor without utensils. And even Oggun was in good spirits on this day. When darkness came we were both exhausted. The yubonnas dressed us and once again put us to bed like children.

"Hey Chango, are you awake?" Roxanne called out into the darkness.

"Yeah, I'm awake."

"Are you scared about tomorrow?" She asked.

"You mean the Ita? No, I don't think so."

"Oh yeah, you do that stuff for a living. Do you see it all the time? The future I mean."

"No, it's not like that. I only see it if someone asks me to. And even then, they only show the future if the person needs to know it. You know, maybe to prevent something bad from happening."

"Does it? Prevent something bad from happening, I mean?"

"Truthfully, I can't seem to prevent anything at all. That's the bad part. It's so frustrating, knowing what's going to happen and not being able to stop it. That's why I'm here, I think. I'm sure it can be done. I just don't know how."

"What if your wrong? What if it's just a destiny thing and it can't be changed?"

"I guess that's where faith comes in. I want to believe it. I want to believe that we chose our destiny, that were not just victims of it."

"I guess it all depends on what your destiny is." She resigned. "But we're going to find out tomorrow, for better or worse."

The next morning, Roxanne was chosen to go first. I waited for several hours, wondering what destiny held in store for me. From what I understood, *Ita* was like a spiritual DNA. And, just as DNA in the body can foretell ones propensity towards certain diseases, these letters would foretell what problems would most likely enter my life. They would help me to fortify certain vulnerable areas. They would help me to identify major catastrophes and hopefully spell out their prevention. This was the map I would follow for the rest of my life. I only prayed it will not be too difficult.

Several hours later, Roxanne finally returned. Her face was stained with tears and she glared at the man who walked her back to her throne in the corner. Maybe she had been right to fear what they might have to say. Was I really prepared to hear everything?

I was brought to a patio outdoors where several Santeros were seated. They were the ones selected to witness my reading. My Godfather was seated on a straw mat on the floor resting his back against the building. It was explained that the numerical letters or signs would be recorded in my libretta for me. While I cannot reveal most of the entries on this day, I can share with you some of the warnings I was given. As they have already manifested and come to pass. These are the words that were spoken to me on that day:

"Jeanne Marie, you come into this world with all the blessings of Chango. In this life you are a clairvoyant. The veils were lifted from your eyes by birth. This vision, the ability to see without the restrictions of time and space is Chango's gift to you. It is for you to use for solving problems. Do not give this gift away so freely. Be careful who asks you for this gift. There are many dangers before you. Remember this gift is your strength, but every strength has equally its inherent weaknesses. But this is a lesson you must learn.

The day will come when you will leave my house. Do not forget what you have learned here. The day will come when you, a child of

Chango will be called upon for this strength, your vision. Believe half of what you see and none of what you hear. Do not forget where your vision comes from. Your spiritual mother is Yemaya, the mother of the ocean and the mother of all the *Orishas*. You, Chango and Yemaya are *Okana Oni*, of one heart. The day will come when she will bring you the greatest love you will ever know. Remember she will always love and protect you, but a flame cannot live in the ocean, and the living cannot live in the world of the dead."

Then there was silence and I sat very still. He began to speak again. "There is a *patiki*, a story with a message, in English…" He looked at me for the word.

"A fable," I answered.

"Yes, a very important fable. In this patiki, it is Yemaya, the mother of the earth who speaks. It is her sign, her signature in the universe. Some people in this world hide from death. It cannot be done but they try. In the same way you Jeanne Marie, have tried to hide from life. But this is all behind you now. In this religion, you will learn to touch the blood and body of this world. Then he reached over and grabbed a handful of dirt. "This is the nature of the earth, this is her body. This is where you live." He emptied his handful of earth. "This is the story of how burials came to be. It is called the *odu* of the hole that is dug for the first time.

A long time before anyone of our house remembers, people did not bury their dead as they do now. When their spirit left their body, they were instead respectfully wrapped in a white shroud and placed under the sacred ceiba tree. Now there was a woman who had both a husband and a son. She was bored with her husband, and wanted more from life. She was bored of her life, such as it was and it was not long until she met another man. Now, this man had a wife who cared for his house, but he looked for another to take care of his business at the market. The market was an interesting place, filled with colorful people and events and this looked to be a far more appealing way of life. Now this man certainly desired the woman, but she was married already to another.

One day as she peeled the vegetables, as she did every day, she thought of way to escape her tedious fate. Quickly she finished the chore at hand and ran out to explain her idea to the man. "I know a way I can leave my husband and become your second wife," she began. "There are some herbs that when mixed together can cause a sleep that could be mistaken for death. When my husband brings me shrouded to the ceiba tree, you can come and take me to your house. Then I can live with you."

The man of course, who desired to have this woman, agreed. That night the woman drank the herbal mixture and with great sadness the next morning she was wrapped in a shroud and taken to the sacred tree. The man waited until the darkness fell over the sky. Then he came to take her. Everything went exactly as they had planned. Until...

One day the woman was working in the market, as she did now every day, and her son came into her store. As there was no mother in the boy's home, it had become his chore now to buy their food at the market. He spotted his mother immediately. "You are my mother," he screamed in anger and fear. "You are not dead!"

"No, the woman answered," I am not your mother. "Now go away."

But the boy was not convinced. He went home and told his father what he had seen at the market that day. The father who could not believe the story but did not disbelieve his son decided to see for himself the very next day. He got up the next morning and went to the store. Now the woman was busy, sorting the vegetables and she hadn't noticed her husband who had just come in. He looked at the woman and gasped, "You are my wife, but you are dead."

She looked up at him now in terror. She could not speak, and she could not run.

"You died in our house and we placed you at the foot of the cieba." His voice grew loud with fear and anger, gaining the attention of all that were there. "Why is it you did not stay where you belonged?" By this time many people gathered, and the man fed by the growing crowd grew in his anger at this great betrayal. "As you have already died, it is not fitting that you go about the business of the living, and unconscionable that you should live with another man." The crowd nodded in agreement. "You are dead and you did not stay where you belonged, this is a problem that I know how to solve."

With that, he grabbed her up and tied her into a shroud. Then he took her outside and began to dig a hole, a very deep hole. He threw her in, assuring the crowd who stood nearby, that a person should die only once, and this she had already done. He then covered her living body with the newly exposed earth he had dug. The people knew then that the dead must be kept in this way from trying to live in the wrong world."

When all the oracles had been revealed I was taken back to my throne. I was told to meditate on all the things that I had been told. I thought about the story, of what it could mean in relation to my life. I knew metaphorically it spoke of a woman's sexuality. It represented the first sexual encounter for a woman. This is when the hole is opened for the first time. It is the death of childhood in a woman's life. I remembered the rape. It had been the death of my childhood. How could an eleven year old be expected to go from childhood to womanhood? I had missed some valuable transition in my life. Perhaps somewhere deep down I had never fully accepted my womanhood.

It was said that if a woman had this sign, she must never have two men at the same time, or she will die. A man will bury her, sometimes alive. When Yemaya speaks this sign to a woman, she will want more than one man. She will desire more than one husband, but she must always respectfully leave one before taking on another. They say this is the sign, through which death and betrayal were first born. It is the sign of the living dead.

Perhaps I had betrayed life in this way, living death again and again, and never fully remaining in either world. Perhaps it was death I betrayed, by conducting its business with the living. I thought of all the lost children I had tried to help through the years. I thought of Jennifer, the other little girl whose death had eluded her burial. The child who had been brutally raped and murdered, she had been so young, and so brave. Yet she had asked for nothing but warmth, and clean white bones. How many times I had prayed for her peace, and for the purity of her white bones that now rested safely in the earth's dark womb.

I knew deep down, there had always been a child inside of me, a little girl who could not die. She had tried, long ago when she was opened for the first time. She had begged through the old stones for the earth to open and swallow her up, to keep her warm. But the stones would not allow her passage and the shadows of the dead refused to let her stay. But she had not been brave. She had asked for death because it was safe, because it was easy, so much easier than life. Life demanded courage, and I had been afraid. This I knew was the real betrayal of my saint and guardian.

8

Gray Shadows

It had been almost seven years since the day of my initiation. I was still learning the ways of a Santera, the ways of a saint. I worked hard, and I learned a great deal during those years. I learned to speak to the wind, the rivers, and the ocean. I learned to listen when they spoke to me. I learned to watch the patterns and interactions of nature for the answers to my questions. Most importantly, I learned that all the things I had come to understand were no more than a drop in the ocean of knowledge.

My Godfather had been right. I left his house a little more than a year ago. The letters of my *Ita* had indeed spelled out this destiny. Why I left, even I was not sure. It was not as if we had a disagreement or that either of us were angry about anything. The last time we spoke was at his house. "I am taking some lessons," I said proudly. "There is a Santera in Miami who gives classes. She is teaching me to read the shells."

Oba glared at me. "Be very careful whose house you enter. There is too much you do not know. "They will teach you," he said. "But they will expect you to do something for them and you will not be able to refuse. These are my people. I know them well. You will pay more than you think for what you learn."

"No," I tried to tell him. "She only teaches a class and I pay a small amount for each lesson. What would they ask of me anyway? I am still a child in this religion."

My Godfather looked into my eyes and resigned. "I am only trying to protect you. It is a sad day when a father must let go of his child.

You will go to your classes. I can only warn you and tell you that now you have finished in my house. You have received already the things you came here to find. Take them with you and do not ever forget where your strength or your guidance comes from. You are a daughter of *Chango*."

After six years of his love and guidance, I left his house and this was a very sad day. It had been foretold, but never really expected. It was not something I had prepared for. I missed Oba and Iya. They had been good to me. I would always love my Godparents, but I would respect them by leaving without words. I knew I could never again return to the safety and familiarity of his house. It was time for me to grow.

I sat next to the window, fidgeting with the bracelet on my wrist as Iya ordered the drinks. There was nothing particularly charming or quaint about this cafe. It was a rather generic little place. It had a small mica counter with wooden stools and several tables covered in yellow gingham plastic tablecloths. Each small table was adorned with a cheap glass bud vase containing a red carnation and a few sprigs of baby's breath. Apart from the local scents and Latin sounds of Little Havana, it was a simple diner that could be found in any older neighborhood across the country.

"Do you see them?" Iya asked.

"No, I don't see anything," I answered bluntly.

"The man in the white to the left of us. Look with your other eyes," she demanded.

She was right. I was looking from the wrong eyes again. I was grateful to know I had two sets of eyes as she called it. Iya was one of the elders in the religion. She had taken me under her wing after I left my Godfather's house. It was Iya who had taught me to appreciate the ability of seeing from both worlds, of knowing that they both were equally essential components in a priest's pursuit of wisdom. I learned how earth and spirit live together, how they fed one another and how they spoke through the rhythms of their interaction. If not for this wisdom, I might have spent my whole life seeing only from empty eyes.

All of my former life I had thought of myself as some translucent being with hollow eyes. I had only known this world from the eyes of others. It was a unique perspective, but it tended to offer little more than an essentially elusive life. I had the ability to relive the events of other people's lives, their joys and their sorrows, but all too often it was through their deaths that I truly lived. It was through the experience of actually living the deaths of others that I most significantly experienced life. I felt their lives. I knew their pasts and glimpsed into their futures. Such was the life of a clairvoyant, so much vision and so little substance. My learning in this world as Iya explained was in reverse. I had to learn to navigate in this world from the inside out.

"Do you see them now?" She was unusually patient and I knew the monotone in her voice was a means of calming her own emotions. Her expression did not betray her apparent disinterest as her eyes swept around the small familiar cafe.

I must have been blind not to see them. "Yes, I see." I too spoke without expression and sipped the tiny cup of cafe Cubano. I tasted only the sweetness of the dark bitter syrup. She had told me earlier that there was not much time and I understood now what she meant. The first time I looked I had only seen a gray haired Latin man sitting on a stool at the counter. He was probably in his late sixties or early seventies. He was not over weight but his stomach protruded and pulled at the buttons on the white embroidered shirt. He wore silky white dress socks and thin leather shoes with an open weave, the kind they must have worn in old Havana too. He was well groomed and looked like ninety percent of the older Latin gentlemen in Miami.

The second look was not at him. The second look was at what hovered around him. I had seen them before in the clinic. I knew they fed on addicts and long time alcoholics, those who suffered a painful spiritual death. Never had I seen them quite so thriving, so seemingly robust. It looked as if they could leap out at any moment and survive on their own, survive without their host!

I knew this man had been a powerful man in the community. He was not just a priest; he was a priest of priests, a *Babalow*. I could not imagine that such a man could be besieged by these dark soulless parasites. I knew not to ask questions, but I wondered how this had come about and why. I knew that she showed me this man for a reason, and this was all I knew.

Iya left change on the counter and the dark haired woman with appreciative eyes and too much facial hair nodded thank you. We walked out of the open-air cafe that had at least been cooled with shade and paddle fans into the harsh light of the hot Miami sun. Calle Ocho is the main street in Little Havana. It is one of the oldest and culturally richest streets in Miami. The markets are small and filled the heavy scents of tobacco, coffee and decaying produce. There is a candle burning and a saint standing with a small offering at their feet near the front entranceway of every Latin store. The streets are alive with the old and the young together. The old ones come to reminisce about Cuba. For them it is a place. The young ones come and talk about Cuba, because for them it is a state of mind. There are not many Anglos in this part of town, especially ones who do not speak Spanish, but for me it was a foreign country just twenty minutes from where I lived.

I loved the familiarity of foreign places. I loved the sounds of far away languages. I grew up that way, a foreigner in a foreign land. I had been an American in Europe and a European returning to America. Miami had been the home of my parents, but during the years they spent abroad their hometown had become another country. The people they remembered when they returned no longer inhabited it. The place no longer resembled the home they had etched into their memories. For me this was not a disappointment, not a shattered memory, only another faded Christmas story of things long ago. I loved the colorful country Miami had become.

We walked in silence to Iya's house. It was only three blocks away. The scent of gardenias lingered in the heavy air and humidity rose as the sun baked the small lawns. There was stillness in the city. It was hard to describe but it felt as if we were somehow suspended in the eye of a hurricane. It was a perfect quietness, a surreal stillness, a moment of perfect order in the midst of circle of chaos and destruction. Whatever was stirring was subterranean. It was not visible. There would be no maps to chart its course, no warnings of its predicted path, not even a name to contain its being. If this was indeed the eye, the first half had already silently passed over us. The second half was yet to come.

Iya opened the chain-linked gate and neither of us spoke, in that kind of heat it just seemed to be an additional effort to talk. Even the key did not want to work as she jiggled the door handle to loosen its grip. These little houses had no central air and Iya did not believe in it anyway, she thought it was unnatural. She was probably right about that too. But if there was one thing I had learned in America, it was about comfort. It reigned in this country. Technology and luxury were not so far apart and in that respect it was good to be an American.

"*Agua?*" Iya called out from the tiny kitchen.

"*Si*, thank you." Water was one of the few words in my limited Spanish vocabulary. I didn't know exactly why I could not seem to retain this language. Perhaps I was afraid it would take away all the mystery and music of its sounds. Or perhaps I feared that understanding the language would take away all the familiarity of its foreignness and leave me with nothing but words. Iya brought two mismatched glasses of ice water and set them on the table in front of me. I selected one and pushed the other to her as she sat down in her chair.

"So, tell me Yawo, what do you think of this?" She asked. She was relaxed now, at home and genuinely interested in my observations. She still called me Yawo. I assumed she would always call me that. For someone else it would be an insult, but for me it had become a term of endearment. For the first year every initiate is called a Yawo, but after that year they become a priest and earn the title of Santero or Santera. I had long past this stage. For Iya however, I was an eternal wide-eyed Yawo. I knew that this was the part of me she spoke to most often and that was fine with me. This question was not directed to the Yawo however; it was presented to the Santera.

I didn't know where to start. We had never discussed this before. I only knew of the gray creatures because I had seen them. I had never shared this with anyone. Truthfully I had never even thought about discussing them. When you see what is for most people invisible, you learn at an early age to keep it to yourself. Reality becomes personal and at the same time very impersonal, as there is not much need for communicating personal observances. My personal experiences were simply not relevant or understandable to most people. People could neither validate nor share in my experiences. I had come to terms long ago that my life was a lot like death. No matter how many people were with you on this side or the other, ultimately you went through the journey alone. I assumed it was the same for all those who could see through other eyes and as I looked at Iya's softening face, I wondered how many things she too omitted as irrelevant conversation.

"I have seen them on addicts," I began. "At the clinic I saw a lot of them. I worked at the aids clinic down town for a while." I sat back remembering my failed efforts before I continued.

"Not long after my brother's death, I went to work in a clinic that offered counseling to people with aids. It seemed an appropriate job for me. Everyone there was facing death. I thought with my own experiences, that I could somehow help.

It was at that clinic that I began to understand a little more about the gray fog. I saw it often on the victims of that terrible disease. When I looked at them closely I realized, that it was not really a fog at all. It was more of veil, made up of small gray shadows that gnawed like rats through human auras. I assumed these are what people of all cultures describe as demons.

"Demons," I lowered my eyes to the table in front of me. "I found out they're not at all the tall dark and alluring creatures Hollywood loves to portray. They're not witty or intelligent. I saw them, they're small and low to the ground, primal creatures that exist for the sole purpose of survival." I pictured the disgusting shadowy creatures. " Truth is, I can't actually say that they look grotesque, because their form seems to lack any real precise definition. Even their shadowy essence is in tones of gray. Not black, they don't have any of the depth of blackness. Maybe it's the irregularity itself that gives that impression of ugliness. You know, like an animal whose fur grows without direction in varying lengths with no allegiance to any given color. Then again, it might be the erratic vibration itself that makes them so inherently grotesque."

I thought for a moment, but I couldn't put into words what I knew. I knew they didn't feed on blood. It was the other life force they devoured. They thrived on the very substance of the soul, the invisible energy that lives in the fluid motion of the aura. It was this elixir of life that was their food, their only substance for survival. They were the primal disease of humankind. They gnawed holes in our natural protective system, our aura. When this system was pierced we lost a portion of our immune system. We became vulnerable not only to diseases of the body that cause physical death, but also to diseases of the soul that could destroy our very essence.

I looked to Iya, who folded her hands, waiting for me to continue. "Most of the people who came to the clinic were also drug addicts. I didn't have much luck in counseling because of that. Most drug victims are not searching for answers. They're so captivated by the elusive promises of oblivion, that they can't seem to focus on anything else.

I guess the worst case I saw was a young artist. He was from up north, Minnesota I believe. He was born and raised there. He was so beautiful, but he had given up on his life some time ago. Even worse he had given up on death as a release from it. When I met him he was already sick from the virus and the over dose he prayed for seemed to elude him. I remember the first time we talked. He told me about the monkey he carried on his back.

"It's not a figure of speech," he assured me. "It's real, I swear to you I wake up sometimes at two or three in the morning and I feel his teeth in my neck. I think he's chewing my flesh but I can't really feel the pain. It's like an itch when you can't scratch it. I want him to bite through; even the pain would be better than the numbness. I don't feel any more. Sometimes I think the drugs will make me feel something. Sometimes I think they will make me not feel anything. They don't though, they don't do it either way." He stared blankly out the window.

Then he continued, telling me about his art. He described his gallery in Minnesota and how much he had tried to give back to the community he lived in back home. "I supported drug rehabs for juveniles and donated most of my personal work to aids research. Ironic isn't it. I am dying of aids and addicted to ... oh hell what ever I can get. And, I don't even have a place to stay. But I can't face any one back there. About the only thing I can leave them now is a memory. I want it to be in tact, they need that. What little is left of me needs that."

My heart ached for him, but I knew it was too dangerous to tap in and try to help him. There was not enough to grab hold of to try and pull him back, and those things, those shadowy parasites they were all over him. He was right. There was a huge one perched on his back, gnawing at the base of his neck, sucking the life force right out of him. I left soon after that. I didn't know how to help, and I couldn't bear to watch the suffering any longer."

I thought of my brother Raymond, I had not understood at the time why my brother had tried to leave his body that night. It was not fathomable to me why he did not wish to fight to remain in this world. I did not understand how rudely I had interrupted his escape from the gray shroud. I did not know what dark consuming beasts it contained. It had been his soul that was trying to leave, desperately seeking to preserve itself from the evil things it no longer wished to feed. I did not know his spirit was literally being eaten alive. I could not conceive how painful it must have been for him. It is no wonder he sent me away the second time, preventing me from unwittingly pulling him back again. I am only grateful he made it out of those dark shadows. I am thankful that his soul found a way to survive the devouring gray demons.

I prayed that God would forgive me, for leaving all those suffering souls behind me. Still, I did not know why. Why had he given me this cursed vision in the first place? Why did he show me all these terrible things if they could not be changed, if I could not help?

"The only way I could help at all, was if I could somehow get them off before they had completely pierced through the aura. You know it takes them a while to eat through it. In that respect, I think it is like a disease. You have to catch it early. This is all I know Iya. What about you? What do you know about them?"

"The first time I ever saw them was back in Cuba," she smiled as she thought back. "My Godmother was a woman of few words. One day she came to my house and told me to get dressed, all in white, like a yawo. She took me on a bus, I had never before been on a bus, can you imagine. We went a long way, to another town. I was only in the religion two or three years at this time, and I knew nothing but cleaning floors and washing pots. Knowledge was difficult to come by in those times. It was earned...very slowly. We all knew that knowledge of any kind would not only protect us, someday it would put food on our table. This day she needed an assistant to help with a cleansing. It was the son of a prominent doctor. I remember being terrified to go into such a house. It was a palace to me and I was afraid of such important people, but I was more afraid of my Godmother," she smiled.

I carried the supplies we brought in a bag made from an old piece of white cloth tied up with a torn strip of bright red cloth. I tried making this job look important, but my knees were shaking and I was too afraid to look around at so many rich things. The servant took us to the boys' room. It was larger than our whole house. When I saw him, I forgot everything else. He was about thirteen or fourteen. We were about the same age. His eyes were so big. Even now they haunt me. He was nothing but skin and bone and eyes nothing else...and the shadows. At first I thought it was a single entity like a great dark cloud that dimmed the light of his soul. His eyes stared aimlessly there was no light in them. He was one of the living dead. I had never seen anyone die, so I thought maybe the aura turns gray maybe this shadow was what was left behind when a person was dying. When I looked closely I could see it moving, not flowing like the aura, moving, swarming like insects it was horrible. They had consumed the boy's life force, and while the body lived, the boy was gone. I had never seen my God-mother nervous before, but I knew she was. She hesitated, and she was not yelling orders. I knew she was not sure what to do.

'Look,' she finally said. 'Look hard and remember what you see. This is a curse that has finished its deed, and now it is a curse without a master.'

She told the servant to bring the boys father to the room. When he came she told him she could not help the boy, it was too late for that. She went on to explain that a ritual cleansing must be done immediately or his wife would become ill and die. She told him that he must do, what needed to be done. He didn't question her. No one ever questioned her, not even a wealthy doctor. She was a powerful and well-respected Santera.

I took the basin from the boy's bedside and asked the servant to bring us fresh water. I knew the herbs would have to be prepared. Next I untied the cloth bag and began setting up for the ceremony. I laid out the herbs. There were eleven different herbs. They were the herbs of San Lazzaro. I knelt down to proceed with the blessings and for the first time, my Godmother named each herb as she held it up for prayer. I knew then that she intended to teach me the ceremony. You must understand, this was a great privilege, especially for one so young. She did not often give away her trade secrets; many of the elders did not know them. I paid close attention as she put more of some and less of others into the basin. I watched carefully which part of each plant went into the mixture.

As I began cleaning the large stems from herbs in the basin, she sang to *Osian* the spirit of all herbs requesting that he allow each one to release its power into the brew. I sat on the floor and began kneading the herbs as she dipped a small gourd into the bucket of water and poured it over my hands. She cried out the African prayers to one powerful spirit after another, I joined in the choruses as I twisted and squeezed the juice from the herbs into the water. My little hands ached; she was long winded and knew a lot of songs. The liquid got darker and darker until she finally finished her repertoire of songs and I squeezed the last of the pulp from the herbs into a ball and set it down beside the basin.

Next she took out the little ball of powdered eggshells and drew a cross first on my forehead and then her own. She dipped both arms into the basin of herbal mixture, splashed some on her face and then cupped her hands filling them with the liquid and applied it to the base of her neck. Moving aside, she motioned to me to do the same. Again she picked up the little white chalky ball and proceeds to draw crosses on the floor one in each corner of the room. She then sprinkled a mixture of sweet waters and holy water in each corner. In the center of each cross she placed a small white candle and lit each one with a prayer for protection from the four winds. Without missing a step, she turned the boy over exposing the back of his neck.

'Do you understand?' She asked me. 'There is no *ori* to work with here. You must feed the *eshubako* the place of the ancestors. We can only hope to protect his family.'

It was true, the boy had no *ori*, no opening at all at the crown of his head, the place that we would normally work on. It was completely closed nothing at all could pass through. There was no light, no spirit and no guardian; his life force had been extinguished.

'We must act quickly, with this you cannot be too careful. The curse is looking for a master.' With this warning she reached into a deep pocket in her skirt and took out a white pigeon. She quickly dipped its feet and wings into the bucket of water, held it up for prayer and quickly twisted off its tiny head poured the warm blood over the back of the boys neck. 'This will last until morning,' she said. 'Get the servant and tell him we must have a small ram and the boys mother must be here first thing in the morning. You may also ask for a blanket to sleep on, I will sleep on this mat.' She pointed to the rug beside the boy's bed.

The next morning she was up before the sun. I woke up with a start as I realized that she had stared me awake. When I looked at her face she let me know with a look that she had grown impatient with my laziness, it must have taken her a few minutes to wake me up. I looked down as an apology, and she motioned to get on with the work at hand.

I quickly folded the blanket I had slept on and watched as my Godmother repeated the ritual washing in the basin of herbal brew. I followed her lead and when I finished she looked down at the bucket to let me know I needed to get fresh water. The servant arrived at the door bringing a tray of coffee, bread meat and cheese. I was starving but the old woman gave me a look to tell me I had work to do first. When I got back with the water, she had already eaten and was swallowing the rest of her coffee. She pointed with her chin to the table beside the bed. There was a sea sponge and a little piece of brown soap. "The boy," she wanted me to bathe the boy. I was afraid to touch him, afraid that the shadowy curse might come off onto my hands. I turned and looked at my Godmother, then again at the boy. I decided to take my chances with the boy.

The dark film covered him, and it wasn't really so terrifying until I saw it move. It seemed to nestle in a large heap at the base of his neck; there it moved, in an indescribable manner. It was truly horrifying; it throbbed like a thousand evil things trying to break loose from an invisible sack. I felt my skin begin to crawl and I was sure I would have vomited if my stomach were not so empty. I tried not to let her see my fear and reached down and gently lifted his head to begin washing him. It seemed to be only a layer of shadows; they did not stick to my hands or arms. When I finished dressing him I combed his hair, and his eyes never changed. He occasionally blinked but stared perpetually into some place of empty nothingness.

My Godmother stood up and nodded permission for me to eat. I ate so fast that I tasted nothing. I cared only to fill my empty stomach. Then I filled the little cup all the way to the top with coffee. I held it on my tongue for a long time just savoring the sweetness. I took little sips and warmed each one in my mouth before I slowly swallowed. My Godmother was on the other side of the room pounding some herbal mixture with a stone. I realized now why she had allowed me this little luxury. She looked up and motioned to me to turn around. 'This you cannot watch,' she almost sounded apologetic. 'You have not yet received *Asowanna*,' she explained. 'When you do, I will show you.'

I knew this to be a big ceremony. It took many priests and almost two weeks to complete. Everyone had to be fed during this time and it became very expensive. I was poor and there was not much hope of my receiving this saint anytime soon. I did not receive Asowanna until almost twenty-five years later. My Godmother had died long before that. She had never been able to reveal this secret to me.

There was a knock at the door and I opened it to a barefoot boy holding tightly onto a rope. He handed the rope to me and I pulled a very beautiful but stubborn ram into the room. My Godmother had completed the herbal mixture and rolled it into a ball. She placed the ball onto a white plate next to a piece of rolled hemp twine and sat down on the stool again. My Godmother was not a patient woman, she did not like to wait for anyone and the boy's mother had not yet arrived. I tied the ram to the back of the bed and busied myself straightening the room. I was hoping to avoid becoming the focus of her displeasure. Luckily, there was another knock at the door and two women and the father arrived.

The father began in a very polite way to introduce the women to my godmother, but my godmother cut him short ignoring his flowery introductions and walked directly to the mother. 'This woman is your sister?' She asked the woman bluntly. She looked her up and down and quickly assessed that it was okay for the sister to stay. My Godmother was very guarded about these things, sometimes for their protection, sometimes for hers.

The mother held tightly onto her sister's arm. She was clearly frightened and it looked as if her sister was holding her up. The father was not used to being spoken to in such a harsh manor, but it was the way of things then. Even an important doctor kept his place in the presence of a powerful Santera. He was so sad, he knew what the Santera had told him was true but he did not know why and this made him powerless. He could not help his son. He had tried everything he knew, he had brought in colleagues and experts from Europe and America, but no one knew. Unfortunately, this was his last resort, but he knew now that he had waited too long, that he had only succeeded in keeping the boy's body alive, he had lost his son long ago. He had won a battle but lost the war. The image of his son lingered now in an uninhabitable body protected by a gray shadow veil.

My Godmother did not waste time. She went to the side of the bed, picked up the white plate and handed to me to hold. She grabbed the ram's mouth as it was partially opened and preyed it further open. She shoved the moist ball of herbs into its mouth and tied it shut with hemp twine. Next she motioned for the mother to come. The sister led the mother reluctantly forward.

'Present her to the ram,' she ordered me. I handed the woman a small piece of coconut with a guinne pepper on top. I told her to chew it but not to swallow it. Then I explained that she must blow a little into each ear and into the eyes of ram. While she did this she must thank the ram with all her heart for exchanging his life for hers. I then placed the woman's forehead to the forehead of the ram. I held it there firmly for a good connection. I then motioned for her to bend down so that I could place the ram's forehead to her breast.

When this was finished, my godmother reached for the ram's horns and pulled him toward the boy's bedside. 'Present the boy to the ram,' she commanded. I sat the boy on the side of the bed and placed his forehead on the forehead of the ram. I pulled the ram's head down to touch his male parts to the forehead of the ram.

'Now,' she said, 'The *eshubako* you must present it to the ram.' This was not something normally done and I was not sure how to hold the boy so that I could place the back of his neck on the ram's forehead. The father who could see what I was attempting then picked the boy up and held him in a position that allowed me to carefully place the back of his neck firmly on the forehead of the ram. 'Hold it there,' she told me sternly.

The gray mass began to stir. It jumped and thrashed chaotically. It bulged as if it was ready to burst, and in a second, the dark shroud was torn open. They poured into the ram's aura like tiny rodents running from a sinking ship. 'Hold him,' my Godmother yelled. I was frozen with amazement; I could not let go if I wanted to. Even my intense repulsion did not distract me from my gapping amazement. When the flow subsided, she motioned for us to lay the boy back down on the bed. She nodded to signal me to grab the horns of the ram. Then she picked up her sharp knife and cleanly slit the animal's throat.

The mother's knees had given out, and the sister struggled with her weight trying to allow her to gently melt onto the floor. I knew she had fainted from the sight of the blood and the release of emotions. She had no idea of what had really taken place, it was all invisible to her and that was probably just as well. How much after all does a mother need to bear? Her husband who just now reacting to his wife's response, started towards her when my godmother caught him by the arm.

'He will die now, within three days.' This seemed to be more than he wanted to know, but it was what he needed to know. She pushed further with specific detailed instructions for the disposal of the animal and burial of the boy. It seemed at first cruel but it was this harsh momentary distraction of reason and duty that brought some semblance of order to this father's shattered world. It forced him to rely once again on his old familiar ways. This required logical thought and determination and this he could do. It was some assurance that not quite everything had been lost.

Our work was done. This was my first experience with them." With that she stopped abruptly and waited now for my response.

I stared at the puddle of water forming from the condensation on the glass. She had obviously recounted this story with a purpose. In this religion every story has both a history and a lesson, and if you look carefully enough, they usually contained an answer. The answer was the antidote. The answer was the cure and this I did not know.

"There are so many foreign things here," I replied. "So many things I do not know."

"Miami has long been the Gateway of the Americas and many good things have crossed our threshold. These are strange times coming now, something very unwelcome has entered our gates." She paused and I wasn't sure whether she was waiting for a response from me, or simply pondering the possibilities.

"It is sad growing old in a new world," she began again with a sigh. "When the old ones die the old ways will go with them. Much of their knowledge has been passed on, but their ways will die with their memories. For many years now I have repeated prayers to the names of the elders from my house. Only now do I know in a small way what those old African priests must have felt passing their religion on to the children of their white captors. But, we Cubans were their only hope for survival. They were wise and saw beyond their own image. They too knew they would die in their new world and the religion could no longer survive on the bloodlines of the houses alone. There was a great struggle between the elders in those times and ultimately, the houses divided. Only half chose to integrate their house with a bloodline that would become a ritually symbolic one. This is the time when a godparent began to serve in place of a birth parent. These were priests that looked beyond color and culture; these were the priests who saw with both eyes. They choose the initiates carefully, in accordance with their spiritual potential and abilities.

We Latins are a superstitious breed. It is our nature. We believe in the mysteries of the church. We follow the priests because we know there are many things we do not know. When the priests did not have answers for certain problems, it was not unnatural to seek out another priest who did. When a mother has a sick child, she does not care from whose hands the cure is delivered. She is grateful. Many of these children were dedicated to the spirit in nature who had saved them. They became the Saint's child. There were only two ways to enter the religion. To offer one's life of dedication in exchange for life or health or…one was born with destiny for the priesthood. Perhaps they are only two different paths to the same destiny. At any rate, they had to be blessed with ache on their head. Ache, the essence of spiritual grace above them. In these times, apprenticeship meant growing up in the house of your godparent. This took many years and you did not leave until it was decided that you were ready to go out and build a house of your own. Building a house was necessary, the spirit of the godparent would need a place to live after their death. The godparent would become an ancestor, and in this way, they would go on.

These were the beginnings of my house. These are the ancestors that live through the continuation of our house. Once again we find ourselves faced with the same decision, and the same division. The ancestors who came as slaves to Cuba have survived for over four hundred years through ritual blood sacrifice, through the Cuban Santeros. Now, we too look for our survival. We too find ourselves on foreign shores. We cannot survive on the bloodlines of our houses alone, and once again there are those who cannot see past their own image. They cannot see past their own race and culture. Generations breed blood lines, but blood, like a river only carries and nurtures life. Rivers are not the source of life. The source is much larger. It is the ocean, *Yemaya* who is the mother of all rivers. This is the nature of Yemaya and Ochun. *Ochun* the river is very beautiful, but she can so easily be carried away by her own vanity. She is after all *Santa La Carridad*, the patron saint of Cuba. You understand what I am saying?"

"Yes, Iya, I understand." Santeria was a colorful religion. It was a mixture of ancestors, saints and nature, which at first was confusing. It was at the same time filled with the simplicity of poetic beauty, the complexity of natural physics and the contradictions of human nature.

Each aspect of nature in this religion, the ocean, the river, the air, fire, earth, metal was filled a unique life force, a specific energy, and a source of living *ache*. The word *ache* itself was literally translated as the spiritual 'grace' of life. This ache had to be known and understood by its priest. The duty of a priest was to convey this ache to help those who did not understand how to know or use its power. In order to truly know this energy, one had to know its spirit, a spirit that lived with physical, psychological and spiritual attributes. Each one had positive and negative qualities. They were both male and female in accordance with their natures.

Yemaya was the name given to the spirit of the ocean. She was the mother of all life on Earth and the source of deep spiritual awareness. As such, she was the mother of Ochun. In accordance with her nature, Ochun embodied the rivers who carried the fresh waters to the earth. This was her job. Moreover, in accordance with the nature of the human body, she was the veins though which our blood flows and the birth canal through which we all entered this world. In this manner, bloodlines and rivers are connected to the same spirit; they were guided by the same energy. These were the energies that channeled the flow of life.

It was however, also Ochun who provided man with the first reflection of himself, in her sweet waters. It was said that many are blinded by their own image; they fall in love with this reflection and never see through it to find her true nature, which is love. In the new world, the Spaniard's looked into the mirror for their reflection and so the Saint La Carridad who represents Ochun always carries a mirror in her hand.

Reflections, whether they were from a mirror, a river or a bloodline, could be deceiving and so it is with the nature of Ochun.

I knew she directed this little piece of history to prepare me. Iya was a priest of Ochun, I knew it was for the respect and not the lesson of Ochun that she directed this story to me. I was an Anglo, and there were more than a few who were uncomfortable sharing "their" rituals with an American Santera. In truth, I felt like Iya that I was in fact a symbol of an unwelcome necessity. Miami was their home now. Their children are no longer born Cuban. They are born American of Cuban decent. The religion was undergoing a second synchronicity. Just as the African culture was forced to merge with the Latin culture, it would now merge again into the American culture. There would be additions, substitutions and losses.

No culture melts gently or willingly into the great American melting pot. This was the perpetual struggle between the two great warriors fire and metal. *Chango*, the spirit of fire fights to defend the growth of the future brought about by rapid changes. The nature of Chango is lightening, he is electricity and unless he is properly channeled he can strike with quick and unpredictable results. *Oggun*, the spirit of metal and industry, fights with the strength of iron to protect the things that work, like the time honored tools that till the ground and feed the people. Ogguns' nature, like tempered steel is resistant to change. Progress will always fight status quo in a fiery battle.

There are many colorful stories in the mythology of Santeria describing the battles of these two brothers in eternal war. One of the most heated debates I had ever heard among the Santeros was over who established the first house in America, Chango or Oggun. The importance of this being which one is considered to be the guardian spirit of this country. It seems to me a technicality as whenever one arrives the other is not far behind; an iron rod inevitably attracts lightning.

Oggun was the eldest. It seemed more likely that it was he who had arrived first. I understood a little more about Oggun. I understood the necessity of a dark warrior; Chango could not be a warrior without him. Only Oggun was fierce enough to pull the anger of Chango down from the sky. It was Oggun who brought Chango to the earth. It had been Oggun, disguised as the men in my life who had finally caused Chango to stand up in me. He was indeed my brother, even if he was a dark one.

At all this new found knowledge, I continued to marvel. I was the eternal Yawo, I watched, I listened and I learned. Iya knew this. She also knew that I had great respect for all these things, but I knew there was something more. "Iya," I asked finally. "What is it you want me to do?"

"There will be a funeral soon. The Babalow we saw today will die and what ever happens between these times, you must attend the *Itutu*. I will let you know when."

The *Itutu* is a ceremony done for a priest three months after their death. I did not question why I was to attend but I nodded to let her know I would be there.

Iya looked tired, and I knew she carried much more than her own concerns. It was time to leave and I thanked her for everything she had shared with me, hugged her and kissed her cheek. I walked away, with what I assured myself was only a small portion of the weight she carried. It was heavy nonetheless. I needed to think on all that had been said, I needed to stop feeling all that had not been said. I wanted to go home, to my own quiet house.

I was home again. I was only thirty minutes to the Town Davie. I loved Davie. My friends all laughed when I moved here. It had a red neck, good ol'boy in a pick up truck kind of reputation, but the truth was it was a little piece of country charm nestled between Miami and Ft. Lauderdale. It was miles from the gateway, and the people here tried to keep things simple. There was no pretense in Davie. It was originally horse country and the two blocks that constitute downtown Davie had a rodeo and still maintained the hitching posts outside the restaurants, Griff's feed store and Rosie's Saloon. On some level everyone knew it was only an illusion, but it was such a pleasant one and in these times, such a necessary one, that we all simply choose to keep it.

I glanced at the mailbox but thought better of it and decided not to look. It was the end of the month and there would only be bills anyway. The plants in the front planter were drooping and grass was beginning to look like straw. I would try to water it tomorrow. I was just too tired. Maybe it would rain tonight and I wouldn't have to. I opened the door to my little gingerbread house. The paint was already beginning to peel. It had only been a few years since it was painted. I remembered when it was first painted, pink. I painted everything pink inside and out. I don't know why. I just liked it at the time I guess. My neighbors dubbed it the Barbie house. It was Barbie pink with white trim, but it has faded at least three shades lighter in the harsh Florida sun. That part was an improvement.

Cool air escaped through the doorway as I entered and I felt the forces of hot and cold collide as I closed the door behind me. Here there was stillness and the only thing that stirred within was me. I sat down in the center of the sofa. It was soft and laid my face to the side to feel its velvet touch against my skin. I was about to be pulled in, into some unknown subterranean soup. There was no way around it. I somehow belonged even though I had not the faintest idea of how or why. I was certainly not the most knowledgeable, nor was I the strongest or most talented. I simply had vision, which seemed to be both a curse and a blessing.

9

Call of the Dead

"Si Iya, I will be there." I knew it was time. It had been several months since my visit to Iya's house. The first service would take place at sunrise at Santa Barbara's. There are several Catholic churches that extend a sort of professional courtesy to the Santeros in Miami, but this one was my favorite. Not only because it belonged to my saint, but also because it had a kind of old world character. It is not big or beautiful to the contrary it is very small and rather poorly garnished. It truly belongs however, to the people who cherish it and it is filled with their faith and hope. A traditional mass for the dead would be said before the rituals of Itutu could begin. It would begin Friday morning and finish sometime Sunday evening. It would be a long weekend and I was not sure what I was to prepare for.

The alarm went off too early, for me anyway. I hate getting up when it is still dark outside. I was grateful that I actually prepared my clothes the night before. I did not want to be late arriving. It would be difficult enough trying to beat the traffic even at this hour. I dressed all in white as every ritual required and began putting on my elekes the necklaces worn by priests. This in itself is a ritual, as they must be put on in a certain order, depicting the hierarchy of the natural powers. The first is always Elegua, a string of red and black beads representing the power of connections. He is the keeper of the gates. This is the power that opens one thing to another, without whom, no other powers could be accessed. All of the priests have at least five elekes but as new problems arise so new powers are needed and additional ones are added. These all come with their respective ceremonies gifts and responsibilities.

Their power is in the dedication and knowledge that comes from these experiences, but they are considered sacred and no one other than the owner is permitted to touch them.

I would have to walk two blocks. The streets were filled with people most were priests. I knew this Babalow had many friends and many godchildren and judging by the numbers in white attire, I would not see the inside of the tiny church on this day. I hurried across the street and as just as I stepped up from the street to the broken sidewalk there was a man leaning against his car watching me. I am used to standing out a little at these events, as I am typically the only Anglo Santera. This man was however, beautiful! He was not tall, but at five two, tall is not a prerequisite for me and he was gorgeous. He had dark wavy hair pulled back into a ponytail, a square jaw and dark eyes that were absolutely captivating. He was dressed very sophisticated but under-stated, a typical Miami look. His suit was casual, light, but not white and he wore a collarless knit shirt underneath. It was obvious that I had seen him, so my immediate reaction was to look past him. I was hoping that it might not appear quite so apparent. Before I could avert my eyes in any particular direction however, he sort of caught them. For an unnerving few seconds our eyes seemed to lock. Neither of us spoke and I was a little uncomfortable. Then I considered that he might have actually been looking at me out of attraction and not so much out of distinction. I felt a little better. Mindful of my not so flowing movements, I followed the lead of the elder priest and walked up to the doorway. I quickly crossed myself with holy water when a hand suddenly reached through the doorway and pulled me through the crowd into the building. I knew by the grip it could only be Iya.

"Come," she plowed through the crowd pulling me behind her. The mass had already begun and she pointed to the corner of her eye motioning me to pay attention and see everything. I knew there would be questions later so did as she requested.

I started to look around the room. Some of the faces were familiar. I had seen them at ceremonies throughout the years. Others were total strangers. Then again, I was looking with the wrong set of eyes, as Iya would say. I couldn't really see much individually as we were packed into such a small place so I began to look over the tops of heads. Some gray emanating from a man standing near the front, he would die soon. I did not know who he was, he was elderly and it did not look unusual. To the far right, closer to the back I sensed something. I knew this is what she was looking for. I could feel the man who stood there but I could not see him. The crowd hid him. It was an unnerving feeling, powerful, a little mysterious, and somehow vaguely familiar. We were on opposite sides of the room but he was closer to the door than I was. The mass would end soon and I knew that if I didn't get to the door before he did I would miss something important. I was pretty much trapped. There was no way to move. I could pass out cold and still be standing up in the same position. Perhaps he would be at the house afterwards.

I drove up behind Iya at the house. "He was there?" She asked.

"Yes," I answered.

"Do you know who he is?"

"No," I confided. She tightened her lips and said nothing. I wasn't sure now whether she knew who he was or not. It was not likely that I would know someone of significance in the religion that she did not. She knew a lot of people and not just in America.

"When we go in, eat! You will need your strength." She shook her head disapproving the weight consciousness of Americans. "No food, no strength." She pinched at my waist. "Nothing," she exclaimed in disgust.

Inside everyone moved quickly. Preparing the breakfast table with white cheese, ham, bread, guava paste and an array of pastries filled with meats, jellies and cream cheese. Café Cubano was brought out in shifts, as it would be for the next three days. Everyone would be awake and moving until exhaustion set in sometime on Sunday.

The plate for the Eggun had to be prepared and presented before anyone could eat and this was being done as the food was being set out.

The Eggun were the ancestors of the house, the spirits of the dead who must be fed before the living. They are honored with the first plate of food as their ancestral position affords them this respect. It was the Eggun who brought the spiritual wisdom to one's house. For this reason they must always know they are as welcome in death as they would be in life. Every house had a place for their Eggun. It was always on the floor, close to the earth. A glass container of water, a candle and an Eggun staff were kept in this place. Every house was a little different, some require three goblets of water, some seven, they could be very simple or outrageously elaborate but every house maintained a space for this purpose. Every priest knew the value of this wisdom, and every priest knew the responsibility of this wisdom. Someday their godchildren would call upon them for their wisdom. In this way we were all assured that the wisdom of the ancestors would not die. The next three days would be dedicated to preserving and facilitating this ideal.

Over the years, a priest acquired a variety of tools and implements used in the trade. Among them was a collection of plates. They were for the most part ordinary white dinner plates. Some of the plates are decorated slightly, but all of them on a white background. These plates were used extensively in ceremonies and a busy house required many of them. When a priest died, the plates, as well as all his other ceremonial possessions, must be taken care of by the members of his house. The first breakfast after his death was served on these plates. It would be their last ceremonial use. After the breakfast was over, they would all be broken.

A large hole in the same dimensions as a grave was dug in the back yard. The hole always faced East to West. Nine colorful candles contained in glass jars were placed around the hole and lit. They would remain lit until the end of the ceremony. Nine wooden poles were decorated with hibiscus and colorful satin ribbons were staked into the ground. The Santero's staff, which he used in his lifetime to call upon the dead, was the only thing that remained standing before the grave. A glass of water and a plate of food were placed before the staff reminding the deceased Santero that he now joined the honored dead. He would be for the first time fed as an ancestor. It was a profoundly sad and simultaneously beautiful portrait of an honorable death.

One by one, the Santero's religious articles would be ceremoniously broken and placed into the hole. It was a long tedious and complicated process. Each item had to be washed in herbs, prayed over with long mournful African songs, consulted with the use of oracles and sadly broken. A black chicken and a white lamb were finally sacrificed and buried along with the remnants of his most sacred possessions. It was a somber day.

On the second day, a large pig was sacrificed inside of the house. A small amount of his blood was caught in a gourd and placed aside. It would be poured on the grave outside. Most of the blood however, must be poured through a drain inside of the house. In this case, it was done in the back bathroom. This pig was a large animal and the space was too small for so many people. It was hot and stuffy; the pungent odor of blood permeated the air. The priest was skillful, but I could still hear the pig's eerie squeal and I felt a little sick as his throat was sliced. Itutu was the only ceremony that a pig was ever sacrificed and it was the first time I had watched up close. I hoped it was the last. The carcass was carried out to a table where a team waited to butcher it. The next day, the meat would be roasted and served for dinner. I would never look at pork in quite the same way.

On the third day, the drums began in front of the grave. They would continue to play for the next five to six hours. One was required to show their respect by dancing. Once you began however, you were not permitted to stop until the drums ended. It was a long and exhausting circular dance. People cried, sang and wailed out loud. Some swayed to the rhythm, others swayed from their own sorrow, but everyone moved to the beat of the sacred drums. As the sunset, the drums became more and more intense. This was the time I knew when the saints came down and possessed their respective sons and daugh-

ters. It was said that the Saints mounted their horses when they came
to visit us on earth.

Even the old priest drew a second wind for this final episode. The
drums began to beat faster and louder and the chorus echoed from the
crowd in shouts of ecstatic energy. The priest in front of me began to
jerk as if some invisible hands were suddenly grabbing him. No one
stopped moving. He continued to spasm until his whole body shook
uncontrollably and hit the ground catching himself incredibly with
both hands. In a single almost indistinguishable motion, he turned
propping his head up on one arm and placing his hand on his hip with
the other. He broke into a large grin and began laughing, cackling
actually, more like a witch than a woman. Two women ran up to him
and began taking off his shoes and rolling up his pant's legs. A man
tied a multi colored skirt around his waist and handed him a black
horsetail beautifully studded in colorful beads and shells. He stood up
and began to spin waving the tail and talking wildly as he spun. I could
not understand what he said, but I knew this man was the child of
Oya, the spirit of the wind and guardian of the cemetery. I also knew
the drums would not be over until she appeared I was grateful she had
decided to come down without too much delay.

The drums finally came to an abrupt and final end. The grave
remained lit only by candlelight and the grounds were suddenly silent
and still. I turned to retrieve my purse from the room inside when a
strong hand caught me by the arm. I looked up to see the face of
Fernando as he smiled.

"Two weeks," he said. "In two weeks the drums will be played to
Yemaya it will be very nice. You need to come, there is something you
need to see." He pointed to his eyes in case I had not understood his
English, which was heavily accented, but perfectly clear. "I will expect
you there. Iya will call you with the address, *Belision*." He hugged me
and kissed me on both cheeks.

Another three days, of ancient rituals and blood sacrifices have
ended, nothing out of the ordinary. It was a typical working weekend

for a Santera here in the sub terrain of South Miami. There had been no sign of him, or them. Whatever it was that I had felt at the mass. He was not at this house. There was no word of or about him, them or it. Only a long strenuous participation in a time honored method of elevating the dead. I was completely exhausted. I had no idea what I was even there for but I was too tired to care. I just wanted to go home, back to my quiet little house in Davie.

I thought of the long drive home, a hot bath and maybe some soup for dinner. There was no food in the house. There was not even any milk for my coffee in the morning. I didn't want to go to the Publix in Davie. I just didn't want to see any one I knew tonight. I remembered the little market just before ninety-five. I would stop there and pick up a few things.

The market was practically empty. I picked up the milk and a not so fresh loaf of Cuban bread but I did not see the soups. When I turned the next corner I saw two men standing aimlessly while a young pregnant woman tried in vain to get a box on the top shelf that was just out of her reach. She made several attempts, both of the men were obviously tall enough to retrieve the box but they just stood there in a daze. I started to walk closer when I saw them.

The gnawing gray creatures, they were covered in them. I looked again at the woman; on her left hand she wore a bracelet of yellow and green beads. I knew this was worn when one needed to protect himself from death. I looked over her head. Her aura was worn but not pierced. She was not a priest, but she practiced the religion. It was not difficult to tell that none of them had been in this country for long. Her basket, however sparse, was filled with the ingredients one used for offerings not with the food one prepares for dinner. I knew I was staring, but the two young men were completely oblivious and the woman was so intent on gathering the items she needed she did not notice. I spotted the soup cans just behind them. I did not want to walk too close to them. The sight of those ugly gray parasites turned my stomach. I was not really afraid, just tired, too tired to struggle with anything tonight. So I turned to walk back to the counter, I had lost my appetite anyway.

As I approached, I saw the profile of the man I had seen Friday morning before the mass. I was sure it was him. He was a man I had definitely noticed and that was something in itself that was out of the ordinary these days. He paid the man at the register and turned his head in my direction. Our eyes met once more, he nodded in acknowledgment and walked out of the store with no groceries. The woman and her two vacant escorts stepped up to the register before I could and the grocer pointed to the door, he told her in Spanish that it was paid for. She asked some questions, but I couldn't understand much else. Obviously, prince charming had paid for the peculiar trio. He had also remembered me. I was flattered, but too tired to play speculation games. I needed to go home. I needed to sleep. I would think about it later.

Driving home, my mind began to wonder on its own. I wondered who the man in the store had been. What connection he had to the odd trio. He was very attractive to me and I wasn't sure why. Looks were not usually the thing that drew me to a man. I wondered if that was really the thing that attracted me to him. But there was something about the way he looked, perhaps his expression or his eyes. Yes, there was something about his eyes. I wasn't sure exactly what it was, but it had been his eyes that caught my attention on the street, and now again in the store.

Attraction always blocked my inner vision. It was a temporary block, but a very complete one. I had no insight about him what so ever. It had been awhile since I had been so attracted to a man. Relationships were as illusive to me as visions of the other side were for most people. By this time I was sure they would probably never really exist for me. I remembered just after my initiation, when the women of the house first told me, about the relationship between a Santera and her guardian. What it meant to the woman to be dedicated to and protected by a male Orisha.

It must have been in my second year, because I was working in the house. This is a term used that meant I participated in the ceremonies to initiate others. I knew most of what took place now as the Yawo was born into this new world. I knew how a Saint was made. Some of it was still a mystery. Some of it always would be.

On this day, we were washing the objects in the basins, after the sacrifices had taken place. This was a sort of rest time, as we all knew this was the last chore of the day. We each got our last little boost of energy from the high-octane coffee and relaxed as we carefully washed the Orishas. Each basin contained a different guardian, a specific source of energy that would be used by the new Santera or Santero. There were always two sets Orishas. One set that had been presented to the new Yawo and one from the godfather who gave birth to them. Each priest picked up a basin of these sacred contents and carried it outside to be cleaned. There were at least a dozen, depending on the needs of the initiate, but there were more than enough hands available. I picked up a basin not knowing what was inside because by this time it was filled to the rim with coagulated blood and herbs, sometimes a head or two of birds or turtles.

The first time I had picked one up I thought I would pass out. It took everything I had to reach into the gross concoction to retrieve the tiny cowry shells. I plunged my hand into the basin, but when I brought it out again, it was not a shell I was holding. It was the tiny head of a decapitated turtle. It was everything I could do to maintain my self. I wanted to scream, throw up and pass out all at the same time, but I didn't. And in time, I actually leaned to perform this task with some proficiency. I actually looked forward to this chore, to the strength it gave me, both physically and spiritually. These ceremonies began at sunrise and it was a long day of hard labor for everyone. We all appreciated this part, washing the Orishas was a relatively light job and you could do it sitting down. It was usually around sunset, all the Santera's talked at this time and if I was lucky someone spoke to me in English. Most of the elder priests did not. They could not. They communicated to me with hands and eyes, as we worked together. I watched a lot. I knew my education in this religion would never be learned in words.

At this particular initiation, there were two women who spoke English. They were both second generation Cubans. I plucked the tiny shells from the basin and placed them into a small round bowl made from a dried gourd, dipped the second one into the fresh water and carefully poured it over the shells. The shells were then stirred in a circular motion with the fingertips. This took quite a while as the blood is difficult to remove from the crevices and running water is forbidden in the process. It was said that all of the ache would flow out of the objects if this were done. So, many hands were rhythmically stirring. As it had been for thousands of years, talk and laughter began at this time to release the intensity of the day. Also, as it had for thousands of years, the subject of men, sex and marriage arose among the women.

"You are omo Chango?" The first woman asked. She was asking if I was a child of Chango. She said it with a little question in her voice, as I did not have the outward characteristics of a priest of Chango. His priests were generally, a bit more electric. They were usually outright flamboyant. They loved to be seen and tended to be a bit hot headed from what I observed. I did not appear to be either, so people were generally curious when they saw me. It was understandable.

"Yes," I answered. "I am omo Chango."

"You are not married." The other one inserted.

"No," I shook my head and shrugged my shoulders.

"Ah," she smiled. "Your guardian does not often allow his daughters to be with men."

"What do mean?" I asked. This was the first I had heard of this and it did not sound good.

"Oh, yes." The other one piped in. "My godmother was an omo Chango. She had many children, but she could not keep a husband. Chango can be very possessive, hers certainly was."

"It is very difficult for a woman to have Chango. For a man it is easy, but for a woman…" She shook her head in sympathy. "Didn't your godfather tell you that?"

"No," I answered. I wondered if he had, if it would have made a difference in my decision to be initiated.

"Well," the first one sighed. "That's probably because he has Chango himself, but he is a man."

They went on telling stories of other Chango women and their inconceivable difficulties with men, sex and marriage. The women described how one daughter of Chango had resolved this problem by never marrying or having sex with men. She was said to have been very content with nightly visits from her guardian himself. She was so content with her divine lover, that she had not ever felt the need for a man in her life.

I tried to keep my mouth closed so they would not notice my reaction as I contemplated the implications. This was not one of he problems I had considered, and I was hoping that I was not told because perhaps there was a loophole, some kind of exception. It had been known to happen in some cases. I thought about this for a week or so. I had to prepare myself for the answer. I did not want to ask until I was ready to know. Finally I went to my godfather to ask if this was true.

"Yes and no," he answered. I knew by this time that my godfather was rarely diplomatic about things. It was not his style. I knew this was not an easy answer for him to give me. It was not an easy question to ask knowing this.

"Yes you can get married," he continued. "But, because of the nature of your guardian, it is not so easy to stay that way. You must remember that your guardian is the essence of male virility. When this essence is given to a woman directly from her guardian, it is not likely that a man can give her this also. How can any man compare to an Orisha? She cannot long be satisfied with a man; she will desire the qualities of her guardian always. Chango is strength, virility and passion. All these things he gives you. He is the source and the patron; he demands to be recognized as such. You see in man, Chango is channeled much to the delight of himself and his women. In a woman, it is different."

"I understand," I uttered sadly. Truthfully I listened to everything he said but I did not understand. It sounded like another gift with internal thorns. It was another gift that made my heart bleed. It seemed to be the only kind I received in this life. I was granted unlimited passion, sexual encounters that transcended the boundaries of space and time, but I would be deprived of any meaningful relationship with a man. Did this mean I could not have a mate? I was heartbroken at the thought of always being alone in this life, but I knew this too was a non-returnable gift.

I knew there was truth in what he had said, and I assumed I would have to give up on my marital illusions. I had to somehow accept this explanation. I thought of Saint Barbara. She had died fighting, not for virginity, or marital status. It was something more, something much deeper. She had known somehow who guarded her, where the divineness of her true being had come from. And she fought to remain true to her essence, true to herself. She had been courageous. In life she did not win, but through her death she had preserved her truth. In the end, she gained her peace and her power. She had become one with the very energy that guided and protected her.

I resigned myself to the fact that I could love. I just couldn't hold on to anyone forever. I suppose that ultimately, this is a truth for everyone. For me it was just much quicker. For an omo Chango, life in general was quicker. We were the children of the lightning and Chango struck as well as guided, with quickness.

I tried to convince myself that if my love life could never amount to anything more than a series of lovers, that I was no longer interested. It was a lie, and no matter how many times I tried to repeat it to myself, it refused to turn into the truth. I loved, and I loved passionately, but I seemed always destined to love the passion more than the man. For me, the very act of sex itself had become a sacred thing. It was the only time that this ecstatic process of life became a tangible thing. Sexuality became a touchable, almost attainable essence of the elusive electrical energy that charged my life. It was the sublime act of an unbridled expression of sensuality. It was my connection to this world. I could touch and hold, even if it was only for a moment. I became and simultaneously exuded the fire of life that I both loved and desired.

Sex was a profound moment, a portal in time through which the rapturous guardian of passion himself possessed me. Making love was not a loving affair. It had little to do with love or emotions. And it had even less to do with the man. I was destined to be seduced by a passion that would always overshadow the man. My godfather was right, in a man, this powerful energy becomes an extension of himself and this is a fortunate thing. It enhances his love for a woman. In a woman it is different.

This was a difficult obstacle for me, but not hopeless. Every Santera was dedicated to some powerful aspect of nature. This aspect reflected their own internal strengths and weaknesses. Some of the elements like the ocean or the rivers seemed gentler, maybe easier for a woman but each one had their lessons. And this one, no matter how unlikely it appeared, was mine. Thunder and lightning for the Anglo Santera who preferred to be silent and unseen, was not so understandable, but every priest had their own bridge to cross. Each was difficult and perilous in its own way. Perhaps one could cross this bridge in their present lifetime. Perhaps their own element would then lighten its grip on them. Was it possible for the possessive nature of her guardian to give way to the integration of another nature that might somehow bring a balance into her life? This I did not know, as no one had ever spoken of it, but it did seem possible.

They say when you cannot resolve things with your father; you must go to your mother for understanding. So, I began to look to my spiritual mother, Yemaya. She lived in a blue and white ceramic ginger jar. It was a deep jar and I was told to keep it filled with water from the ocean. This was the only thing I had really done to care for her. I did not know her. Inside of the jar I knew there were the dark stones that held the essence of her life force. I knew there were several silver symbols, a mermaid, a sun and a moon. I did not remember what else rested at the bottom of her small ocean house. They were her symbols. They must be able to tell me something of her nature. I went to the kitchen and took out a clean white dishtowel and spread it across the floor. Next I picked up the jar and set it down carefully on the towel and removed the lid. I hesitated for a moment, because I did not know if I was about to disturb her in some way. I then decided that if she were my mother, she would understand that I was only a child and I did not know any other way to learn.

With that, I reached into the narrow mouth of the jar and began removing its contents. The first thing I pulled out was a large key. I hoped it was a message that I was on the right track. I placed each metal symbol gently onto the towel. I realized they were not silver. They were heavy like lead. As I removed each piece, the small cowerie shells on the bottom rattled like bones, I knew I had awakened her. One by one I held each of the smooth dark stones in my hands. I wanted to feel her essence. I wanted her to know, that I needed to touch her, to know her. There were seven stones, for this was the number sacred to her. Perhaps it represented the seven seas, or the seven days of creation. These were both integral parts of her nature. She was the ocean and the mother of all creation.

I looked carefully at her symbols, a key, two ores, a ship's steering wheel, a life raft, an anchor, a mermaid, a sun and a moon. I would have to think on these things. Tomorrow I would go to the ocean. I decided to take her a small offering and ask her to help me to understand. Perhaps my plea would touch her heart and she might even help me to find someone on earth I could love and be with. I did not know what else to do.

The next day I went to the ocean, sat on the coral rocks that jetted out to the water. I poured Molasses over the water, and began my prayerful petition. I asked for understanding of her, of my father and of my path. I asked that she help me to fill my heart. I asked that she not allow my father to sentence me to a lifetime of aloneness. I told her I needed more than passion from a man in this world. I let the fruits drop into the water, seven dark plums, grapes, pieces of melon and seven silver coins. It was calming. The act of prayer itself is peaceful and whether she granted everything I asked seemed almost secondary now. I watched her soft waves washing the shore, wetting my feet. I breathed the humid salted air. She had touched me, filled me and maybe that was all I really needed.

So much was never spoken of in this religion. So much of the information was strictly maintained beneath the veils of mystery and silence. I worked in the house of my godfather for five years after my initiation. I began as the youngest of the house, cleaning the blood of sacrifices from the floor. Carrying buckets of water for bathing and cleaning and all the other mundane chores that were required in the performance of ceremonies. For two years I was told practically nothing, just to work, watch and learn. Verbal instructions were precious few, and questions were kept at a minimum. Generally the answers led only to more unaskable, unanswered questions.

In time I began to understand this. I began to understand that it was not information that brought wisdom; it was the ability to understand its patterns. There were patterns in rituals, patterns in nature and patterns in the synchronicity that existed between the worlds. Knowing these patterns, their contents and their behaviors was the key to all the mysteries in life. These were the secrets that the old ones, the wise ones knew. They were not secrets that could be passed on in knowledge, in spoken words. In order to receive these lessons, one had to know that it was not enough to experience the five senses, in this world alone. One had to master the ability of seeing, feeling, smelling, tasting, hearing, inside themselves, in the greater nature of the world, and in the invisible other world. Only then could one be prepared to perceive the patterns, the secret codes of nature. These codes provided one with the recipe of their being. It provided a map of its movements, its habits, likes and dislikes. If one knew all these things, one was in a position of power. This was a dangerous thing without the wisdom of cause and effect, but this was the responsibility of a Santera and she knew this as she began.

I had not gone to the house of my godfather looking for power, for this is the thing I valued least in my life. I went looking for wholeness. I knew something was missing, but what it was I did not know. I was told once that there are two sure ways for things to go wrong with your guardian, one is to be too close and the other is to be too far away. I believe there is wisdom in this. To be too close is to live the life of your guardian, repeating the exact patterns of their nature in your life. It is enjoying all their strengths, but also suffering all their weaknesses for both strength and weakness come with equal intensity they are the front and back of the same thing. There is no balance and no growth in a life such as this. The other is to avoid the one who calls for you or to minimize their value in your life. An offended nature can become an angry shadowy one, a dark and powerful one. It can strike out with fury and take everything in your life away just to get your attention or appreciation.

It had taken me many years to understand this small piece of wisdom. I knew now that I had indeed offended my guardian. I had been avoiding him most of my life. I had unquestionably handed my power over to others who wanted it more than I. I had always given it unconditionally to the men in my life. I had never valued it, never missed it. I had always enjoyed the fruits of its existence without bearing the responsibility of its being. My hands had never been soiled. Power for me had been so easily given away. How difficult it had been for me to learn that power was strength, and it was not so easily regained.

At my initiation, it was not difficult to remember what I had asked of Chango. From Chango, the very embodiment of power and prowess, of change and progress, I had asked for only one thing, stability! I had asked the nature of lightning and fire, for stability!

I understand now the insult, at the time, I did not. I did not understand the ways of nature, how could I comprehend the power of it. Of all the Orishas, Chango was the most difficult for me. I have come to understand that they choose us, and they offer us what we need in life, which is not necessarily what we want from life. Stability and attachment may never be granted to me in this life, but then again it could be that I am simply too close or too far away to find it.

10

Rhythms of the Heart

Two weeks had passed quickly. It was fall in Florida. One season is all but indistinguishable from another in Miami, but seemed as if time somehow began moving again. Iya called me on Friday with the directions to the drums. Sometimes they were exciting and sometimes they were not. For me, they were always interesting.

The address was somewhere in east Hialeah. I was not sure if it was in a house or a banquet hall. This time it was a hall. I could hear the drums as I got out of my car. I knew they had just begun; there was an order of rhythms that were strictly adhered to. It was crowded. These events usually were. As I walked in, I noticed the stage on the other end of the large room. I had never seen such a lavish presentation of the Orisha being honored. It was beautiful. The entire stage had been artfully draped in what must have been hundreds of yards of shimmering satins, rich brocades and elegant laces. On the floor in a magnificent design created of thousands of pieces of fresh fruit were the large ceramic urns containing the implements and essence of the Santero's Orishas. On a great throne of royal blue brocade, topped with a cloud of iridescent white lace sat the guest of honor, Yemaya, in a blue and white ceramic urn. The entire scene was ingenuously lit by thousands of tiny lights that gave the effect of ocean waves softly rolling through the sea of colorful tropical fruits. It was without a doubt the most beautiful throne I had ever seen.

To the right was a doorway to a smaller room and inside I knew the new Yawos sat nervously waiting to be presented to the drums for the first time. The guests who attended were not all priest, but everyone

243

would soon know who the priest were as the drums called them one at a time to pay tribute. No one uninitiated could dance, and even then, if they had not undergone the ceremony of presentation to the drums, it was forbidden. Each Orisha had a rhythm. Each Orisha had their own dance. Each one was played and danced as a reflection of their role in nature. The drums always began with Elegua. It began in a childlike simple repetitive rhythm. Then gathering momentum it escalated into a quickening series of complex but powerful beats that led to a frenzy of movements that were all but impossible to follow. Each respective rhythm mimicked the energy it aspired to attract. Elegua's rhythm opened the way for all the ones that would follow.

The drums and the dance belonged to Chango. The drums were the sound and dance was the movement of life. It was Chango's heartbeat and an active expression of his passion for life. I knew the rhythm as it began, the dance of Chango may be passionate, but it was the dance of a warrior, not a romantic. Each of his priests were required as a sign of respect to dance their way up to the drums alone. They had to prostrate themselves onto the floor in front of the lead drum. They would proceed to donate a small offering, cross their arms and kiss each of the three sacred drums. Upon completion of this duty, everyone in the room knew you to be the child of the Orisha you had paid tribute to.

It was my turn to pay this tribute and as dedicated as I was to my guardian, I could not eliminate my shyness. I did not like the attention. I knew this was viewed by my peers as unbecoming to a priest of Chango, but no matter how I tried flamboyant did not happen for me. The only dance I had ever known was ballet, and even that was many years ago. I was not a dancer and my dance bore little resemblance to a powerful warrior. For this I was reputed to be the Anglo Santera who was too reserved to effectively exhibit her saint, but too ethereal to bring her spiritual abilities into question. I suppose this was not a very approachable combination. I was always treated with respect, but it was always tempered with a hint of distrust.

For some unknown reason on this night I closed my eyes and as I began my approach, the beat of the drum became my heart. My body moved with some faintly familiar rhythm resonating in some other far away but comfortable space and time. I did not recall the crowd of people. I could not remember the hall I was in, only the rhythmic call of some primal rapture that carried me forth. When I opened my eyes, I was faintly kissing the drum of Yemaya. I looked around, startled at the quickness of the change in my perception. I wasn't exactly sure whom or what had performed this ritual of the drum within me, but I was the one who was now turning to face the room full of people.

Alcohol was never served at these events. The combination of spirits could be dangerous. There was an open bar in the back serving sodas and waters. I walked as casually as possible to this bar. I did not watch the rest of the tributes. I never did pay much attention to who was who at these events. I recognized the last song. It was to Yemaya, the patroness of this affair. It was the rhythm of the ocean, and its dance was always beautiful. Her dance reflected the waves and the movements of the sea. Next, there would be a colorful pageant of the new Yawos.

The small room to the side was filled with the godparents and attendants busily dressing the Yawos for their entrance. The first one brought out was a young girl, an omo Yemaya. She wore a long peasant dress of white cotton, a scarf covering her hair and a white lace shawl over her arms. This was layered on top with an ornate crown of royal blue peaked with the feathers from an African parrot. She was draped over one shoulder in a large braided rope of blue and white beads. In one hand she carried a large stalk of bananas while holding on firmly to the feet of a live rooster in the other. All these things were heavy and not so easy to carry, I remembered. Two attendants, walked beside her to help direct her to the drums.

Everyone watched, as this was the equivalent of a sacred but joyous kind of coming out party. The Yawo was brought a few steps towards the drums and then a few steps back again. At this point other priest joined from behind. It was a ritual step of coming close and backing away with the drums leading the pace. The bananas and rooster were then offered to the drums and the Yawo threw herself upon the floor in a salute to them. She was then helped to her feet and introduced to each of the three sacred drums. Each drum was adorned with an elaborate satin cover in the colors of its patron. The Yawo was then led to the center of the floor where she would perform her first dance to her guardian Orisha.

It was difficult to dance with all the heavy necklaces that hung on her almost to her knees. Despite the heavy garb, the girl moved elegantly with the rhythm of the ocean waves. She began to smile and just as she began swaying in delight, the attendants grabbed her on either side and began to spin her around and around. In this dizziness the girl was then swept away back into the small side room. She would not come out again until everyone had left for the night.

There must have been five or six presentations that night. The dancing did not begin until all these things had been completed. When the last Yawo was seated back into the room, the drums broke into thunder. Every priest was now beckoned to dance to the honor of the various rhythms of nature. No priest wished to risk offending any of the powers that be. It is during this time that many of the Santeros are 'mounted by their orishas'. Meaning they become possessed by their saints. This was something that could happen at any moment, to any priest. It was a sudden and sometimes a shocking transformation.

As the dancing began, the drums called one saint after another. The Santero next to me began to jerk convulsively. His eyes rolled back and he fell to the floor. As quickly as he had fallen, he jumped up. His eyes were wide and wild. He seemed to fight the possession, but it was too strong. He began taking giant steps, as one would do when their perception had suddenly changed. I knew it must be like putting on very strong eyeglasses and moving in accordance. The size of the world for him had changed. Everyone circled around him to keep him contained. I knew to be careful not to touch him with my hands, as they reacted very unpredictably. The crowd moved in shoulder to shoulder to center him. At the appropriate time, two attendants began to take his shoes off, roll his pant's up and dress him in the costume of his saint. The costumes were usually very elaborate, made of colorful satins and brocades, decorated in beads and gold or silver trims. His personal jewelry was removed and handed to someone to protect as it could easily get lost, broken or given away by the Orisha in possession.

No theater on earth could compete with this show. Cuban's have a flare for the dramatic. They have a style that is uniquely their own and the drums were the instruments that brought it all to life. This was the stage where the Orishas expressed themselves on the earth. Sometimes, they performed amazing acrobatics. I had seen one do back flips across the entire room filled with people. I had seen them make jumps in mid air that would have made Baryshinikov envious. I have heard them sing out unearthly sounds that were completely astounding.

One of the most important aspects of this flamboyant display was however, the message that the Orishas delivered during this possession. Throughout the remainder of this event, the saints walked among the priests and the guests and delivered messages, cures and prophecies. This was a seemingly random selection. They simply walked up to a person and began talking. Sometimes, it was profound. Sometimes it was disappointing. Some Santeros were better channels than others.

On this night, a Santero who had been possessed by Yemaya spotted me from across the room. He cocked his head like a proud woman and lifted the corner of the blue skirt he was wearing. He stood like a statue for a moment and then bolted towards me. He literally dived through the air landing at my feet. I was so stunned. I forgot what I was supposed to do. After what seemed like a very long moment, he/she stood up. I reciprocated the honor by saluting her in turn. As I lay prostrated on the floor, she tapped my back with the traditional blessing and completed it with the words *de dae*, which meant stand up. I had not fully come to a stand when she grabbed me in a heartfelt hug and began sobbing.

"Little child of Chango," she cried. "You have come to your mother Yemaya." She held me tight and I could feel her warm tears on my neck. "We are *Okanna Oni*, of one heart," she sobbed. "I will bring you what your heart is asking for, because I have heard your prayers and I love you very much. You think your father is very hard because he brings you too many visions. Do not be arrogant, and do not think that everything you see is necessarily the way you see it, or you may not see at all. Be careful, the waters of the ocean are very deep. They are infested with sharks. They are dangerous and you Chango my child, could be eaten trying to cross them. Your father cannot protect you there. I will be close by to protect you, but you must not lose your head. Everything will depend on this. You understand?"

"Yes," I replied. I understood the words, but I did not have a clue to their meaning. He could not have known that Yemaya was my spiritual mother. He could not have known that I had just made a petition to her. Nor that I had many visions, but the sharks and deep waters I could not relate to. I would be careful not to lose my head, but I did not have much of a temper so even this was not too relevant, but I thanked her for the message all the same. Then as quickly as he/she had taken hold of me, she released me, and in a gale of laughter she went on to someone else.

I stood there in a sort of daze. Then I was suddenly pulled out of the way of a large man who flailed his body about in erratic uncontrollable jerks. He could have crushed me. As I looked up to thank whom ever had saved from this bull, I could not believe my eyes. It was the prince charming from the market. I strained out a barely audible thank you and smiled. He smiled back, and as he did he took my hand and led me through the crowd. I did not know if he spoke English, I did not know where he was taking me to and I felt faint at the mere touch of his hand.

"Would you care for something to drink?" He asked. His English was perfect, with only a slight, very sexy Latin accent.

I tried in vain to cover my shyness, but it worked no better now than it had ever worked before. Fortunately my mouth that occasionally worked on autopilot managed to answer, "yes, thank you," but I knew my face blushed all the same.

"If I had not seen you dance to Chango," he said. "I would have thought you belonged to Oshun."

Oshun was Santeria's equivalent to Aphrodite. He was beautiful and charming. I had nothing witty to reply, so I smiled. I could feel nothing but my heart beat to the seductive vibrations of the drums that tirelessly pounded out their primal rhythms. My mind stretched for something rational to say. I needed words to put into some orderly thought before he deduced I was some simple minded mute, but nothing came out.

He smiled and rescued me once more. "So you are very shy. Yet you come to Hialeah, to the drums alone?"

"I was invited by Fernando," I answered gaining a little confidence. "Do you know him?"

"For many years," he replied. "So, you are not from Miami, and you are not Latin. How is it that you came to be?"

"It's a long story," I answered.

"Then we must make time for you to tell it. The drums will be ending soon, perhaps you would join me for some coffee after." He saw the hesitation in my face. "The café is just next door," he assured me.

"All right," I agreed. It was late and the coffee would be good before my drive home. Not to mention the fact that I was incredibly intrigued by this man.

The last of the rhythms was being played. A woman now picked up a bucket of water that had been carefully placed beside the drums before they began. She began swinging it around and around as she made her way to the door. Everyone backed up as she passed and shouted as the water was splashed out onto the street marking the official ending of the ceremony.

We were not far from the door. He grabbed my hand and gently pulled me through it. I laughed out loud at the sudden change in intensity, at the deafening sound of silence. It was only a few steps to the café next door and as he opened the door, I knew I was stepping through yet another threshold of reality.

"Whatever you would like, it will be my pleasure to give you," he smiled as he gracefully motioned to the menu.

Every charming man began in the same way, and it was always wonderful. I loved it. I could think of a lot of things that would be a pleasure to receive from this man, but I would ask for coffee. "Espresso would be fine," I answered.

"The same for me, two espressos," he nodded to the man behind the counter. It was late and there were no waitresses, only the man behind the counter who interrupted his nightly cleaning ritual and began making our coffees. "Now, as we have not yet been properly introduced, please allow me to introduce myself. My name is Miguel Javier Hernandez." He extended his hand.

"It's nice to meet you," I extended my hand also. "My name is Jeanne Marie, Jeanne Marie Antoinette."

"Very beautiful name," he kissed my hand. "It suits you. So, what is it you do when you are not dancing?"

I had always dreaded that question, but I had decided some time ago that for simplicity's sake I would answer only that I was a counselor. Which is exactly how I answered before returning the question to him.

"By profession," he said, "I am a physician. Personally I am a priest of Yemaya." He smiled. "My father was a physician and his father before him was a physician for many years back in Cuba. There was not much choice involved in selecting my profession."

"And becoming a priest, when did you choose to do this?" I asked.

"Well, to be honest I may not have exactly chosen that either. I was initiated long before I can remember." The man at the counter set the espresso cups in front of us and he continued. "Actually I did not know about this until I had completed medical school. My mother died when I was very young. It was my aunt who told me that I had been dedicated to Yemaya when I was very young. She raised me. She told me that before I was born, my mother had lost her first son to some terrible illness. My mother, she told me had grieved inconsolably for the loss of her child. My father sadly became a man of few words after the death of this son, a brother I never knew. He was not a great comfort to her.

"She went to the Santera to console her?" I asked.

"No, it was my aunt who did this. She could not bear the unhappiness in the house, so she went to find help from the only hope she knew, an old Santera she had once met. This Santera was very well known in these times, she was very well known in Cuba. The Santera told my aunt what needed to be done to bring new life into the house. My mother was terrified of the woman, but my aunt insisted she follow her directions. She did, and soon after I was born.

"So, your mother dedicated you to the Saint in appreciation for this?"

"Not exactly," he smiled a little and sipped the coffee. "It was told to my aunt that the next male child born in the house must be initiated to Yemaya, as soon after his birth as possible. She warned that this was the only way to protect his life, as well as the lives of those who lived in the house. It was said, that death would be knocking on the doors of our house if this were not done. But my mother wanted no more to do with these things. She was content now with her child and refused to go through the initiation.

Soon she gave birth to another child, this time a girl. My aunt begged her to initiate me before some tragedy struck again. My mother was an educated genteel woman, she knew nothing of this religion and dismissed it as superstitious nonsense. Her sister reminded her that they had both seen first hand the evil things that could consume the health and ultimately the life of a child. My mother refused to remember and adamantly refused to discuss it at all. My father spent more and more time away from home. Perhaps he feared getting too close to another child he might lose. My father knew nothing of the situation.

A few weeks after her birth, my infant sister died. My aunt was beside herself in fear and grief. She begged my mother once again to listen to the old Santera before another tragedy struck. My mother grieved again, but she believed it to be a natural death, and this was probably true. A few months later my mother was diagnosed with cancer. At that time, this prognosis was a death notice. She took me for the initiation and dedicated my life to the service of Yemaya... She died two years later. So," he looked up. "You see everyone has a story that brings them to the place they are in this world."

"This is true," I replied, "but my story is not nearly so captivating, or so romantic. I am just a sort of misplaced clairvoyant. Actually, by trade I am a counselor, but in reality I am a psychomotrist. I touch inanimate objects and see the lives of those that have touched them before me. I try to help people in the process. I spend my life looking for the soul of things, the invisible life that hides inside of them. That's how I found this religion, it's what I was looking for. Every thing and every place has a soul. Santeria as I see it is the soul of Miami, it is the life force hidden beneath the city, and I needed to touch it."

We continued to talk into the small hours of the morning. I did not want it to end. He had gently kissed my hand as he tucked me into my car. I took a deep breath and drove away as my heart still beat with the rhythm of the drums of the night.

I met Miguel the following week for lunch in a small Cuban restaurant. It was on Calle Ocho in Miami. He apologized for the location. Explaining that his work schedule had been extraordinarily heavy lately as he spent most of his time volunteering at the clinic on the next block. "The people are poor," he told me. "Many of them have nothing but their new found freedom, and for that they are grateful. Others have lost their hope and succumb to the parasites of the streets, consuming copious amounts of drugs in a futile effort to feed the dreaded diseases of the soul. There is a new breed of this dark disease, it is increasing daily, and Miami is the gateway through which it enters. But you saw this, that night in the market."

I don't know why it struck me all of a sudden that he too knew of these things. But he did know, and he knew much more than I. Of this I was fairly certain. "Yes," I assured him, "I remember, but it was the girl you were helping, the other two were surly beyond anyone's help?"

"There may be no cure," he corrected me, "but no one is beyond help. That young girl was taking care of both of them. She knows they are dying. One is her brother; they brought her out of Cuba, where she lived a life not worth living. Now she cares for them, and prepares to care for another. She still has hope that she can protect her child."

I wanted to ask more questions. I wanted to know exactly what he did, but I did not. He obviously thought I knew more about the disease than I did. Even Iya did not know too much. Why would he assume that I knew more than someone so much older? But, he had heart, he cared for people and I did not want to think of anything so disturbing as death and gray demons right now.

He continued to tell me bits and pieces of his daily life. He was passionate as well as dedicated to what he referred to as his children. The clinic treated many of the new arrivals to our city. Some legal and some not, but they were all people in desperate need of help. He focused on the children who came. They came without families, without support. Sometimes, he told me, their own family gave everything they had to send them here on risky boats with few provisions. They send them with the hope they might be able to prosper and someday bring them over as well.

They were children he told me. They were sometimes no more than thirteen or fourteen, in a strange country with nothing, with no one. They usually became children of the streets, recruited by unsavory benefactors who worked them for sex and paid them with drugs. They feared the streets, but they feared the government more. If they were caught they feared they would lose the freedom their families had sacrificed to provide for them. They feared they would be locked up or sent back, in disgrace. There were so many fears, and they were not even aware that nothing could ever be as abominable as the reality they lived. "Someone," he said, "has to look after them, care for them, and do what ever small things can be done. People do not want to see them. They do not want to know about them. On paper they do not even exist. They have fallen through the cracks of bureaucracy. They are simply the lost children of the city."

When he was not at the clinic, he spent his time working on staff at the children's hospital. There he cared for the privileged sick children, the ones with parents, homes and hope. This was his professional life. In his personal life, which seemed to be severely limited until very recently, he liked to spend time in the Islands. He had many friends in Jamaica and it was an escape to a much needed other world for him. "This is the time," he said, his voice soft and melodical. "When I wake up in the morning and fill my eyes with her, from the top of her mountainous breasts to the endless ripples of her ocean body. I eat her fruits, I listen to the music of her waves and I inhale all of these beautiful things until I think I will burst from my love of Yemaya... And, this is the time, when I remember, how blessed I am to be here on this earth."

Soon, Miguel and I were spending every spare and precious moment together. We spent afternoons at Bayside milling the shops in the marina. We talked insatiably over long lunches and drank too many glasses of red wine. We strolled South Beach watching the sunset and the moon rising. We ate in the trendy beach cafes and walked barefoot in the white sand. It was a beautiful romantic dream, and I prayed that this was the thing that Yemaya had so graciously sent to me. This man was wonderful.

Miguel did not make love. He was love. Chango was the fire of life, but I discovered through him that Yemaya was the eternal fluid of life. Lightning could strike the ocean ten thousand times, and she would merely smile at his arrogance. She was an immense power of nature, and only now did I truly realize her power and her beauty. She had shown me all this through Miguel. Life was full and I did not want any changes.

The holidays were a busy time for Miguel, but we spent as much time together as possible. Somehow we made it to most of the parties, and I was glad. I had many friends who invited me to their elegant homes every year, but I rarely went. With Miguel, I felt radiant and beautiful and I wanted to be seen that way. Everyone complimented me on this new radiance. Everyone was happy for me and I was beginning to feel like Cinderella. If only, midnight would never come.

It was Christmas Eve. Tonight, I was convinced, would be that special night. It would be the passionate culmination of all the warm and tender collective moments we had shared so far. Miguel had been patient, he was always more patient than I. "If you dive into the water too quickly," he said. "All your fire will be gone. Do you understand this?" He caressed the top of my head with both hands and gently kissed its crown. "This is what you must respect."

I knew what he meant. My head belonged to Chango. I knew he was right, but it did not ease my desire. And, as much as I loved my guardian, I would have succumbed to it all in an instant. But, Miguel had not allowed it to happen, and in spite of myself, I had been respectful. I loved him for that. He had called me from the hospital that morning. "I've arranged everything, my work is covered and I want to spend the entire evening with you. Tonight we share something very special, something I could not share with anyone else in the world." Tonight would be the night, and Christmas would become a new memory, it would be whole and beautiful at last.

I had changed clothes three times, from white chiffon, to black velvet and finally to deep claret red silk. It felt right. The dress was simple but elegant, sleeveless with a low cut back and slightly flared at the hem just above the ankles. The dress called for my hair to be up, but I would not comply. Tonight it would be down. I would scrunch it up with my fingers as it dried and allow it to be full and a fall where it wanted.

By seven I was dressed, had the wine chilled, lit candles and rearranged the coffee table a half a dozen times. Miguel would not be there for another half hour. I poured myself a glass of wine and turned on the stereo to relax and listen to the season's music. Silent night played softly and I could not help but to look up at the angel who adorned my Christmas tree. I looked at the pretty golden curls that framed her tiny angelic face and I thought of Sunny, of Jen and of all the countless others whose faces I had forgotten. I thought of Nuremberg and the window of the store filled with all the beloved little daughters of some nameless man who had given them wings. They had all been loved. The father in Nuremberg had loved his daughter, even when he could not reach her anymore, even when she left, he had loved her. Tears rolled down my face, splashing onto the crimson silk. I couldn't do this. I felt a sudden sense of panic. I wanted to run. Bolt out of this place like an immense shaft of lightening and vanish into the night sky. I could not be with Miguel, not tonight, maybe not ever.

"Jeanne Marie," I was startled by a voice; someone was tapping on the window beside me. It was Miguel. I didn't know what to do. It was too late to hide, too late to cover tears or dry my dress. I had to open the door.

He gregariously scooped me up and kissed me several times. Then holding me firmly by both shoulders, he pulled me back to look at my face. "What is this, what has happened to my beautiful angel?"

If I cried, I knew he would only pull me closer. He would try in vain to comfort me. No, I would not cry. "Nothing, it's nothing, I was just sitting here and…it just happened and it's all silly, look at me. I wanted everything to be perfect when you got here. Now look what I've done. Look at my dress."

"Perfect things are not real ones. You are beautiful." He wiped the moisture from my chin and then kissed the wetness from my cheeks. "Come," he took me with one hand and picked up my wine glass with the other. "Tonight we celebrate, all good things," and he filled a second glass to the brim with Chablis. "To the saints, and all the beautiful things they have given us."

We ate dinner outside at the French Cafe on Los Olas. The colonnade was bountifully decorated with boughs of greens and filled with the glitter of twinkling Christmas lights The streets were lined with grand date palms outlined with thousands of tiny white lights. Elegantly clad people in holiday motifs peered into the windows of galleries and small exclusive shops. But I kept my eyes on the table before me. Miguel had ordered some wonderful wine for the occasion, and the waiter had kept our glasses full.

By the time we got home, my mood had softened, to a comforting malleable blur. Miguel took the key from my hand and opened the door as we arrived. "No more vino, for you tonight."

I walked over to the sofa and kicked the uncomfortable heels off my feet before I sank down. "Why, do you think my decision making abilities might be impaired? That I might be in a position to be taken advantage of?"

"Yes, I am worried about that." He knelt down in front of me and nuzzled his head into my lap. I could feel his warm breath there as he spoke. "You are making me crazy. You know that don't you?"

"I don't want to make you crazy. I just want you to make love to me," I said.

"I know you don't understand why. I'm having trouble with that myself right now, but you have to trust me. It has to be complete. It must be at the right time or it will not last. I love you, not just today and tonight. I love you, and it goes much beyond that. We will make love, I promise you and it will be so much more than one passionate evening. It will last a lifetime. It must last a lifetime."

I said nothing. I loved him, and I could not possibly comprehend what he was talking about, but I would wait. Miguel handed me a small oblong box wrapped in shinny gold paper. I untied the gilded ribbon and opened the box. It was a beautiful gold bracelet delicately set with seven aquamarine stones. It was beautiful.

"You should never be without an offering for Yemaya," he told me clasping it around my wrist. "If the time ever comes that you find yourself too deep in her waters, you will always have something on your arm to help you."

I cried, and I loved him for that too. Then he handed me a little envelope containing an itinerary for two weeks in the Islands. We would begin in Ocho Rios in Jamaica. The plans were to leave on the last day of January. We would return on Valentines Day. It was all a wonderful surprise.

It was all so perfect, everything fit and for the first time in my life. I actually experienced a moment of contentment, but it was fleeting. I was blissfully happy, and deeply afraid. I was terrified something would take it all away. There had to be some way to secure these blessings with my guardian. Surly he knew how much I needed Miguel.

But my guardian was thunder and lightning. He could be heard and seen, but never grasped. His energy was powerful and intense, but it was not an attainable thing. By the time one saw the flash and heard its proclamation. It was gone. The nature of Chango was magnificent, but like all the natures of this world, his energy was not selectively packaged. I was at the same time blessed with an eternal luminous flame and cursed with the desire to hold it.

The energy destined to guide me did not possess a tangible form that one could readily hold on to. Unlike the waters, the earth, metal or mountains, Chango was not touchable. His form in nature is electricity. In the other world this is a kind of spiritual friction, but in humans it is passion. Chango is a stimulation of life, rather than a thing of life. My path was directed it seemed, not in what came between life and death, but in the transitional process itself. This path required so much from a Santera, so much from a woman, too much from me.

I was a woman, and attraction to an unattainable passion was not enough. I craved attachment. I wanted a love I could keep. Attraction to this in a man had always scrambled my psychic reception, it blurred my vision, but attachment I knew could block it altogether. It could blind me. It could cause me to lose my insight, my perception and my abilities. But this did not prevent me from wanting love, from wanting Miguel. Like everyone else, I desired to have and to hold some of the things of this world. I thought about all these things, and it did not matter. I was attracted to so much more than passion in this man. I was in love and this was the strongest attachment in life. I could be blinded by it. I could lose my energy. I could lose my life source, but I did not care. I did not want to live without this man. I wondered what would happen if my guardian abandoned me. I remembered an incident several years ago when I had witnessed this very thing.

The first of the year marked a special occasion. For every Santero, it was a time for consultation with the Babalow. Every priest came with their small bag of seventeen shells belonging to their guardian Orisha. The Babalow would cast these shells and their message interpreted. No one knew what forecast or responsibility this would bring. If it was a warning, one needed to prepare for what was to come. They might be able to lessen its impact if they could not prevent it. Sometimes it brought news of good things to come. Sometimes it was merely instructions of what one should focus on in the coming year. It was not a thing one could know until the shells had spoken.

I waited as always a bit reluctantly for my turn to see the Babalow. Just before me was a Santero in his mid thirties, he was a priest of Obatala. I knew of him, I had seen him at some of the drum ceremonies, but I did not know him. It was said that he was a very wealthy Santero. Rumor was that he had all of his Orisha's implements made in solid gold and that they all lived in huge magnificent porcelain urns he had imported from China. He was known for the lavish gifts and parties he offered to his guardian Orisha. It was also known, that much of his money came from the drug dealers who sought his aid in protecting them from the law.

Now this did not seem to be an appropriate choice for a Santero to make. Especially if one happened to be a priest of the Orisha who was the very nature of purity, respect and law. It is not the place however, of any priest to make a judgment regarding the path of another. Judgment belongs to the divine. It belongs in particular to Obatala who owns the position himself. Santeros, just as every other group or organization is made up of the same thing, people. Some are good. Some are not. The first lesson that every priest must learn is that the world is neither good, nor bad. The nature of the world is only to be, and so it is. One cannot have vision until they learn to see from this distance.

On this day, I watched as he opened his beautiful silvery silk pouch and poured the small shells onto a white plate to present them along with a generous offering to the Babalow. The Babalow lifted the shells in his hands, said the blessings and gracefully threw the shells onto the straw mat as he had for the numerous Santeros who had gone before him that day. The room was suddenly still.

I knew what sign had fallen, but I could not conceive of the severity of its silence. I knew the pattern meant that the Orisha did not speak. I did not know it also could mean that one's guardian had abandoned them. No one moved for several seconds, then the Babalow scooped up the shells, like dried bones that were no longer alive and dropped them back onto the plate. He did not touch the offering. He nodded to the Santero without expression motioning him to pick up the plate.

The Santero then burst into a loud rapid succession of words that I could not understand. The Babalow would not answer. He would not respond to the provocation. The Santero finally in anger grabbed the shells and the money, stuffed them into the silver pouch and stormed out of the house. It was not until later that day that I was able to ask Iya what it had meant.

"He will die," she said simply. "He was told before that he could not buy the favors of his guardian. His guardian loved him, so he granted him many favors. He mistakenly thought he had paid for them. It will cost him his life. He is without protection, a child abandoned to the dangers of both worlds. He will die." She said matter of factly.

Several months later, I heard the Santero had been killed in his own home, in the room of his saints. It was assumed that one of his clients in the drug trade had murdered him. They had paid him for a protection that they did not receive.

The ways of the Orishas was a predictable pattern. People however, did not always predict this pattern correctly, especially, when there was a personal interest involved. This is why the priest went to the Babalow. It was a sort of preventative spiritual check up, but this always opened the risk of being told you were sick, needed an operation or were terminally ill. Some things could be prevented, some things could be cured, and some things could not. If you came to ask, you had to be prepared to listen, to all these things.

It was time now for the annual visit to the Babalow. Iya had called to remind me. If I had been reluctant before, you can only imagine how it was now. I did not want to see, I did not want to hear, and I did not want to know. I just wanted to be happy forever in the arms of Miguel. I feared the advice, instructions, forecasts and warnings of my guardian Chango.

I thought about the drums on the night we first met and the Yemaya who spoke to me with the warning. Were these the deep waters? Were these the dangers she warned me about? No, Chango would never be spoken of as shark infested waters. I would not lose my head, and the other thing about seeing things as they were. Things may not be as I saw them or I might not see at all. I could not quite remember exactly how she said it. Was this a warning of losing my vision?

I didn't want to think anymore. I wanted Miguel to hold me, and take me far away from here. I did not want to see anymore. I had seen enough for one lifetime. There would be no more ominous visions of sharks, blindness or death. In a few weeks we would leave for the Islands. We would drift away to an unknown place somewhere in the Caribbean. We would love and it would not end.

11

Preparing for Destiny

It was just after the new year, the second week in January and my appointment was scheduled for noon. When I arrived at Iya's house, there was no place to park on her tiny street. I knew her house was full. She sponsored this event annually. I sat down in the living room there were three waiting before me. I was informed that he was just beginning. This was expected, as Babalows did not seem to have the same time frame as the rest of the world. If I saw him before three or four, he was making good time, but I did not mind waiting. I was never eager to know these things.

It was a little after three when I was finally called into the room. I took out my little red satin pouch and poured out the small shells onto a white plate. They were called the mouths of the Orishas, and it was these little mouths of Chango who would now speak to me. Beside the shells, I placed a small offering of fifty dollars for the Babalow to interpret their message. Their message would come in the form of two letters, they were actually two numbers and this combination was known as an odu. This odu is between the Orisha and their respective child. It is never to be revealed to anyone else. So I cannot say specifically what odu was given to me, but I can tell you what was told to me that is yet to come.

"Ah, the spiritist," he began. "I am afraid you will have to listen very carefully, my English is not too good. But I know you can understand more than the words I speak." He looked at me and smiled.

"Your English is fine," I assured him.

"First you cannot fear your own guardian, he is your father and he loves you very much. He is there to protect your head," he tapped the top of his to indicate the crown. "You understand this?"

"Yes," I nodded affirmatively.

"Very soon, you will be crossing the waters of Yemaya. I would tell you not to do this, but it is something you must do anyway sooner or later. Some things you cannot prevent. But, even Yemaya cannot prevent every tragedy in your life. She will remain by your side, but she may not be able to save you from your own head. Your eyes have seen many hidden things in the past, these things you will see again. You have seen too much of the dangerous things who live in these waters. Sometimes what lives at the bottom of the ocean, it is better we do not know, or see. Do you understand?"

"Yes," again I nodded again. I understood the words but could not relate to what he said.

He tilted his head and drew a large breath of the warm air as he thought. "Do not let your eyes deceive your mind, your eyes can betray you." He thought for another moment before he began again. "You will need to do an ebbo to strengthen your head before you make this trip. If you don't you are in danger of loosing it. Do you understand?"

"No," I questioned now. I did not understand. What was supposed to be beautiful and romantic was now becoming ominous and terrifying. "What do you mean I must strengthen my head, what ebbo needs to be done?"

"It is not a simple ebbo, but you do not have a simple path, you have difficult things in front of you." His voice lowered now to express his sympathy.

Truthfully, I was angry. I was not sure whom or what I was angry about, but I was. The only consolation was that he had not told me I would lose Miguel, only my head. "I am going on a trip to the Islands at the end of this month," I resigned. "What is it I need to do?"

He touched my hand now and began to speak like a father to me. "I would prefer to stand in front of a train that is coming to run me over, than to do this ceremony. It would be an easier thing to strike a blow at me." He held one hand up and hit his fist hard into it making a loud smacking sound. "This is something I have only done a few times in my life, and I am an old man in this religion. But, we all have things we must do, and this is the thing I must do."

It was not a question of whether I would or would not do the ceremony. The ebbo would be done. I did not know how or when, but it would have to be soon. I was instructed to see Iya after everyone had left for a list of items that would be needed. The list in her handwriting is still in my libretta: one Chiva, a goat, two guinea hens, a rooster, two white pigeons and a large metal tub. There was also a list of herbs to make the omero, honey, and eggshell powder, white clothes and three Santeros. I was told this had to be done in my house. I cringed a little at the thoughts of this. Davie was not used to these ceremonies.

Everything came together on time. Miguel was working hard for his time off, and I would prepare my head now for the future. Iya and one of her godsons showed up on time. No one ever came to my house for these things, and it was nice for a change. The Babalow was a couple of hours late but finally arrived with the animals in small cages. I did not know if this could be done too discreetly, but it had to be done. I had worn old clothes, as I assumed there would be a cleansing involved and they would be torn off and disposed of. Everyone was in good spirits and we sat out on the open patio and began making the *osian*, the herbal liquid for the bath.

This is a ceremony in itself. The youngest of the house spreads out the straw mat and kneels down as she hands the herbs one bundle at a time to the Santera who says the blessings for them. They are then passed to each person in attendance to strip them from their stalks and throw the leaves into the basin. Songs are sung to raise the vibrations or the life source of the herbs, to soothe them into working together. Water is added as the song calls for it, and the herbs are rubbed together with hands until it becomes a thick green liquid. The Santera in charge adds the last ingredient. Several pieces of coco butter are bitten off chewed up and spit into the mixture. This must come from her mouth, as saliva carries with it her *ache*. This entire process takes a few hours to complete, and this herbal concoction is used for bathing as well as drinking. Omero is the elixir of the Orishas.

A straw mat was thrown in the middle of my kitchen floor, the large basin placed on top and a bucket of water placed beside it. The Babalow brought his own stool, which he now sat securely in front of the basin. He shifted the seat a little as if he were checking to see if he could brace himself and then nodded his head that he was ready and I should take my place. I knelt down in front of the basin.

"Now," he began. "Hold onto the sides of the this tub with both hands, put your head down and keep your eyes closed. No matter what, do not open your eyes. You understand?"

"Yes," I was a little nervous, but I was ready. I don't know why these things are so disorienting, but they always are. My head was first washed ritually with herbs and black soap. Chanting began, and I do not remember the birds, only the sound of those loud guinea hens as they squealed. Songs got louder and I remember hearing the goat, his muffled cries. I always hated that sound. It was too much like the cry of a child. Then I felt the warm gush of blood flowing over my head. I heard a loud cry from the Babalow and then silence. I waited, my head was spinning but I held on to the sides of the pan. The singing began again, honey was poured onto my head, then cold liquid, I was not sure if it was water or omero. I could hear the tin sound as it hit the metal basin.

My arms were frozen in place and my eyes were glued shut. After what seemed like forever, I could feel the hands of Iya wrapping my head with a towel. I was told I could now open my eyes; they opened directly to the dead eyes of the goat that had just lost his head. The head had been set in front of me. "Pick it up," the Babalow instructed me. I hesitated for a minute, gathering strength. Then I reached down with both hands and picked it up.

"Tonight you must clean it, because this head is what will save your life." He relayed to me in great detail how I was to remove the brain from the skull and boil the meat away. He proceeded to tell me how the skull was to be prepared and where it was to be kept. I listened carefully, feeling a little weak in the knees as the warm blood from the severed head I held in my hands, trickled down my arms. He and the other Santero then turned abruptly and walked out the side door to the patio.

Iya motioned to me now to put the head down and step into the basin. She unwrapped the towel from my head and began pouring cold water over me. Next she took a sharp knife and cut the top edge of my shirt and skirt for an easier start at tearing them. Clothes could not be cut off, they had to be torn with the hands and I watched them drop to bottom of the tub and redden as they fell into the bloody mixture.

"Tonight, she said. "You can wash your body but not your head. You cannot touch your head until tomorrow." With that she wrapped my sticky blood soaked hair with a clean white cloth and tied it securely. I was still standing there, wet and naked. She then handed me a towel and told me I could get dressed. I put on fresh white clothes and she called to the men to come back into the room.

I was a little dizzy, but I knew everyone must be tired and thirsty. I went to the cabinet and took out the glasses for cold drinks and turned on the stove to make the Cuban coffee. I was glad I had prepared the little coffee pot earlier, I only needed to turn on the burner and that was about the extent of my energy anyway. The three of them busily cleaned the blood from the floor. They had already neatly removed the animals. I was not allowed to help clean. I was told to rest and stay quiet for the rest of the day and that night. So, I sat a little uncomfortably as they worked.

When everything was clean, the Babalow stood in front of the kitchen window, with a glass of ice water in his hand and began to speak. "You have a very unusual path, no one will ever know why this is, why it was born to you, but it is enough to know that it is." He sighed and then perked up his tone. "Now, you must not drink any alcohol for three months. No drugs, no alcohol," he accentuated this loudly. "Nothing that can take away from the control of your head. This is very, very important. You understand?"

"I understand," I assured him. "I will not touch anything for three months."

"Good," he growled. "And even after that you must always be careful of these things. You cannot be around drugs or anyone who takes them. It can bring terrible things into your life, many tragedies," he shook his head. "A little drink socially, is okay later, you know what I mean." He softened a bit and smiled. Then became serious again. "You must never in your life get drunk, or lose your head to a substance. Be careful of addiction of any kind, stay away from it, or anything to do with it, stay away from addicts. You have a grave warning here."

I assured him once more that this was understood. I did not know why this should be such a major warning for me. I was not much of a drinker, and never had been. I did not do any type of drugs. I seldom took even aspirins which was the only medication I had in the house. The only thing I drank was a glass of wine in the evening, which was certainly not a problem to eliminate from my life for a few months. I certainly did not need to be warned to stay away from addicts. That was a given, but I listened all the same.

Soon, my house was quiet again, and I was alone. I wanted to sit down and rest like they said, but I knew I had one task to complete before I could do this. The head of the goat had to be prepared. My stomach tightened at the thought of this, but I knew well that some things just had to be done.

I had not heard from Miguel in several days. I stayed quiet, contemplative. I told myself everything would be all right now. I had done what I was supposed to do. Soon we would take our trip and be happy together.

We spoke on the phone, but I did not see him much before the trip. I knew he was busy with his work. I told him I had done an ebbo, but

I had not told him the full extent of it. We would have plenty of time in the Islands to discuss everything about it in detail. The flight left early in the morning, so I planned to stay at his house the night before. I was happily packing all my little things when he called. I knew something was wrong. It was not so much what he said, as how he sounded. I could hear it in his voice. I assumed he could not speak freely. I knew he was on his shift at the hospital when he called. He asked me if I could meet him at the clinic the next morning. He said there was something he needed my help with before we could leave. He would say nothing except that it was very important that I get there early, before six. It was Monday. We were leaving on Thursday. I could not imagine what he needed my help with at the clinic. It was an odd request to say the least. I was not exactly knowledgeable in the medical area, but I agreed to meet him there by six the following morning.

The top of my head still felt open from the ceremony. It's hard to describe, but the crown of the head is somehow sensitized when something like that is done. It is not exactly painful. It just feels open. I knew I should cover it, especially going to the clinic. My head was vulnerable, almost as much as it was just after the initiation. I threw a white scarf in my purse just in case. It was early, four thirty. I had no idea what traffic was like on a weekday at anytime in the morning. So I figured I had better give myself an hour.

There was no traffic. I was early but I saw his car in the back as I parked. Everything seemed quiet except for the rattle of the air conditioner suspended in the side of the small stucco building. I knocked on the door in the front, I wasn't sure if he could hear the knock over the noise of the air conditioner, so I tapped again on the window. He lifted the edge of the closed blinds and peeked through before he opened the door.

I slipped in the opening, which was not too wide and put my arms around him. "Who were you expecting at this time of the morning," I laughed. But he did not smile back. He just took me by the hand and led me to the back room. So many images are engraved in my mind.

Sometimes I wish that I could somehow send them away, because I know they will never just go away.

My eyes were still adjusting to the light when I looked down. The two men from the market were lying on the floor, dead. Their bodies were pushed so close together that their heads touched and a thin white sheet was spread beneath them. The young pregnant girl, who now looked like a small child herself, sat cowering in the corner on a small wooden chair. My knees started to give out on me and Miguel caught me by the arm to steady me. The room was spinning. It was a nightmare. I prayed it was a nightmare. I looked up once more. It was still there, all of it.

I wanted to scream at him. What the hell is wrong with you? How could you bring me here, show me this. You must be crazy to think I can even look, much less do anything. I had only dealt with the visions of death, not the physical part, not the bodies. But no words came, only a horrified gasp.

He took a deep breath now that he was aware of my reaction. "I am sorry, I am so sorry, but you must understand I need your help."

I still could not respond, not in the slightest. I could not run. I could not speak I could not even fall down now. I was just too afraid. He continued to explain to me anyway. "I need your help or the girl and her child will die. The disease that consumed these boys must be destroyed. You can see them. I need your help. Carlos died last night. I could have managed it myself, but I did not expect that the other would die so soon after. He died within the hour. I did not have time. You see what has to be done."

For some reason, his words brought me back. I was standing of my own volition again. I looked once more at the pathetic duo twined together on the floor and saw beyond their skin and bone. The ghostly gray rats still gnawed, on what I did not know, but they swarmed over both bodies without distinction, without boundaries. Their auras had been permanently extinguished. I understood what Miguel meant now. Without the containment of the auraic film the beasts were free to roam. They were free to find a new host. I put this in these words for lack of existing terminology. There are no terms to describe them. These vaporous gray demons have no definition to eyes that cannot perceive them, but he had greatly over estimated me. I had no idea of what needed to be done. "Miguel," I said finally, "you will have to tell me what needs to be done."

He looked relieved. I was resigned. This was much too much for me, but there was no choice. "Come with me, we need to prepare," he said simply.

I followed, like a first year nursing student might follow a brain surgeon into the operating room. I knew nothing. He handed me scrubs to put on. I knew what they were, but not how to wear them. I put on the pants and shirt and covered my feet with the paper boots.

"Make sure you cover your head," he reminded me.

Oh god, I had forgotten my head. I covered it now, but it was probably too late. Then he handed me one of those things that doctors wear to cover their mouths during surgery. I assume to protect the doctor from germs, or to protect the patient from his germs. I wasn't sure which way it was supposed to work. I slipped on the gloves like he did, minus the grace of practice. I had no idea what we were preparing for.

"Are you all right?" He asked. He sounded so genuinely concerned.

I just looked at him. How on earth would anything ever be right again? No, nothing in this world could be so wrong. But I said nothing. He had to know what I thought. He came close to me and held me in his arms for a few seconds. It was a bad move. I started to melt again so I pulled away before I lost myself in this temporary safety. What ever it was that lived, feasting on the two people who died, was in the other room, waiting.

"Everything is pretty much prepared," he spoke to me as he picked up a bucket containing an herbal mixture and we started into the other room. "Hold on," he said as he stopped to set the bucket down on the floor.

For one cherished moment I thought he changed his mind. Maybe he thought better of this whole thing. Maybe he remembered it was me he was with. But he said nothing. He just dipped his hands in the bucket of liquid herbs and rubbed this moisture over the back of my neck and then on my throat. Then he dipped another handful of liquid and bathed both of my arms. Leaning forward, he reached his arm into the room where we had been standing grabbed a little ball of eggshell powder and drew a cross, first on my forehead and then on his own.

"Now," he said. "We are prepared."

I only hoped that he was as confident and knowledgeable as he acted and sounded. We entered the dreaded room. It reeked of death. I never smelled death before, but I was certain now that I knew this scent like every other living thing, by instinct. I had not noticed the cage before. It was sitting next to the girl. As he walked over to the cage I noticed the counter had been set up for a ritual, all the necessary items were there. The ram did not leave the cage willingly. I did not blame him. He grudgingly stood up and bucked his head a little. This was not a small ram.

"There is a rope on the counter, and a plate. Bring them over here," he asked as he held the ram by the horns.

This part at least I knew. I waited for him to open the mouth of the ram so he could put the ball of herbs in. The animal was not too cooperative. He finally prodded his mouth open, then slipped the ball in and closed it again. I helped him tie the rope around his mouth as he held it closed. He took the ram now by the horns with both hands and told the girl to stand up. I picked up the piece of coconut with the small black grains on top and handed it to the girl. As I handed it to her, he explained to her in Spanish that she needed to chew it up in her mouth and hold it. When he was ready, she was to blow it into the eyes and ears of the ram asking for his blessings, thanking him for exchanging his life for hers.

"You will have to help her present herself," he began to direct. "It is very important that her scent is on the ram, make sure she makes good contact."

I pulled the girl's head towards the rams and rubbed her forehead firmly against his. I knew how important this connection was. Then I pushed her shoulders down a little so her breast would rub against the same spot on the ram. I held her shoulders for a moment to make sure her scent had been transferred. This being done, I led the girl back to her seat in the corner.

"No," Miguel interrupted. "You must take her to the other room, it will be too dangerous for her in here."

I did as he asked, trying not to anticipate what the next step was. But it was not hard to figure out at this point. I walked in and he looked up at me with apologetic eyes. In the years since my initiation, I have done so many things I did not think I was capable of, but this. This was beyond anything I could ever imagine. I knew what had to be done, but I could not even bring myself to look down again. I had to figure out a strategy.

"You're going to have to stand at the other end." He broke into my dreaded thoughts. "I can pull the ram's head down, but only to a point. Your going to have to lift their heads together, the point of contact has got to be strong and you cannot let them separate."

I knew he was right. The shadowy shroud that covered them could not be separated. I did not know what could happen if they were, because I did not know the behavior of these revolting crawling things. I only knew it could be very dangerous.

I looked down now, trying to ease my fears of the corpses. They were not men. They were boys with only the height of men, children. Neither of them could have been more than eighteen. I wondered where their mothers were. Would they never know what had happened to their children? Their bodies were tall but they looked so small, people look smaller when they die. Our auras may be invisible, but they seem to take up space. They make us appear larger than we are. Without it we look very different, small and empty.

I walked around the sheet now to the other end and knelt down. My hands shook as I slowly reached down. He was positioning the ram so I did not have to lift too far. I knew I had to pass my hands through the dark vaporous creatures before I could touch their heads. It was every disgusting horrific thing I could possibly imagine. I did not know if they would crawl up my arms as I reached into their midst. I was afraid if they jumped as I held on to their heads I might drop them. But I had to stop thinking and do. I reached in quickly grabbing up their heads and Miguel held the ram tightly.

The ram began to buck as the things began to pour into the small opening in his aura. Miguel must have made it. I did not know how it was done, but the shadowy vermin ran like rats from a sinking ship into the field of the ram. I watched in amazement, almost forgetting what revolting thing my hands were now holding. I knew the ram took all his strength to hold, but he held it tight. The gray blanket was shrinking, but I did not know how much longer it would take, or even if they would all go.

I could not ever tell you how long it took. Except to say, it was forever and a little while longer. I did not think I would ever feel clean again. At this point, I was far beyond emotions. Even repulsion could no longer come near me. The bodies were now wrapped in clean linens and I finished cleaning the rest of the blood from the ram. Miguel had done almost everything. He worked circles around me. I was in some shock-induced autopilot. I just wanted to clean, everything.

"The girl lives only a few blocks from here, we will take her home and then we will go to my house so I can take care of you."

I was mechanical. I helped the girl into his car and then got in myself. I don't remember the ride back, only that he walked the girl to her apartment and an older woman took her from there. I remember taking a bath, washing my hair and putting on his robe. He had gone back to the clinic. I know there were other things that had to be done.

I did not ask what they were. I did not want to know. Then he came back home, showered and held me until morning. We did not speak.

The next morning he had to go to the hospital to work. I went home. He called every spare moment, checking to see if I was all right. I lied, there was nothing else he or anyone else could say or do. It was all just a long terrible event. It would somehow subside and life would go on. We would go away soon and maybe we would forget. Maybe all the ugly things I had seen would somehow go away too.

We arrived at the airport early. I knew I should be looking forward to getting away to the Islands, but I could not. Miguel had held me all night, but he knew that I was slipping through his fingers and he could not hold onto me. His body no longer comforted me. I was sure that no body ever would again. I had enough of this world of blood and bones. I wanted to go back to the other world again. I wanted to go back to the cool cobble stone streets of my old walled city. I wanted to beg the children who lived there to let me be with them now. I had been to the new city. I had helped the lost children. I had done what I was supposed to do. There was too much blood in this world. I did not want to feel it any more. I wanted to come home now. I wanted to slip through the cracks in the stones and live safely beneath them. But that was all so far away and I was always it seemed, on the wrong side of the world.

On Air Jamaica, everyone did their best to set the mood for a carefree beginning. They served champagne and played music filled with simple rhythms and cheerful lyrics. I could not drink, but I could drift into the music. I could feel the bustle of the energy around us and enjoy the motion of taking a trip. I could dream of arriving in a magical Island paradise. I had to forget, even if it was for a little while. We were on our way, everything terrible had already been. I looked down at the little bracelet on my arm. Yemaya was beside me, she loved me and she would see to it that Miguel and I were happy now. We would begin again.

12

Crossing Dark Waters

We landed in the small Island airport early and as soon as we came through customs, Rudy met us. An enormous Jamaican man with dread locks and a well warn white beret on his head. He was very friendly. I loved the colorful way he spoke, and he was genuinely happy to see Miguel. "Hey my brother, it's good to have you back, you been away from us too long. Too much doctorin ain't gonna do you much. Ahh but maybe the young lady's helpin you out now. Savin ya from yourself. I'm happy for ya, mon. I'm happy for the both of you."

Rudy took us on a wild ride to the cottage. Miguel had not prepared me for the harrowing driving experience here in the Islands. If he had, I might never have gotten into the car. It was strange enough that in Jamaica they drove on the left side of the road. It was worse as the cars sped around the narrow mountain passages. It looked each time as though they would plow right into us head on.

Rudy only laughed, "Why do ya think they give ya all that booze on the plane mon. It's so the tourists can survive the ride to their hotel."

As we drove through the countryside I marveled at the tropical virgin forests. Banana trees and wild papaya just sprang up on the side of the road. There were many unfamiliar trees, heavy with plump ripe fruits. I wanted to know what they were. I wanted to stop, look at them up close, pick and taste them all. It was an exotic visual elixir, and as my eyes continued to drink it in, I noticed splashes of color. Beautiful tropical hues of color provided by the numerous flowering trees were delicately mixed into the vivid green wildness. I had never seen any of them before. "What kind of tree is that?" I pointed to the side of the mountain to a flamboyant red flowering tree that caught my attention.

"The name of the tree is an African Tulip, but we all know it here as the Flame of the Forest. It's a beautiful thing. All the lovers know that tree." Rudy smiled and with a little laugh he continued. "Everyone know when they're young, go to that tree and make love." He smiled again, as he thought. "Yea mon, that tree is for passion, they say if you make love under it, nothing bad can happen. Young girls don't get pregnant and young men don't get caught."

Miguel smiled, first at his explanation and then at me. The Island was paradise. We had crossed the dangerous waters and safely arrived. Rudy turned off the main road and drove through an old stone and wrought iron gateway covered in bright pink bougainvillea flowers. Grand old trees lined the driveway and it felt as though we were entering another time, some elegant but much older world.

There were several little white cottages over looking the ocean. Rudy drove directly to the one on the end. Miguel opened the door for me and helped me out of the car. My legs were a little rubbery from the ride. It was breath takingly beautiful. Miles and miles of ocean shore rested at the foot of the majestic Blue Mountains. I could understand why he chose to come here. It was everything he described.

We settled into the small white cottage. It was built in an English colonial style, with a subtle tropical island motif. White painted lattices divided most of the inside space from the outside world and it provided an airy garden like atmosphere. It was charming. It was from another time and place in history. I loved it. There were several cottages nestled closely but each was positioned in the lush foliage to provide for maximum privacy. Each was built on a different level, hidden from full view, creating a vision of pictorial charm.

"It's beautiful, I can't believe how beautiful this is!" I ran up the stairs marveling at everything. It was so quaint and so incredibly perfect.

Miguel only smiled. "I'm glad you like it. And, because this is your first visit, you get to decide what we do first. I could try to influence you." He reached his arms around my waist and began kissing the back of my neck. "But of course that would be cheating."

"But of course, that probably wouldn't stop you."

"No, it probably wouldn't." He scooped me up like a child in his arms and carried me to the canopied bed. I sank down into the feathers of the white linen comforter and looked up into his face, into his eyes. I loved this man and I wanted nothing more than to be with him.

"I brought you here because I wanted to surround you with love, here, right now is everything in this world that I love. Everything is complete, and I want to make love to you, beautiful, beautiful love to you." He began gently kissing my forehead. He released his grasp on my hands, which he had been holding firmly over my head and proceeded to run his fingers down my bare arms. I was paralyzed. I couldn't even lower my arms. I just lay there, mesmerized by his every word, entranced with his every movement, and allowed him to undress me. He stroked and caressed every infinitesimal part of my body as he gently peeled away the clothes, and I responded to his touch like warm resin. He kissed each of my breasts, my throat and ultimately my yielding mouth. Then he gently parted my legs. Before I could utter a sound of objection, beg him to please not do anything that might bring this to an end, his entire being had slipped into mine. It had to be some form of divine ecstatic sorcery, some profound sacred alchemy. I had transcended every world I had ever known. We had become a single entity, with one magnificent aura that glowed without color, a sheer reflection of only the purest essence of light. At last I understood, at last body and soul had merged. This was love, and it would never end.

Heated love was followed by cool water. As we showered, washing away the residues of passion and love, I knew they were forever forged together, like fine tempered steel. This powerful covenant could not be broken, and I silently said a prayer in gratitude. Everything had changed, forever changed and it was wonderful. Why had I been so afraid? I kissed his wet shoulders and hugged him as I pressed my breast against his back. "Now, it's my turn, let's go for a walk and find food, I'm starving."

"All this, and it's not enough? You want food too!" He laughed and began kissing and caressing me again.

"No, food first." I pushed him away and jumped out of the shower grabbing a towel as I ran to get dressed.

There was a dining room just up the path. I had seen the front of it when we first drove in and as we came closer, I realized it had a beautiful gazebo with a few tables overlooking the ocean. We walked down the little footpath lined with the ample red spikes of ginger flowers. Miguel selected a table and pulled out a chair for me. It was all a wonderful fairy tale and I never wanted it to end.

I must admit I did miss the glass of wine. If there were ever a time and a place for it, it was definitely here and now. A bottle of wine just seemed appropriate with the baskets of bread and trays of tropical fruits and cheeses. I remembered the warning, but I did not want to bring up any of those things, not here and not now. I did not want to think about anything other than this magical place. After lunch we walked in the woods, everything was so luxuriously green. We lived in the tropics in Miami, but Jamaica was different. The plants that grew here were all oversized and filled with brilliant colors of exotic fragrant flowers. The ferns were magnificent. I felt dwarfed like I was walking through some prehistoric forest where dinosaurs still roamed. It was magical, wonderful and gratefully so far away.

That night we laid down in the sand of the deserted beach in the moonlight and let the waves softly roll over our bodies. Nature could be very beautiful. We made love, bathed again in the warm fresh water of the tranquil pool and made love again. I woke up in his arms, and I was content. I assured myself that everything before this moment in my life had only been a bad dream.

For seven glorious days, I ate slept and breathed all the pleasures of the natural world. We walked through secret woods and discovered their hidden lagoons. We reveled in the mysteries of the Blue Mountains and lavished every evening in the waters of our benefactress Yemaya. If there was a heaven on this earth, surely it was here.

We had gone to breakfast early. Miguel was taking me to meet a friend of his who lived nearby. "You should know, that she is not well, health wise I mean," he began. "She is dying of cancer among other things. I try to help her when I can. She is a very close friend, I have known her for a long time."

I did not know what to answer to this. He was a physician. It was his nature to take care of people. I assumed that he did not want this visit to bring back any distress from the event in Miami. "Is she in the hospital?" I asked.

"No, she is in a small house," he explained. "There is a woman there who cares for her."

It was a plain little house, a very heavy set Jamaican woman sat on the front porch watching the empty street. She stood up when we reached the front step and nodded hello. "Mister Miguel come to see you Miss Marion," she sang out as she walked.

I followed Miguel and the Jamaican woman into the side bedroom. It was small and plain, but very clean and well cared for. Miguel walked to the side of her bed and took her hand. She was hooked up to some sort of drip, from a bottle that hung by her side. Her eyes were sunk and dark circles were beneath them. Her thin dark hair covered her right cheek. Miguel gently pushed this hair aside and gently kissed her cheek. There was a large ugly scar crossing her pale skin. I glanced around the room, trying not to feel like I was intruding on a private moment. There were pictures of a very beautiful young woman. She was obviously a model. These were studio shots from a portfolio. Perhaps it was her eyes, I don't know, but it hit me very suddenly and I gasped out loud. Miguel looked up now, not surprised, rather slowly like he had been waiting for me to realize who she was. The room began to spin. I couldn't remember where I was.

Someone was gently patting a cold cloth on my face. I felt sick and I did not want to open my eyes. Miguel was looking down at me, and then I remembered. "Who are you?" I screamed and I did not care how loud I screamed. At that moment, I did not care about anyone or anything. I did not know what was going on. I did not know why he brought me here. The only thing I knew was that it was all his fault. All the terrible things, he was somehow making them happen.

"It's okay, it's okay," he said lowering his voice trying to calm me. Then he tried to stoke my face.

I jerked away as if he were trying to strike me. "You knew, you knew all along. You lied to me. What do you want from me?" I was still yelling.

He looked at me, with a genuinely surprised expression. "You don't understand." He shook his head like he couldn't believe it.

"Understand," I replied sarcastically. "Oh I understand. You used me. I don't know what you want yet, but you used me."

"But you remember Marion?" He asked sincerely.

I was beginning to think I was in the twilight zone. Didn't he think that this was all a bit strange? How could he have known that I recognized her? I was too angry to think rationally, so I kept screaming. "Why did you bring me here? Why do you know this woman? Who is she and who the hell are you?"

"If you stop yelling," He lowered the sound level again. "I will explain everything to you."

"Explain what!" I screamed. "There is no explaining this. You think your Ricky Riccardo now; you're going to splain this. You can't. I hate you, I hate everything to do with you." I knew I was about screamed out. The tears were falling down my face and my throat was closing up.

He calmly sat down in the chair across from me. "Do you care to listen now?" He asked in a tone that a teacher might have in speaking to a badly behaved child.

I just glared at him. I would be quiet now, but that was the most I could manage. I would still hate him.

He composed his words carefully. "The first time I saw you was at the mass for Gustavo, Do you remember?"

I nodded my head, reasonably certain that I would receive only half the truth if I received any at all.

"Do you know why you were there?" He asked.

This was not sounding like much of an explanation. I was answering his questions, but I needed to know what was going on before I lost it all together. "No, not really. Iya had asked me to go," I answered.

"She did not ask you to look for anything?" He asked skeptically.

"I don't really know what I was supposed to be looking for," I told him. "She just asked me to let her know if I saw anything ... strange."

"You had no idea," he asked incredulously. "You did not know what you were looking for?"

"No, I told you. She just told me to go there and let her know if I could see anything unusual. I had seen the Babalow before he died," I volunteered. "I had seen the..." I hesitated. I did not even know what to call them. "The things that were killing him, but I only saw him for a moment."

"And did you see anything when you were at the mass?" He asked.

I was so confused. I did not know whether to trust him or not. He seemed so surprised that I did not know what to do. I was not sure of anything anymore. There was little to lose at this point. "I knew the man they were looking for was on the other side of the room, but it was crowed and I couldn't reach him before he left, I never saw his face."

"And you have no idea who this was?" He reiterated.

"No, I told you I didn't see him, I just knew he was there. I could feel him," I said adamantly. "But none of this has anything to do with Marion. How do you know that I knew of her?"

He clenched his lips and thought carefully for a moment. "Eight years ago, maybe a little longer now. I received a call from Marion, she was very afraid. She told me her life was in danger and asked me to help her. As I told you, I have known her for a very long time. She was very beautiful when I knew her, but she wanted everything in life, and bad always comes along with good, sometimes in greater proportions. On this night, she called me from Key Largo and she was certain she would not live to see the next day. I believed this because I knew she was with many unscrupulous people, I had helped her out of trouble before. By the time I arrived, she was on the yacht she had been staying on, very drugged. I could not believe how terrible she looked. She had been so beautiful, but the life and the men she had chosen had battered her inside and out, and this was apparent. She could not even walk, so I knew I would have to carry her. When I leaned over to pick her up, I looked into her eyes."

"Me!" I jumped up. "You saw me, it was you. You saw me and you tried to kill me."

He paid no attention to my outburst, "Are you going to listen?" He asked calmly.

It's not like I had a choice. There wasn't exactly anywhere to run on this Island. "Go on," I resigned.

"Yes, I saw you," he said simply. "I knew someone was looking for her, I also knew someone wanted her dead. At that same moment, she called out *"tiburon,"* shark. The man she had been with was standing behind me. She had seen him. This is a very cruel man. He cares for no one. Human life is nothing for him. It was said that he fed his women to sharks when he finished with them. This was one of the many things she feared." He lowered his eyes and his head now remembering.

I too began to remember, more recent things, the Babalow. The vision he had told me that I had seen before, and I would see again. This was it, and I tried to remember the rest of what he said. He had told me that the things I had seen were not as they appeared to be. There was something else he said, about my eyes betraying my mind. I couldn't exactly remember it anymore. Maybe I had misunderstood everything I had seen. At the risk of sounding as incredibly naive as I was, I blurted out, "I thought it was a name. I thought it was the man's name."

"You know what the sharks are?" He asked now, expecting at least one answer that would not disappoint him.

"No," I said earnestly.

"They are the disease that we cleaned from the boys in the clinic. That is what all this is about," he sounded exasperated.

"Who did you think I was when you saw me?" I asked.

"Someone who had a very unique ability," he sighed. "But someone who was helping the wrong person. You were like a child. I was not trying to hurt you, only to warn you."

"But the DEA agent, he was trying to help her," I defended.

"What do you know of this agent?" He asked.

"He had asked me to help find her because he knew she was frightened, and in the hands of unscrupulous people. That she had witnessed a murder of one agent by another and he felt that she was a victim. He came to me, with a plea from her family, her mother and her son. I felt sorry for them, for everyone involved." I shrugged my shoulders. "He told me he had been fired from the department because of this. That he wanted to make something right from all the wrongs that had been done. He was a little obsessed, but sincere, I thought he was trying to help her."

"You were not aware that he was the one who killed the other agent?" He did not look up now.

"No, I didn't know," I said simply. "Why?"

"The man he killed was the partner of the man Marion was with on the boat. Among other things, they were importing drugs from the Islands. The agent you spoke with was backing out of something. He could not go through with things he was about to do. I do not know exactly how it happened, but Marion watched everything as it took place. You can understand why she was afraid of him. She had only two choices, bad and worse. She chose worse, she ran to the dead agent's partner for help. The agent who killed his partner knew he had sentenced her to death."

"Did this man really feed women to the sharks?" I asked.

"Not the kind that swim in the ocean," he looked up in dismay, "but he has fed many people to the sharks, the kind you have seen on the addicts."

"How, did he do this? How do you know it was not from the drugs they took?" I asked.

"It took me a long time to discover this," he confessed. "The only thing worse than an evil person; is an evil person with knowledge. The Babalow, Gustavo who died in Miami, was his godfather. Gustavo was a very old and very knowledgeable Santero. He was well known in Cuba, many people came to him for this knowledge and it was not given freely. He was careful whom he taught his secrets to, but one never knows who will choose to become evil. He taught his godson the procedure we did in the clinic, so there would be more hands helping to cure this disease. He taught him of their patterns, their movements, their likes and dislikes. But eventually the godson saw this knowledge as an opportunity for his own gain. Once he knew that he could transfer them to a ram, he also knew how to transfer them to people. He had the power to infect as well as cure.

But the infection kills fairly rapidly, and the people were poor. Too many could not afford the cure and they died. He soon left Cuba and came to America, the land of opportunity. He was unfortunately as intelligent as he was opportunistic and Miami was the gateway to it all. The drug trade was a lucrative business, but like all things in America, it was competitive. Central and South Americans had a strong hold on the market. So, he decided to create an edge, to build his own trade.

He knew that once a person was infected with the devouring disease that he now understood and controlled, that they would crave copious amounts of the drugs. When a human spirit was being depleted, the body could be temporarily fed with this substitute. Drugs prolonged the life of these sharks and people consumed massive amounts when they were infested. He decided to start the fire and profit from the fuel that would keep it burning. Infecting people however, was not such an expedient method. Drugs alone took too long for him. The only other way was to puncture the protective layer of the aura and implant the thing. Then he learned the secret of how they procreated. He discovered their eggs, seeds that can remain dormant for long periods of time, sometimes for years. This was the curse that emerged through the generations in a house. The old ones knew of this. They knew the nature of this evil. They knew the dangers of this knowledge.

Gustavo lived to see this knowledge, abused in the worst imaginable way. He spent his life trying to stop the curse he had unwittingly unleashed, but he did not succeed. It is only recently that I fully understand his grief, that I comprehended the full extent of his godson's atrocity. It is the eggs. He plants the eggs in the drugs he sells on our streets."

"You understand now the dangers, the immenseness..."He could not finish.

I thought for a long moment, it was a terrifying thought. It was worse because I knew it was true. Everything he said made sense. It filled in most of the gaps, but I still did not know why he had brought me here. What was it that he wanted from me now. If he didn't know before, he certainly knew now how little I really knew about any of this. There had to be so much he wasn't saying, but I couldn't even think of the questions to ask.

He looked softly now into my puzzled face. "*Porisita*," he hugged me. "My poor little Chango."

"I don't know who I am," I cried. "Or what I am. I don't know anything anymore."

"A Santera," he said as he wiped the tears from my cheeks. "A Santera, with the gift to see through the eyes of another. A Santera that I am in love with."

On the ride back, I was sorry that I had yelled at him. We were both quiet, too much had been said at one time. I could not comprehend how large it was, how great the effect all this had on so many people. I had only thought of me. I was still thinking of me. I remembered a story my godfather had once told me of Yemaya and Chango. Perhaps it reflected my nature, and his. We all react after all perfectly within the pattern of our making.

Chango had been away from the shores of his birth for many years. So, it is understandable that when he first saw the beautiful mother of the ocean Yemaya standing on the shore as he arrived, he did not recognize her. In keeping with his charming but somewhat womanizing nature, he invited her onto his boat boasting of all the natural beauty he would show her there. Being his own mother, she knew full well who he was, but she decided to show him who she truly was. Soon they were far out to sea, and he was ready to make his most irresistible sexual advance. Suddenly, this most beautiful of female creatures lifted the hem of her dress and began to fan ever so slightly. As she did great waves began to rock the boat, the waves crashed over the sides and Chango looked at the woman in terror. "You do not recognize your own mother Chango," she asked.

Chango now stepped back in fear and humility. He realized his arrogance as he recognized his mother. For as far as he could see the angry ocean waves were rising. His little boat was no more than a matchstick and he no more than its flame in midst of her vastness. "Please forgive me Yemaya my mother," he begged.

"You can be very arrogant Chango, but I am your mother and I love you," she said. "I will forgive you, but do not ever forget this lesson."

What a tiny little flame I was in this world. What could I possibly do that would matter in such an enormous situation? All this time I had no knowledge, only vision, now he was giving me his knowledge. I didn't want it. I hadn't asked for it. I had only tried to help, childishly, stupidly, blindly tried to help.

The silence became deafening between us. We walked to the beach, maybe for some semblance of normalcy. It was a repetitious act, something that might conjure up familiarity. I longed for an exercise that might expel the demons of the day. We sat in the sand, watching the sunset. A ball of fire swallowed up by the ocean.

We don't often remember how minuscule we really are, not until we find ourselves in the shadows of the greater natures of the world. "Miguel," I sighed, "I love you, with all my heart and soul, I love you"

"I know my little one, I know you do," he reciprocated.

We sat, for a long time. He wrapped his arm around me until the waters became dark and only the luminous white caps of the waves shun in the moonlight. If only there were only one world, one place and one time, everything would be all right. Miguel was here his arm around me, holding me, we were one, and everything was all right.

The next morning we both woke up early. He looked at me sadly, "You know there are things I must do, my love. Not everyone is blessed with time."

"No, no more things to do," I pleaded. "You have done enough. I have done enough, no more. I want nothing but you."

"There are many lives at stake," he tried to explain. "There is still too much you don't understand." He rolled over in the bed and stared up at the ceiling.

"Your right, I don't understand, I don't want to understand," I pleaded.

He took another exasperated breath. As though this would be the last time he would attempt to spell it out for me. "If these things are not done," he began, "this man will come looking for you."

"For me!" I exclaimed incredulously. "How is that possible? I don't know anything, what could he want from me?"

He spoke now with sober words and little expression in his voice. "What is it you do not think you know? What is it you do not understand?"

I stopped now in an effort to sober up my own emotions. I would have to back up, try to think orderly. I tried to remember where we had left off. "The man," I said. "The man on the boat, how did you get Marion off of the boat?"

"He let me have her," he said dryly. "I am sure he assumed she would die sooner than she could talk."

"But he was waiting at the bar for the agents that night, he had sent the boat away. How did he know they were coming?" I asked.

"He was waiting for the police," he said. "He sent the boat ahead, because he did not want any excuse for a search, for a detainment by the police. He was sure I would send them. He was expecting Marion to die. Someone had to come. This was an old game to him."

"But she didn't die. Did he know this?" I asked.

"Yes, he had been watching her mother and her son, and the agent who had betrayed him. While he watched, the DEA watched them all, everyone waiting, everyone looking for Marion. He knew she would not return... alive." He added.

"I don't understand," I said. "The DEA wanted the agent, or the drug dealer?"

"Both, and Marion was the key, and her mother and her child became the bait," he said matter of factly.

"She has never seen them again?" I asked.

"No, she knew that if she returned, everyone would be killed. She knew why her son was still alive. The agent you met, he did stay with her family. Maybe for the reasons you believe, he did become very protective of them. But, the agent disappeared about two months ago. Foul play was suspected. Everyone believed, that Tiburon had finally killed him. Perhaps he grew tired of waiting for Marion. Perhaps he thought she had died after all. The agent had remained adamant that she was still alive, but he never found her," he trailed off. "By this time, as you saw Marion is too ill to go home, too ill to even remember she has a son."

"The agent is gone and Marion is no threat to him," I recapitulated. "Why would he come looking for me? He knows nothing of me."

He looked at me and shook his head, then ever so patiently began. "Miami is a big city, but we are a small community. He knew that you were looking for him. He knew you could see him. It was only a matter of time before you found each other."

"What are you talking about?" I cried out in disbelief.

"Many people know he is a powerful man, a murderer. He is a drug lord. But only a few people knew what a monster he really is, that he murders the souls as well as the bodies of his people. Gustavo knew, and before he died he told this to me. Gustavo had cancer for many years before he was infected. He was already dying. This is why he did not seek the cure. He would not have lived through it. He went looking for this godson, in a last effort to destroy him. You know that the Babalow was an omo Chango, the oldest in this country. This godson had been told in the Ita of his initiation that if he chose to abuse the powers that were given to him, he would be hunted down and destroyed by Chango himself. Gustavo tried, but he failed, and his own godson infected him with the curse he had spent a lifetime trying to lift from this world. But he told his godson then, that he would die peacefully knowing that Chango indeed would hunt him down and destroy him. He told him then, that it would not be a sick old man like himself, an old omo Chango. It would be a young child of Chango, one who could see from other eyes, who would bring him down and humiliate him in the process."

"No," I covered my ears I did not want to hear any more. In this religion, age was calculated from the day of one's birth through initiation. I was only seven, a young child of Chango!

"You must listen," he said. "Everyone knew this, it is a small community. It was given in the letters of your birth. This was your path, and it is not an easy path. They were trying to prepare you, strengthen you. It was only a matter of time before he knew who you were. He would not wait to be hunted. It would be too great a humiliation. Not only are you a child, but you are a woman."

"You knew this all the time, everyone knew." I thought now of my godfather, of his tranquil house and simple ways. I knew he had been trying to protect me. I remembered his warnings when I told him about the lessons I was taking. "They will teach you," his words echoed in my ears. "But they will expect you to do something for them and you will not be able to refuse. These are my people. I know them well. You will pay more than you think for what you learn." He had known.

I never really understood before now. I loved my godfather. He had been a friend, a teacher and a father to me. Why was I supposed to leave his house? It had been forecast from the beginning. A thing destined to happen. Something powerful had called me to venture beyond the safe confines of his house. I thought I needed to grow, to learn, to sink or swim on my own in this world. It had been destiny calling all along. Sadly, I left the house of my godfather knowing I could not respectfully return. Only now did I know the extent of the dangers he was trying in vain to protect me from.

I was supposed to face Goliath. I did not even have a small weapon, no slingshot, no pebble, nothing. But I couldn't even use a weapon if I had had one. I was not skilled. I had not finished learning. I knew all these things now, and I still knew nothing. I did not have a clue of what I was supposed to do, of what needed to be done.

13

Final Visions

Miguel was dressed now. I followed his lead and slipped on some white shorts and a knit top. I was still combing my hair when he told me he had to go back to Marion's house.

"I'm just going to take care of a few things," he said. "It would be better if you waited here at the cottage. I asked Rudy to come by and stay with you until I get back."

"You asked Rudy to come over to watch me," I said. "I'm really okay. I don't need any company. I'm not afraid of being alone."

"Humor me, it will make me feel better. I will try not to be too long," he said putting his arms around me. He buried his face in my neck and gently rocked me as we stood. I was afraid to relax, to feel too much. I knew I would only cry and beg him not to go. Despite what I said, I was afraid. And now, I knew that he was too.

Miguel left and I sank down into a comfortable chair in the corner of the room. I just stared listlessly into a faded tropical print that hung on the wall. I did not want to think anymore. I don't know how long it was. It may have been an hour. It may have been five minutes. I was somewhere outside of time. I heard someone open the door. I assumed it was Rudy. When I looked up, I could see it was a man. But it was not Rudy. It took a moment for this to register, a moment too long. Before I could jump up, before I could scream, he had injected a small needle in my bare arm. I saw the syringe, his hands and my punctured flesh. The fluid burned as it traveled through my veins. I opened my mouth to make a sound, but before it reached my tongue I could not move a single muscle. Everything went black.

When I woke up, it was another time, another place. "Where am I," I moaned. "Miguel, where is Miguel?"

I could barely make out the face of a young black woman looking down at me. "Your gonna be all right, you been away for quite a while now."

I looked back to her blurred image, puzzled. My head was splitting with pain. "Where is Miguel?" I asked again.

"Soon enough," she patted my arm, "soon enough. I am going to get the doctor now," she advised me. "Just rest for a minute now."

She returned as she had promised with a doctor who opened my eyelids with his fingers and shined a little light into them. "Where is Miguel?" I began to cry. I was confused and frightened.

"Someone will be here soon," the doctor now answered gently. "We let him know you are awake now. You have been unconscious for three days. You take it easy now until he arrives."

I was temporarily appeased. Miguel would come and explain everything to me. He would make everything all right again. He would know how to stop this pain in my head. I would wait.

I must have dozed off again. It was Rudy who stood over me now. I could not see him clearly, but I knew his stature and his voice.

"You gonna be all right mon," he assured me.

Why was it Rudy who was assuring me of this? "Where is Miguel?" I asked.

"Miguel, he sent me to take care of you," he answered.

Something was wrong, even through the fog that now engulfed me I knew something was terribly wrong. "Where is he," I demanded.

"Miguel is dead," he answered finally.

His words pierced my already shattered reality. I knew he was not lying, but I did not believe him. I could not believe him. I did not respond to his revelation.

"Miguel was killed three days ago. You have to know, I loved this man like my own brother. I would have gladly died a thousand times to save him. I am doing that now mon, but it don't save him. He sent me to protect you, and I was too late for that too." He turned his head to the light in the window. He could not bear to look at me. "Everybody's gone now. They killed Marion, dyin in her bed, the nurse taken care of her and Miguel when he come into the house. They shot and killed em all, everyone is dead."

"No, it can't be, it's not supposed to be like this," I cried. "This can't happen, it just can't." Someone was patting me. It was not Rudy. It must have been the nurse. I just cried. I did not know what else to do.

I went through the motions of life for a day or two. I don't really remember how many days went by. But Rudy came to the hospital to take me to the airport. I needed to go home, back to Davie and my safe little house. I did not want to ever leave it again. I asked Rudy to take me back to the cottage before we went to airport. I told him only that there was something I needed to do. We said little on the way, but what little was said was more than enough. It was only a comment, an expression of his sorrow. I knew he assumed that I had known.

"Poor Miguel, he aint never gonna see his son, and that's a sad thing. He was always makin plans for that day. Now that day aint ever gonna come." He sighed.

I wasn't surprised anymore. Nothing could surprise me now. Marion's son had been their son. It was just the way of things. He pulled up in front of the cottage as he had the first time when we arrived. I did not wish to enter. I got out of the car and walked down to the beach, to the place we had spent our few happy moments sharing the beautiful things of the world. I took off the little gold bracelet he had given me, the offering for Yemaya. I threw it as far as I could into her endless ocean body, and I thanked her for her son. I could not ask for anything more. I thanked her for giving me love, even if it was only for a little while.

I don't remember much of the trip home. I do remember wondering if my guardian Chango had been offended by my plea to Yemaya. I wondered if I had gone over his head to ask for the things he had not given me in this world. I was grateful that my ocean mother had stepped in. That she had allowed me to know love. At least now I knew a little more of her nature and I was comforted by that. I understood an infinitesimal bit of her pattern. I thought of my godfather explaining to me once that when we tried to comprehend the nature of Yemaya, it was like trying to swallow the ocean. "It should not be attempted," he said. "Because it cannot be done."

I have lived already two lives in one lifetime, and that is probably one too many. I have had two child hoods, one physical and one spiritual. I have been blessed with two sets of parents and cursed with two sets of eyes. So, the second of my childhoods has come to an end and I will miss the process of becoming. I will always miss the innocence left behind at the house of my godfather. I will miss the lessons he taught me as a Yawo. When every question I asked was answered with a story, and every story opened a thousand questions more. I have forgotten many things, but I have not forgotten his words to me the first time I left his house after my initiation.

"You are a Yawo now. Remember first that you are the daughter of Chango, for now and for all your life. You were presented to him as a female and you must always present yourself as a female to him. That means you must always present yourself in a dress when you come before him, also before me. For one year you must wear only white clothes, remember you are just beginning a new life. Remember that you are pure in the eyes of *Olodumare* and must conduct yourself accordingly. Do not wear make up, nail polish or any jewelry other than your *elegie* (religious necklaces) and *ide* (bracelet). For the first three months, you must keep your head covered, for like an infant your crown is still vulnerable and you must keep it protected. For three months also, your shoulders must be covered with a white shawl, to keep death away from you. When you come to your godfather's home, you must first salute your godfather's guardian. Remember the guardian of your godfather is the guardian of all his godchildren. Salute your godfather, this you do always. You will never be too old or too wise to show this sign of respect."

At the time, I thought these things were actually difficult. Now, I longed for the simplicity of these, things that had to be done. I remembered after the first long year, the list of taboos and restrictions are too long to recount right now, but even the small things like the deprivation of color was a lesson. I will never forget the first time I dressed in a bright color after wearing white for so long. I could feel it. I could feel the energy of a color and actually know it without seeing it. I thought this was a tremendous revelation. I understood why colors played such an important part in rituals. I had learned the various energies that colors contained and how they could be infused into the ritual for strength. I understood that even the simplest of actions had a purpose in this religion.

Perhaps Chango had abandoned me after all. I could no longer feel his power, his presence. If the shells were thrown now, I wondered if they would all fall silent. I had not shown much promise in utilizing the abilities and powers my guardian had made available to me. I was certain I had disappointed and offended him once too often. I had gone to my godfather once with this dilemma. I was concerned because I had moved my Orishas so many times, trying to find a place for them in my house, in my life. I was worried because I did not know yet what offering to give them, what their likes and dislikes were. I did not know their patterns, their ways. I could barely remember their names. I spoke to them in my own language. I did not know their ancient tongue or prayers. I figured I had insulted and or offended them too many times. My godfather who was also omo Chango answered with a tender patience that surprised me.

"In your religious life Yawo, you are a child. You will make many mistakes. This is the process of learning. Innocents can never offend the Saints. If you know the right way however and choose to ignore it or go against it, then you must accept responsibility for you have committed a great offense. Children learn from their parents, and in this way you are born into this religion through your godparents. Watch, listen and repeat. These are the ways of knowledge and eventually wisdom. Children do not come into this world with language, it must be learned. Do not be so concerned that these ancient words do not begin with perfect pronunciation. This too comes in time. Chango knows this. He knows you are only a child."

I was not sure how much time was enough time, but I was fairly sure that mine was up. I was no longer a child. I had failed to display the quickness, the strength or the power of his nature, in short, any of the positive characteristics of his nature. I had only displayed his arrogance, his weakness, and the most negative of his traits. I saw so much and knew so little.

Perhaps I had not wanted the responsibility of knowing. There was power in knowing, power in knowledge. Once more I had rejected this power. I should have known better by this time. I could no longer claim ignorance. I had rejected the gift of my guardian. It was only appropriate that he should reject me sooner or later. Chango was not reputed to be the most patient element of nature. He was after all the energy of lightning. Patience belonged to another energy, another pattern and probably another lifetime for me.

I am back in Davie. I am home now. Perhaps you can understand, why I find it so necessary to write all this. I am struggling in these few pages to write what I have found to be important to me, things that may also be important to you. There is so much I have not said, so much I cannot say. The lights in my eyes have begun to dim, and my vision in this world is failing, but perhaps people are only meant to have one vision at a time. The world is so much clearer that way. Perhaps that's why Reverend Gilman, the old woman in Opa Locka, was blind. I remember Miguel once telling me, that we all have a story, one that brings us where we are to be. I wondered what her story might be. Some stories were so much more romantic than others. I wonder if I should become old, if people would come to see me in my darkened house and I would only see them from a world that was invisible to everyone else.

The top of my head burns. I know the dimness in my eyes is from the shadows cast by the devouring gray sharks who now grow, in my aura. The seeds have been planted and I wonder if the pain will be too great when they begin to multiply. I am not afraid of them any more. I will not be tempted to feed them. I will not prolong their life or mine. I know blindness may be very difficult. It blocks out the beautiful as well as the grotesque things of this world. But I have had enough vision. There is nothing else in this world I care to see, and finally I pray, nothing else I must do.

I am only a little flame. A tiny match tossed into the great ocean of this world. I am no David. I did not topple the giant who threatens our land. I did not hunt him down, destroy or even mildly humiliate him. I lost my head before the battle had even begun. I am sorry for the people who will continue to die. I am sorry for all the people who have already died, and I am sorry for myself, for my failure and my grief.

Miguel died, our life together is over and I never even saw it end. His body was cremated, turned to ashes while I slept in oblivion. I long for his touch. I long to hear his voice. I do not know why he has not communicated with me. There have been no visions, no dreams and no goodbyes. He has not come to me at all. Perhaps it is too soon. Perhaps I am too close or too far away. Perhaps he cannot enter through the shadow of the gray vale that covers my head. Strangely, I am comforted by this dark shroud, and I will wait for death's devouring embrace. I pray that I will find Miguel in the other world and we can be together there. About this, I am not altogether hopeless. Perhaps they will grant me this.

It has been months since my return, and I have not spoken to anyone, not my family or my friends. Some distant phone service picks up my calls. They do not listen to your messages. They only record them. And, I do not hear your questions, as I do not retrieve them. Please forgive me for this. I know you have probably wondered why. So much cannot be spoken. It takes time to sort out what can be said. It takes a toll on the soul of my being to remember all the things that have been. Perhaps now you can understand, then again perhaps my life is only stranger now than it ever was before. You may be looking too close, or from too far away. What ever it is that you see, be grateful. Be grateful that you do not see from both sides at once. Visions can deceive you, they can confuse you and if you are not careful, they can blind you. I can think of nothing else that needs to be said.

When I wrote these words into my libretta, I had intended for them to be my final words. I believed it was to be the end of my story. Who knew it was all destined to begin again? It was Iya, this time, who showed up at my front door. She walked in, without so much as a knock. She came in without her customary sweetness, without so much as a greeting. I was sitting on my sofa. I was surprised, and more than a bit taken aback at her entrance. She walked directly to the large window in the front room and pulled open the verticals exposing the harsh summer sunlight to my dark secluded little living room.

"*De dae*," she commanded raising her arms, gesturing me to my feet. "*De dae omo* Chango. Stand up, you are a priest of Chango."

I knew by her tone she meant business. She sounded angry. She was a strong woman and a powerful Santera. I was not in a position to argue with her, so I stood up.

"You are a Santera," she spoke harshly but authoritatively. "What lives in your head is sacred, and it is disrespectful to your ancestors as well as your guardian to allow it to be defiled." She continued in the same harsh tone. "Life does not end with a death, and you more than anyone know this. Get up now Santera, there is much that needs to be done."

So, once more I am asked to do something and I cannot refuse. My head was cleansed. They say the ugly curse has been cast out. Once more my head is ritually prepared. My physical vision is still not clear. This damage may be permanent. I am not sure. They say I will be back to normal. For the first time in many months I smile, and tell them. "I don't know how this can be. I have never been normal before."

I wait, because it will take time they say for my strength to return. I prepare now to do whatever it is that needs to be done. I prepare now for a new beginning or a final ending. I do not know which one it will be. I do not know even if there is one at all. I look at my libretta once more as I write. The sign of my guardian remains as it was given on the day of my Ita, unfinished. I do no know what this means, but they say once this pattern is set in motion, it cannot be changed. I do not know if this is true, but there is so much I do not know, so much that remains to be seen.

One thing is certain, as my godfather had tried to teach me when I first began. Mr. Disney did not create this world, and all the little animals are not singing on the forest floor. They are hunting, killing and eating one another, because this is the nature of the world we live in.

14

Circle of Hope

A year has come and gone since these words were written in my little book. I am back among the living. And, I try as best I can to remain there, etching out a meager living from my work. There are no more missing children in my life, no more dead or dying souls to contend with now, just people, ordinary people with ordinary problems. They are the only ones who visit my home now. I share my visions and my counsel with those who come looking for answers. Sometimes it is difficult, as I have not yet found the answers to my own tormenting questions.

There are still so many painful memories and so many sleepless nights. I do not sleep too often, but when I do I am awakened by the same haunting dream. The aquamarine waters of the Caribbean Sea are stretched out endlessly before me. The white foaming lace of the gentle breaking waves cover my feet, and I remember all the blissful moments shared with Miguel. I look up to the sky. It suddenly turns black and thunder roars through the dark clouds. Even in this darkness, I know Miguel is there. I call to him, but he does not answer. The waves roll in, each one larger than the first until they completely overpower me. I am carried out to sea where the ocean envelops me. The water swallows me, convincing me to release my will. It is then that I hear his voice. I struggle to swim to the surface. Somehow I reach the shore and I begin to call his name. I look for Miguel, but there are only empty beaches and an ocean filled with tears. I begin to cry, tears roll down my cheeks as I call his name. No one answers, no one ever answers and I do not know why. I wake up sobbing into my pillow.

Why does Miguel not answer? It has been nearly a year, nearly forever since Jamaica, since Miguel's death. All the years of my work as a
clairvoyant had not prepared me for my own personal tragedy. I know
the mechanics of emotional loss and separation, but I do not know
how long I can hold on to my own dwindling hope. There is no one to
offer those cherished words from my loved one, and I cannot even
catch one precious glimpse of his angelic face.

Miguel and I had been in love, deeply and inconsolably in love. His
last promise was that our love would last forever and I so desperately
wanted to believe this to be true. As a medium, I was convinced that
even death could not severe such powerful and sacred connection. But
I also believed that somehow he would have contacted me by now. I
know he lives in the other world. That death has delivered him to the
world of shadows. But this is a world I am no stranger to. It is a dimly
blurred and murky place, but I have been there many times. I go there
often, searching, but I cannot find him and I do not understand why
he does not find me. I know I am visible to him. In the world of spirits
I am only a visitor. I am still of this world clumsy and opaque. I do not
move about there unnoticed. Here where the dead reside, I am the
shadow, a white shadow in the midst of its darkness. Here I stand out
the same way I did the first day Miguel saw me in the streets of Miami.
I was the awkward Anglo Santera, trying desperately to avoid your
gaze. Oh Miguel, why do you not find me?

Both my health and my vision have strengthened since that dreadful
day in Jamaica, when Miguel was killed, but I wake up often with this
same dream. I miss him. I long for his touch, his voice. I miss everything about him. Many times I prefer to forget. I want to pretend that
Miguel was the dream, but I always wake up. I rarely venture out these
days. I do not want to see anyone or anything that reminds me of him,
and everyone and everything in Miami is a part of him, a part that I
cannot bear to touch again. I have lost my place in this world. For the
first time in my life, I had belonged somewhere. I belonged in Miami
with Miguel. It had become my place of spiritual birth, my gateway

into a cryptic world of mystery and intrigue. A world filled with the blood and beauty of reality, but reality was a place I did not want to be anymore. I preferred the dream, the dream of Miguel and I making endless love on the shores of paradise.

Perhaps that was the answer. I needed to go back, not to Miami, but to Jamaica. Of course, why would Miguel ever leave his paradise? He told me many times that his spiritual home was in Jamaica, where he was blessed with the love of Yemaya. Maybe he would come to me there. I needed something from him, a touch a word, anything from him. The only tangible thing he had left behind was the gold bracelet, and I had thrown it into the sea. How I longed to touch something physical connected to him, some proof of his existence here on this earth. Perhaps I could find that in Jamaica.

I called the travel agent and made reservations for the following week. I told no one I was going. I couldn't imagine anyone who would understand, or anyone who not try and talk me out of it. Truth was, I knew little of what had actually happened there. I had been unconscious too long. I didn't even know what had happened to his body. They say he was cremated. How could I know for sure if this was or not? I had seen nothing. What had happened to his things, and who had washed the tears from his Orishas. In Miami, I had only been told that everything had been taken care of. Who had taken care of them? Why had I not even been invited to the ceremonies? Maybe in Jamaica I could find some answers.

I had reserved a room at Sans Souci in Ocho Rios. From there, I would find Rudy. I did not even know his last name, but somehow I would find him. I boarded the plane alone. It was the greatest aloneness I have ever felt. A young Jamaican girl with a small child sat next to me on the plane.

"Is this your first trip to Jamaica?" She asked strapping her squirming child into his seat.

"No," I said. "I've been there before."

"Well, it's a beautiful place to come back to. I'm on my way back home there."

"Are you from Ocho Rios?" I asked.

"No, I was raised in Kingston, but Timothy's father is in Ocho Rios and we're goin home to see him. This is Timothy here and I'm Rachel."

"I'm Jeanne Marie," I said turning my head to gaze out the window. If tears welled up, I did not want to explain them.

"Well," Rachel went on. "What resort are you going to?"

"Sans Souci," I said flatly.

"That's a fine place," she said raising her eyebrows. "A lot of nice young men, you won't be alone for long there."

I started to tell her that's not what I came here for, but the truth was it was exactly what I came here for. So, I said nothing. It was not long before we were in the air heading for the islands. The flight attendant came down the aisles pouring champagne. I must have flashed back, remembering the warnings of the first trip, when she asked me if I would like a drink. She was staring at me oddly when she asked the second time. "No, no thank you," I sputtered out. I'm not sure why I refused. It had not done much good the first time.

"Well, you just leave hers with me," Rachel said reaching for the glass. Then she turned to me, "Your goin to the islands girl. Life is for livin have some champagne and be happy."

I had to smile at her, she was sweet, and trying so hard to be friendly to me. "Thank you," I said finally and I picked the glass up and touched it to hers. "To a happy home coming," I said.

"And to your findin whatever it is your lookin for," she added.

It was just after two when the plane touched down. I was supposed to catch a bus to the resort. I had only one carry on bag so I was the first one waiting at the door. A tall man with dark glasses and a broad smile held up a sign for Sans Souci. "That would be me," I said handing him my reservation slip.

"Welcome to Jamaica pretty lady," he said. "You comin here all alone?"

"Yes," I said, "but I'm meeting with a friend here." It would only become a lie if I did not find Rudy I thought.

"Well, I'm sure you'll both have a good time then. You can leave your bag with me. I'll put it right on. It'll be a little while yet, not everyone has their bags from the plane so soon."

I gave the man my bag and proceeded to look for a ladies room. As I stepped out I saw the hat, it was Rudy. He was getting into a cab. I ran to the doorway, but before I could reach him he was gone. He was driving the cab. I was sure it was Rudy, but I questioned myself anyway. What if it was only someone who looked like him? How could I know for sure? It was a long drive to the resort. I sat by the window and watched the lengthy span of beaches next to the endless waters snake by. If it was Rudy, and he was a cab driver, there had to be some way to find him. How many Rudys could there be in town? Surely there weren't be too many who fit his description.

The resort was beautiful. I only wished I could appreciate it, but I had only one thought and it had narrowed my vision to a single bright light at the end of a long dark corridor. In this darkness, his face was the only light I could imagine.

Finally I was alone in my room. I pulled back the sheer curtains filtering the ocean view and there she was. Yemaya in all her magnificence stretched out endlessly before me. I studied the designs the waves created in the vast liquid fabric for some clue to her receptivity. Her waters were calm, and muted hues of blue-green filled her ocean depths. Perhaps she would listen. "I loved him," I whispered through cold panes of glass between us. "Help me find him Yemaya. Please, just once more help me find him. I know you understand how much I need to see him. I need to know… if he's all right, where ever he is. Please, help me," I choked and the tears began to pour down my cheeks splashing onto my bare feet. The thought occurred to me that I should lie down. Maybe I should rest for a while, but I could not seem to move. I stood there, in front of the window frozen in my own puddle of tears watching as the silent sea rolled out her watery arms across the sandy shores below. Perhaps she was beckoning me to come to her. She knew where her son was, mothers always knew. I needed to go to her. Without thinking, I grabbed the key attached to a curly pink wristband, slipped it over my hand and flew out the door.

When I arrived downstairs, I was suddenly aware that the beach was filled with people. My room had looked over the top of a long covered terrace downstairs. I had seen only the ocean waters. I had completely overlooked the entire population below. The sun was still blaring along with a small steel band playing Island rhythms to the tourists. Couples sat around the pools and sipped their tropical drinks. Everywhere there were couples. Some sat talking. Others danced light heartedly moving together in laughter. Hand in hand, eyes meeting eyes, they were all in pairs. I was alone, utterly and completely alone.

I walked down the shore forever. The sun beat down on my head and the sand was hot under my bare feet. I had not thought to grab my hat or my shoes when I ran out. I had not even changed clothes from the flight, but it didn't seem to matter. I just kept walking. There were mountains here in Jamaica beautiful voluptuous mountains. Miguel had called them the breasts of Yemaya. This whole island was sacred to him. Why should he ever think to leave his paradise? His work was finished in the rest of the world and he was here in his adopted island home. I was sure of it now. I had done the right thing in coming here. Dead or alive, he was here and I knew it. Somehow I would find him!

By the time I got back to the terrace, a beautiful buffet containing every imaginable culinary delight had been prepared. The sun was beginning to set and tiny lights began to outline the path to the beach. It seemed like such a long time since I had eaten. Not filled my stomach because it required fuel, but really eaten. Taken in a meal because it was wonderful food and enjoyable to eat. The food suddenly smelled good to me, faintly familiar spices drew me to the table. I feasted my eyes on the colorful presentation of unfamiliar dishes. Tonight I would eat. I grabbed a plate and began to fill it with samples of everything that caught my eye. Then I picked up a glass of wine and carried my bounty up stairs. I opened the glass doors and sat down at the small table on the balcony to commence my little private tasting.

It was wonderful. Each mouthful was a delightful indulgence. The flavor vacillated between hot and sweet, the spices of life. The ebb and flow between love and passion. I filled myself with this small dish of pleasure and breathed the warm ocean air. "She is beautiful," I said finally. "I do see her Miguel, just as you did. Tonight I tasted her fruits and I feel her. I know what you meant when you told me you breathed her. She is here, in the water, the mountains and the sky. She is everywhere in this place. Miguel she was in every bite I swallowed tonight. I know now how you loved her. I loved you the same way."

The dark depths of infinity had become the night sky and ten thousand stars signaled its distance. There was no answer but silence and there would be no more monologues to the night. I wrapped my fingers around the stem of the wine glass on the table and lifted it to silence my lips. Then I filled my mouth with the bittersweet liquid and swallowed it down. It was not late, but I was tired now and all I wanted was sleep.

I had no idea what time it was when I woke up the next morning. The sun was up and its worshipers were strewn lazily along the beach. I wanted coffee but I did not relish getting dressed and facing the world. Room service would take forever but by the time I showered and dressed they could be here. I called downstairs and ordered coffee and fresh fruit. It arrived just as I finished and I was grateful. "You have perfect timing," I said handing him the tip for his service.

"Well, that's not somethin you hear too often around here," he smiled nodding his head to thank me for the tip. "Is there anything else I can do for you this morning?"

"No," I said looking down at the tray. "Everything looks fine. But there is something, maybe you can help me. I am looking for a cab driver here in town."

"No problem, Mon. I can call for one downstairs. Where will you be going?" He asked.

"No, I don't need to go somewhere. I mean I am trying to find someone, a friend who is a cab driver," I tried to explain.

"Well, what is his name? I'm sure he can't be that hard to find," he said.

"Rudy," I answered.

"And does Mr. Rudy have a last name? He asked.

"I'm sure he does, but I don't know it?" The young man raised his eyebrows.

"It's a long story, but I was here before. There was an accident and Rudy helped me out. He might have saved my life. I need to find him, to thank him."

"I see now," the young man's tone became sympathetic. "Maybe I can help you out there. My brother is a cab driver here too. Do you know what he looks like or what kind of cab he drives?"

"He's tall, a big man, very muscular. He wears a white knit hat and has dread locks. I don't know what kind of cab he drives. It was burgundy. I saw him at the airport when I arrived. At least I think it was him. He was getting into a burgundy car. He was leaving, and I just couldn't get to him in time," my voice trailed off. "If you could help me, I would really appreciate it."

"No problem, Mon. I find him for you. You don't worry yourself any more. Nevil will find the man. Ah yes, I am Nevil," he said reaching his hand out to me with a broad smile.

"And, I am Jeanne Marie. It's nice to meet you," I said shaking his hand.

"You don't worry bout a thing Miss Jeanne Marie. Nevil will watch out for you now."

"Thank you Nevil." I smiled as he closed the door. Who knows, maybe Nevil would find Rudy for me. I poured a cup of coffee and carried it out to the balcony. The whole day was before me and I hadn't a clue what to do with it. I did not have a plan. Truth was I never had a plan. Maybe it was time to start thinking in that direction. Miguel always had a plan, and more than anything in world, I wished I knew what it had been. I only knew half of it, and I had to find out the other half. I needed to get out of the room first. This time the answers could not be found inside.

In the lobby were numerous brochures featuring tours to the local tourist spots. I glanced through them but nothing seemed particularly interesting. Then I saw the title of an old plantation named Rose Hall. It looked beautiful, and it had been completely restored. That was definitely the one I wanted to see. I took the brochure up to the desk with me. A dark skinned woman with short henna tinted hair was just hanging up the phone. "And what can I help you with today?" She asked cheerfully.

"Rose Hall, I would like to find out about a tour."

"And when would you be wanting to go there?" She asked.

"I was thinking today might be nice," I answered.

"I'm not sure I can get you there today," she said looking over the top of her glasses. "The gentleman in charge of that tour won't be in until four, and that would be too late. It's a good distance from here you know. Would you be interested in Dunns' Falls? They will be leaving in about an hour. I could check if you like."

"No, I was kind of set on the Rose Hall," I answered. "What about a cab? Couldn't I just get a cab to take me there and back?"

"Well you could do that, how many will be going?" She asked.

"Just me," I said meeting her eyes with mine.

"You might think about waiting for a tour," she said. "Jamaica is a beautiful place, but it is not always the best place for a woman alone if you know what I'm sayin."

I thought for a minute. "Your probably right," I conceded. "I'll come back at four. Tomorrow will be fine."

I spent the day exploring the grounds. They were beautiful, dark green foliage, rainbows of flowers and dozens of small hiking paths, all leading eventually to the sea. I strolled down my third or fourth passage breathing the humid air. It was perfect for the wild orchids and giant ferns but too heavy and heated to inhale, especially while walking. I was ready to quit and go back, but just before the trail ended on the beach I spotted the remnants of an old stonewall. It was curved at the base and the highest point was not more than five feet tall, but it was unmistakably an old fort of some kind. The stones were made of giant blocks of quarried coral. The Spanish had probably built it. A great stone sentinel erected to guard the bay.

My first impulse was to touch them, but for some reason I hesitated. Surely those stones had seen much in their time. Generations had come and gone in their presence. Before they were completely reclaimed by the earth and the sea, perhaps they had something to say, some last thoughts or unfinished business to convey. I knew it wasn't really my business, but I longed once again for the past, for the company others who might have the answers I needed. I walked slowly over to one of the lower parts of the wall and pulled myself up to sit down on top of it. Then I placed both hands flatly upon the stones on each side of me. Within seconds, the world began to spin. I had no idea when or where it would stop. The only thing I knew for sure was that when it did, it would all be different. It would be another time.

I was aware that my body sat upon the wall, at the end of a trail within the resort, but my vision and my mind were elsewhere. The bay was suddenly filled with boats, grand old ships with flowing white sails. "You should not be here," a voice spoke from behind.

"Why not?" I asked.

"Cause you don't belong here," he said. "Should not be where you don't belong. You never know that you might not get out again."

I turned to see who was speaking. It was a young man, not more than fourteen or fifteen years old. He was dark complexioned with a mop of unruly kinky hair. He wore no shirt or shoes, and his feet were badly scarred. They almost looked misshapen. His tattered linen pants were tied with a rope and rolled beneath his navel. There was not much expression in his eyes; they had no light, no life inside of them. "Why are you here?" I asked him.

"Because I have nowhere else to be," he said simply.

"Is there anywhere you would like to be?" I asked.

"I'd like to be on one of them boats," he said pointing with his chin to the bay. "But they don't come for me."

"I don't understand," I said.

"Man say wait for him, right here by the wall. Tomorrow sunrise he gonna take me to the sea with him. I'm going to work hard and I'm gonna learn to sail, free like a bird over the seas. I am here, no easy thing but I am here. I get up early, in the dark before anyone wakes and I run. I run across them fields so fast the canes burn like fire under my feet. Masters field man's out drinkin and ridin wild. He see me runnin. Maybe he thinks I am a wild animal so he come to see. When he sees me, I am caught. He nearly whip me to death. I lay there bleedin and he's still whippin but I know I got to get here. I am here. I wait, and I watch the ships go by, but the man never comes."

I thought for a very long moment. His dark eyes stared but did not move from my direction. "Perhaps there's another way to get to the boat," I suggested.

"Man say wait here," he repeated.

"There's a lot of boats out there," I said. "There must be more than one Captain. The man who was coming for you, maybe he couldn't find you. You have to look for someone else to take you there."

His eyes shifted then he spoke again. "No one finds me. No one speaks to me here. Why are you here?"

"I came to talk to you, I guess. Do you know why no one can find you?" I asked.

"No. I wait and I wait. People come and go for a long time, but no one speaks to me. No one knows I am here. I think maybe someday the man will find me and I will sail free like a bird over the sea."

The night the man whipped you," I said. "In the fields. Your body did not get up again. You came here without your body. Do you understand?"

He glared at me incredulously and then looked down at his feet. "I can see my body. These are my feet, I can see them."

"Yes, but no one else can. That's why the man couldn't find you. Your body died in the field that night. It could not come with you. What you see is your soul body, it's only a reflection of the other one."

"I am dead?" He asked.

"On earth you are," I answered.

"But I am here. Where am I to go?" He asked.

"Anywhere you want. Do you remember that night in the field? You wanted to be here, and so you were. Do you remember walking here, or how you go here?" I asked.

"No," he said thinking back. "I was face down bleeding in the field one minute and the next I was here."

"And you didn't hurt anymore. Right?"

"Right," he looked at me oddly.

"You can be anywhere you want to be now. You don't have to wait on anyone to come for you." I said. "It's really a very lucky thing not to be burdened with a body. No one can hurt you now, and you can go anywhere you want. You are free. Those boats out there, they've been waiting on you. You can be on any one you want."

"It's true. I did not get here with my feet." He looked over the bay. "I want to be on the grandest ship on the bay," he said closing his eyes. "And I want to fly like a swallow over the sea." He inhaled deeply and suddenly my hands were releasing the stones beneath them and rising up as if I had just let go of some heavy luggage. There were no more ships in the bay. There was no boy behind me and I was alone sitting on the stones of the old fort wall. It was time to go back, back to the resort and to the hope that the man I waited for would somehow find me.

When I arrived at my room, the message light was blinking on the phone. I dialed in for the message. It was Nevil. He had located Rudy, but he couldn't get in touch with him until the next day. Now that I found him, I began having second thoughts. What if Rudy didn't want to see me? He probably would, out of politeness or respect for Miguel but would he really want to talk to me? I knew how it usually happened. My face was permanently etched into his mind along with the memory of Miguel's death. Would Rudy be able to separate the two when he saw me? I had come this far, and there was no way I could back out now.

The next morning I ordered coffee and breakfast in my room. I requested Nevil bring it up. In no time at all, there was a knock at the door. "Detective Nevil at your service," he said brightly as I opened the door.

"Ah Nevil, you are brilliant. Tell me how did you find him?" I asked.

"Well, to tell you the truth it was a very difficult case, difficult indeed. When I found that my brother didn't know the man, I asked my cousin, and he did." He smiled, "and he should be calling you this afternoon."

"Great work Nevil. You're my favorite detective in all of Jamaica. Thank you," I said handing him a generous tip for his efforts.

"No, I thank you from the bottom of my heart but I cannot take your money," he said holding his hands in the air. "This was a good deed, and if I accept your payment it will take all the good out of it."

"You can't be serious Nevil," I protested. "I think you deserve a reward for your efforts."

"Goodness has its own rewards," he said. "You let me know how things work out, okay."

"Okay," I surrendered. "Thank you."

At one thirty the phone rang. I could barely speak when I heard his voice. It was suddenly evident that it had been his voice that had delivered the message of Miguel's death. The two things had somehow merged together. "Rudy, thank you so much for calling," I managed to say. "I don't know how to ask you this, but I would just like to talk to you. It's been…" My throat was closing up on me when he broke in.

"Not a problem, Mon. I am working today but tomorrow I can see you whenever you like."

"In the morning, could you meet me at here at the hotel in the morning?"

"Sure thing, I'll be there at eight thirty. Unless that's too early for you?"

"No, no that would be perfect. I'll meet you in the lobby, we can have breakfast or something," I added.

"Good thing," he said. "Don't worry now. Everything's gonna be all right. We'll see you in the morning."

As I hung up the phone I could hear Bob Marley's voice singing those same words. "Don't worry, everything's gonna be all right." Dear God let it be true this time!

I was up and in the lobby by eight fifteen. I was nervous which I assumed was better than some of the other emotions I had been feeling for the past few days. I did not want to break down and cry. If I did, he might not trust that he could tell me anything, especially the truth. I needed to know the truth, no matter how much it might hurt.

It was a good half hour before he arrived, but it was unmistakably Rudy. "Well it's good to see you lookin so well." He held out both hands and I stretched mine out to greet him.

"Rudy, you have no idea how much I appreciate this."

"You got to stop right there. I come to see a friend and I'm happy indeed to see one. So we go and celebrate your being here," he said leading me to the front door. "I know a nice place for food, good for the eyes and for the stomach."

I got into his cab and we drove down the ocean road until we came to a small dirt road on the mountainside. It was a long winding road that looked like we might fall over the edge at any moment. An old red Pinto was coming straight for us and I held my breath, but he began to backup until he found a narrow shoulder to park on. "These roads are made for one car at a time," Rudy smiled. "And the biggest one wins."

"I don't think I could ever get used to driving here," I said.

"You got to love what you do. It's no problem when you do that. I drive everyday, and everyday I love to drive." He rolled his eyes up as if to god. "Happiness is where you find it!"

I smiled hoping to join his ranks of bliss someday, but before I could think of any verbal response, the car turned into a driveway. "Here we are," he said jumping out to open the car door for me.

"It's beautiful," I said drinking in the lush greenery. There were several stone steps that led down to a small grassy opening in front of the building. Trees of every denomination surrounded the little cove. The restaurant itself was a small stone structure with painted wooden bi-fold doors that were pulled back to reveal open walls. Paddle fans turned the mountain air above the small tables. "This is really great," I said still surveying the landscape.

"In its time, this was once an old mill. Over there," he said pointing to a picturesque stone bridge, "is a seventeenth century bridge left by the Spaniards."

We sat down and a heavy set woman in a blue apron set two place settings in front of us. "Been a long time since you was here Mr. Rudy."

"Workin hard and livin good, Miss Mattie."

"I hear that," she called out, bringing us two glasses of iceless cold water.

"This is my friend, Jeanne Marie. She was a very good friend of Miguel."

"It's nice to meet you Miss Jeanne Marie. Miguel was a fine man, a fine man," she repeated.

"Yes he was," I responded automatically. It felt strange suddenly, like a movie or something. It didn't seem real. They were talking about him in the past tense. At last someone was acknowledging him, which was a start but I was not ready to put him in the past tense yet.

"It's a sad thing what happened. I could hardly believe it was true. Mr. Miguel help old Wyman, every time he come he see to it that Wyman had what he needed to help him through. Old man Wyman passed on last May," she looked to Rudy for a few words of comfort.

"I'm truly sorry to hear that Miss Mattie. I guess the Good Lord's got his hands full now."

"That he does," she chuckled. "He was one stubborn old man, but I loved him. Love him still," she said smiling. "So, let me know what I can get for you when you're ready. I'll be in the kitchen."

"She's a nice lady," I said. "Was Mr. Wyman her husband?"

"No, they work together for fifty years. She's been through five husbands and nine children. Husbands die and children grow up, but old man Wyman and her work always been there. Now all she's got is the work. She's a good woman, and she loves her work."

"Miguel used to come here?" I asked.

"Yeah Mon. Miguel come here. When old man Wyman got sick, liver problems," he leaned over and lowered his voice. "Too much rum. Miguel do what he can. Nobody can fix him but Miguel always made him feel better." Rudy smiled thinking about him.

"I've got to be honest with you Rudy. When I came here, part of the reason was because I didn't believe Miguel really died. I guess I hoped you might have lied to me. It's just that when I woke up, everything was over. One minute he was there and the next minute he was gone. All of him, no body, no funeral, I didn't even know his friends. I didn't know anyone else to remember him with. It was like he was never there. I don't know how to explain it."

"Ah, you don't have to explain that. It's a natural thing. Everybody needs to share things in this life, and dying is part of it. I'm glad you came back. When you left, I had no way of knowing what to do. Miguel asked to watch out for you," he said turning his head. "I'm grateful for another chance to do any small thing to…make it up to him."

"Tell me about him, Rudy. Just tell me about him. I loved him more than anything in this world. We just had so little time and I knew so little about him."

"When you knew Miguel, you loved him. That's what the man was. Simple as that, he was love. That's what made him live and that's what caused him to die. It was all about love."

"Love, how is that possible. Rudy do you know all the terrible things that were involved with Marion, the DEA agent, Tiburon and the horrible diseases he planted?"

"It began with love, and it ended with love." He said firmly. "I know Miguel."

"I don't understand," I sighed.

"Then I'll explain it to you. First we eat, cause it's gonna take some time."

"Mattie, you got some coffee back there?"

"I got coffee and I got some fresh bread too," she called back.

"Good thing, we gonna be needin to have a good meal now," he said.

"I know just what you need," she said bringing out the coffee. "It'll be a little while longer, but I promise it'll be worth your wait."

"I know it will Mattie. You just take your time and work your magic back there."

I poured some cream into the black coffee and stirred the liquid until it turned light brown. Rudy emptied several packets of sugar into his. "Well now, maybe it's best to begin at the beginning. "The first time I meet Miguel was to fight. I am young and angry; he's in love and foolish. I have three younger brothers. They're not small, but they're smaller than me. I am always the strong one. Then we are all young and full of trouble, but the youngest one is more trouble than any of us. One day he comes to get me because some white tourist he says had almost broken his arm. So, I go to break his. He takes me to local bar. It's at the edge of town where not many tourists go. I see this white man with a very beautiful woman who is laughing and dancing beside him. He is trying to pull her away, but she does not want to go. I put my hand on his shoulder and ask him what his problem was. 'No problem,' he says. 'The lady has had a little too much to drink and we are just leaving.' But Marion was not ready to leave, she turned to me and said, 'I only want to dance, this is Jamaica and I want to dance. Would you like to dance?'

'Please Marion,' Miguel pleaded with her. 'We need to get back before we have any more problems.'

'Oh I think it's too late for that,' I say. 'I think you have problems already.' My brother stood behind me with his arms crossed waiting for me to drop the man.

'Look, I apologize for any misunderstandings here. But as you can see, I am only trying to protect the lady from herself right now.' I look at the man. Then I look at the woman and the fourteen sets of lusting eyes surrounding her. I couldn't take him out knowing what would happen to the woman. So, I look down at her and tell her there is no dancing here. If she wants to dance, she has to go down the street. Finally she turned around and walked out. Miguel reached his hand out to shake mine, but I did not take it. The next day I drive the cab to pick up a couple for a tour. It was none other than Miguel and Marion."

"Did you take them on the tour?" I asked.

"Yeah Mon, of course I did. The poor man was hopelessly in love with a woman destined to bring him nothin but misery. Every man can understand that. It was love. I drove them to see the sites; then we go by Rose Hall. That was before it was restored. It was all in ruins then, with nothin but tales to keep it alive."

"What kind of tales?" I asked.

"Most of them bad, but all of em true."

"Oh, I would love to hear the story," I egged him on. "Do you really know the real story?"

"I know the story well," he began. "In 1818 John Rose Palmer brought his young bride to the plantation that stood on high grounds of Montego Bay. It was called Rose Hall. Her name was Annie. She was eighteen when they married, and it was said that the romance was never a happy one. They say she was a raven beauty with piercing blue eyes and long black hair. She was English and Irish by blood, but she came here by way of Haiti where she spent her childhood. They say it was there she learned the black arts from a voodoo priestess.

Now in her defense, John Palmer was a brute of a man. They say when he drank he was abusive and cruel. In time, it grew worse, but she got more than even with him. Annie was wild and promiscuous and before long the Mistress of Rose Hall took a handsome slave for her lover. When her husband confronted her about this affair, she poisoned him. And as the man lay there in agony dyin, she taunted him with the details. Then, growin impatient because the poison wasn't workin fast enough, she ordered her lover to smother him to death with a pillow.

The deed bein done, the two lovers hid the body. So well in fact that it's never been found to this day. Not long after, she had her slave lover whipped to death by the other slaves. After that, Annie Palmer ruled the plantation with a savage hand. Two more husbands came and went, by way of poison from the hand of the Mistress of Rose Hall. But husbands alone did not satisfy her lust for cruelty. At night she would dress like a man and ride rakehell on horseback over the great plantation. Any unfortunate slave she happened to come across on these outings, she lashed mercilessly with a whip.

As you can imagine, the slaves both hated and feared their Mistress. One of her personal maids tried to poison her. Annie had the girl convicted in the courts, then demanded that the authorities bring her the girl's severed head. The head was delivered, still bloody in a basket, to Rose Hall. There it was placed on a pointed bamboo stave where it rotted and remained until it was nothing more than a white skull bakin in the hot sun.

Finally, in 1833 Annie Palmer was murdered. They say it was her latest lover, who refused to drink her poison. The household slaves found her strangled, mutilated body in her bed. They set fire to her room. Later they refused to dig her grave. The neighbors finally had their own slaves bury the woman. But even they would not allow her to be buried in hollowed ground. They insisted she be placed beneath two feet of solid masonry in the center of the Rose Hall Garden. Everyone hoped the mortar might discourage her evil spirit from rising up again. With the wicked Mistress gone, Rose Hall eventually fell into ruins and that's how it was when we arrived."

"That's some tale. Is it really true?"

"Yeah Mon, it's true," he said nodding his chin to Mattie who was setting his breakfast plate down in front of him. "Just another part of our notorious history here in Jamaica."

"That's incredible. So, you told this story to Miguel and Marion?" I asked.

"I don't want to be interuptin," Mattie said placing the food down on the table. "But will there be anything else you'll be needin?"

"No, thank you. This looks great," I said picking up a bite of freshly sliced mango.

"Where was I now," Rudy began. "Ah, Rose Hall. Like I told you it was all in ruins. Now, after I told the story to Miguel and Marion, she wanted to go up and see the grave of Annie Palmer. Miguel was not at all in favor of this. He said nothing good could come of an evil life such as hers and he wanted nothing to do with her grave. But Marion loved the mystery and nothing would do until she visited the grave of Annie Palmer. Miguel finally gave in to her pleading and we all went to see the ruins of Rose Hall.

It was a good walk from the road, through all the overgrown weeds and fallen stones. On the way Marion talked incessantly about the spirit of Annie Palmer, laughing about the voodoo priestess and all the silly superstitions. 'Miguel knows all about voodoo,' she says. 'Tell him Miguel, Haitians aren't the only ones who know about that stuff,' she tells me. 'Cuban's know about it too, right Miguel? He's not afraid of voodoo witches.'

'Every man's got a healthy fear of voodoo witches,' I told her. 'Cause every woman's got a little voodoo and little witchiness inside of her.'

Marion laughed and ran up ahead to the stairs of the entranceway. Miguel just smiled and we walked side by side. There was nothing really bad about Marion. She was just young and wild, but when we reached the top of the stairs she had found the garden courtyard and the grave of Annie Palmer. Now Miguel and I both just stood there, frozen in our steps when we saw her. We couldn't believe what she was doing. She was dancing suggestively around the stone marker singing the name of Annie Palmer over and over, inviting her to come back, to come back and be with her.

Miguel grew furious. He grabbed her arms in an effort to stop her. Marion glared at him with pure hatred. I swear it was the spirit of Annie Palmer herself that looked through those eyes at that moment. It was purely evil. I'll never forget it. Miguel released his grip without a word and turned around to walk back to the car. I followed him and finally Marion came running up from behind. She must have known that she really did something terrible this time, because Miguel did not speak again until we arrived back at the hotel. When we arrived there he asked me if I could pick them up the next morning because they would be checking out first thing."

"But they must have stayed together after that," I said. "They had a child together."

"That was the very same time the child was conceived. Miguel and I had many conversations after that. Marion wouldn't hear of marriage and she was angry about the pregnancy. She was determined to succeed in her career. Everything was ready to break wide open for her. She had a film contract waitin for her when she got back. She was very beautiful."

"They never married?"

"The woman wouldn't hear of it. She was furious at Miguel too. She intended to get an abortion, and when he pleaded with her not to she swore the child was not even his. Then she refused to talk to him. He was hurt, deeply hurt."

"But she had the baby?"

"Not by her choice," he said pointing his fork at me as he finished another bite of food. "There was a terrible accident. Truthfully it wasn't really an accident, but Miguel felt better callin it that. All I know for sure is that Marion was mixed up with some dangerous people in Miami. They offered her the world and then came callin on her for their fee. Marion," he closed his eyes and shook his head remembering her. "She wasn't payin no one for nothing, and she told em so too. She didn't have any idea it was the devil's rules she was playin by. A few days later, a man come to her door. When she opened the door he slashed the left side her face several times and left her bleedin on the floor."

I touched the side of my face, remembering that first time I had seen through her eyes and felt the hair she used to cover the scar. "My God, what she must have gone through," I said imagining one side of her face flailed open and permanently disfigured.

"That's when she called Miguel," he said. "He was always there to help. Understandably she was devastated. Her beauty was her life. It was her career and all she knew. Her face was scarred forever. Even the best of surgeons could not repair her flawless face. Finally she surrendered to Miguel, allowing him to care for her. She told him then that the child was his. Now Miguel always believed it was regardless of what the woman said. He was like a child himself for a few months. He was so happy, he had the woman he loved and a new life comin into this world. Only a man in love could be so blind as to what that woman was becoming though. She grew more resentful by the day. She accused him of using voodoo to destroy her career. Now, that was a terrible accusation for Miguel. And it was made much worse because deep inside of the man he had probably wished it so. He had never acted upon it, but it had happened all the same.

This made him only try harder to please her, but she was inconsolably miserable. I shutter to think it, but somewhere inside I knew that it was Marion herself who had brought all this evil into being. She had called upon the spirit of Anne Potter, and set some terrible thing into motion. Poor Miguel, he was just swallowed up into it."

"If it was all evil Rudy, what about the baby?"

"I suppose nothin is ever all evil. And if there was anything redeemin, it would have been the child. Miguel lived for the birth of that child. He wanted more than life itself to be the father to that baby. And Marion bein the spiteful woman she was at that time was determined to deny him of that pleasure. She left Miguel before she gave birth. The man nearly went crazy with fear. There was no way of knowin what she might do, so he feared the worst. Unfortunately, the worst was beyond anything he could imagine.

She had gone back to the very man who was responsible for all her troubles. The one who hired the slasher to extract his fee from the woman's own blood. Now this man was evil incarnate. He didn't need no help from the likes of Anne Potter. He got all the help he needed from the devil himself. This man was involved with every part of evil, but he made his money on drugs and white slavery."

"Tiburon!" I said.

"One and the same," he confirmed.

"But why, why would she do that? No," I retracted, considering her state of mind. "She must have gone to him to hurt Miguel to begin with. But why would this man take her in, I mean she couldn't have been of much use to him in her condition?"

"I'm sure as he saw it, one condition was temporary and the other only omitted her from the publics eye. She wouldn't be a movie star, but she was still useful to him. It's not a woman's face a man pays for in his business. But Marion went to him with another thought. She convinced him that the child was his. But after the child was born, she realized her status with this man was no better than any other woman in the devil's employ. She took the child to her mother to be cared for while she went to work. Miguel tried in vain to find her, but when he finally did, she was beyond his help."

"I guess that's where I came in," I said sadly remembering the first time I had seen through Marion's eyes. "It all makes a lot more sense now. It's hard when you only know bits and pieces of a story. They don't show you much of a picture or give you much of an answer."

"Well I guess that's true. I'm glad I was able to help a little anyway," he said.

"Rudy, you can't begin to know how much you helped. I'm eternally grateful for that too. Thank you, for everything, and if there is anything I can ever do for you..."

"There is one thing. A small but important one."

"Just name it," I assured him.

"Before you go back, there is something I would like to show you. I think Miguel would like for you to see it."

"I would like that, very much. I won't be staying here much longer though. I need to get back home soon. I'm going to call when we get back to the hotel and find out when the next flight is."

"You let me know when that is. I'll drive you to the airport. The thing I want to show you is on the way."

"That would be great," I said getting up and pulling my purse strap off the back of the chair and onto my shoulder. "I really appreciate it."

Rudy drove me back to the hotel and I made reservations at the desk before returning to my room. I would leave at four the next afternoon. Rudy would pick me up in the morning and show me what ever it was he wanted me to see. Life was an intricate never-ending web. At least now I could appreciate a little more of the pattern it had spun around me. Perhaps there had been some divine plan to it all. It was beginning to appear that way, but who knows. I remembered the words of the Yemaya at the drum ceremony, 'believe half of what you see and none of what you hear.' It all suddenly felt so long ago.

This was my last day in the resort. I was not sure why I had chosen this particular place. I looked down at the name of the hotel. It was printed on the pad by the phone, Sans Souci. The words were French, meaning without worry. They suddenly seemed appropriate. Some terrible heaviness had been lifted from me this morning. How arrogant I had been once more; I was undeniably the daughter of Chango and not a very good one at that. How could I have assumed that this whole incident evolved around me? Miguel, Marion and Tiburon had all shared a history together. Long before I had even shown up. Miguel's destiny had been decreed before we had even met. It is not so strange that all the Santeros knew this. Everyone had seen it but me. Perhaps that blindness is a part of love, and after all, isn't that what I had asked for? I stood on the balcony, oddly at peace. "Yes Yemaya, I am learning my lesson. I am such a small flame in your vast ocean."

I spent the day wondering about the grounds of the resort, not so much thinking as feeling. It was good to feel again. I walked barefoot in the sugary sand along the beach, inhaling the warm salted air as the bright sun enveloped me, along with the rest of the world. By the time the sunset my skin had reddened and even after my shower I could feel the warmth of the afternoon sun beneath it.

The next morning Nevil had come up to pick up my bag and say goodbye. "So Miss Jeanne Marie, you're leavin us now?"

"Yes Nevil, and I must say. I'm a much happier woman for coming here too."

"Now that's a good thing to hear, a good thing indeed. It's what this worlds all about, come be happy and go. Yeah mon, that's what it's about and I'm glad you found it."

"I won't forget that you were the brilliant detective who helped me to find it either," I said.

"All in days work," he said with a broad smile picking up my bag as we left the room.

Rudy was waiting in the lobby when I arrived to check out. "Good Morning Miss Jeanne Marie," he greeted me.

"Good Morning Rudy," I said in a cheery voice.

"Wait a minute," he said reaching for my bag. "I may need some identification from you. Are you the same Jeanne Marie I saw just one day ago?"

I smiled, "Yes, that would be me."

"Well I must say," he said approvingly. "This visit has done something good for you."

"You have no idea Rudy," I said signing the check out slip and folding the receipt. "This visit has given me hope, and I'm so grateful for that. It's such a beautiful thing to receive."

Rudy smiled and nodded his head in agreement as we walked outside to his cab. It was another perfect day in paradise. I turned for a last look at the elegant masonry work on the entranceway. The air was perfumed with the sweet scent of jasmine blossoms. Something fluttered past me towards the flowering bush. At first glance I thought it might be a large bumblebee, but a closer look exposed an exotic species of hummingbird. I had never seen anything like it before. It had long shinny blue and green feathers creating a magnificent tail that curled at the end and tiny wings that flapped faster than the eye could follow. The rapid movement of those tiny wings as the little bird hovered beside me seemed to defy logic. How could they possibly hold up his body, much less that long beautiful tail?

"Did you see that?" I asked Rudy pointing to the bird.

"The humminbird? Yeah, there are two more just over there," he pointed out. "Jamaica is famous for those little birds."

"They're amazing. I've never seen them with tails like that, and so many colors. They're beautiful."

"Very important too," he said opening cab door for me. "They say if you put one of those feathers under your pillow before you go to sleep, you'll see the face of your true love in your dreams that night."

"Does it work?" I asked smiling.

"Now I haven't tried it first hand myself. They're fast little creatures and they travel in packs. You know they don't give up those feathers without a fight either. No, I don't tangle with humminbirds."

I laughed, as we pulled out of the driveway and onto the road, not that there was that much difference between the two. One was just longer than the other. We drove past the Trident Castle. An amazing sight, it was a genuine castle poised like a jewel rising right out of the ocean. "I remember seeing that castle when I arrived." I said. "It looks like one of the fairy tale castles transplanted from the mountains in Germany."

"It's a beautiful castle," he agreed. "It's built on its own little island out there, but there's not much of a story behind it. It's actually a new addition to the landscape. All the tourists photograph it, but the tour guides aren't agreeing on a good tale for it yet. Just hasn't been there long enough."

"Everything here has a story, doesn't it?" I asked.

"Yeah mon, and every persons got one too."

"Yeah," I said remembering Miguel saying those very words the first night we met. "Some are just more romantic than others I guess."

"Well it's all a matter of time as I see it. In time, even the very worst of things become romantic."

"I don't think I ever thought about it that way, but I suppose your right," I said watching the panorama of scenery go by. Miles and miles of it passed by as we drove. It began to look vaguely familiar but I could not place the pictures in any kind of order. I had no idea where Rudy was taking me until he turned the car off the road and we drove through the gates. The cottages, Miguel's cottage, it was not visible from the road but I could see it all the same. Mental pictures of its interior began a sequence of unbidden remembrances. Miguel's face, his voice, his very scent came flooding back and tears began to well up in my eyes. I had not even noticed that Rudy had already gotten out of the car. He was standing beside me opening the car door.

"I promise you Miss Jeanne Marie that this walk will be worth all the pain you must be feelin at this moment." He reached down and took my hand to help me out of the car.

"I'm okay, Rudy. It's just..." I couldn't finish the sentence. My throat was swelling shut.

"Trust me on this one," he said. What I want to show you is down here."

Rudy led me by the hand down the path with the giant red spikes of ginger flowers. I remembered the path. I remembered the dark green foliage and the sunlit sands framing the blue waters that rose up at the end of the passageway. I did not need to have my eyes open to see any of this. But I allowed Rudy to show it to me now out of respect for him. I could not imagine why Rudy needed to show me this place. It had been ours, Miguel and I. It had been our sacred place of spiritual fusion. Here our souls had come together to form a single being and the warm ocean waters had caressed the oneness of our bodies. This was the place where our love had been born.

Yemaya greeted us with splashing waves in the bright sunlight at the end of the path. Her waters were magnificent and endless as always. No matter how many times I laid eyes on the splendor of this sight, it never ceased to inspire awe inside of me. "Over there," Rudy said releasing my hand to point. "That is what I brought you to see."

I looked in the direction he was pointing. There was a gazebo, a small white painted structure with carved railings and wooden benches. It was a picturesque addition and it complimented the landscape perfectly. I ran up to look at it more closely. Over the entry was a small brass plaque. It read 'In memory of Miguel, who will live always in the hearts of those who love." Suddenly everything inside of me came pouring out, in great sobs it opened up and spewed out. Rudy gently placed my head on his giant broad shoulders while I cried.

"Let all out, it's what needs to be. Feelin is a good thing, we all need to feel and we need to feel all things, good and bad. That's the only way we know the difference in this world."

"Oh, Rudy," I lifted my head from the safety of his shoulder and faced the open sea. "I guess this is the first time it was really real to me. Miguel, he's really gone."

"Miguel is dead, but he's not gone girl. Look, out over those waters, can you see anything but Miguel there? He's home mon, and we can't grieve for that. We can only be sorry that we miss him as he once was, because he's still here. He's here in your heart and my heart. He's here in the ground and the sea, here in everything the man ever loved and everything that ever loved him. You got to know that Jeanne Marie."

"I know that now, because I can feel it now."

"There's one more thing, and you might want to sit down for this," he said.

My mind raced forward and another expectation of dread filled my face. "Rudy, I don't know if I want to know anymore," I said hesitating to sit down.

"No, no, don't worry it's nothin bad. He reached into his pocket and pulled out a small red silk bag. "I've been holdin on to this for quite a while now. It belongs to you."

I looked at him not knowing what he was talking about. "It belongs to me?"

"Yes, that last day. The day I was comin to watch out for you. I was late. I was late because when I stopped to pick this up, the man hadn't finished it. Miguel had asked me to pick it up on my way. But when I got here…then I wanted to give it to you before you left, but I saw you throw the bracelet into the ocean. I thought it might not be the right time to give it to you. I wasn't at all sure if you wanted to be reminded of anything here, so I just held on to it. Anyway, this is for you from Miguel."

Rudy placed the little bag into my trembling hands. I stretched open the mouth of the small crimson purse and reached inside. It was a ring, a gold band with tiny delicate waves carved around the endless circle.

"You got to read the inscription," Rudy said.

I turned the ring in my fingers reading the message inside. He had sent me a message. I tried to steady my hand so I could read it. It was inscribed, 'with love there is always hope.' It was written in a circle. I turned around, it read continuously. Maybe it was suppose to be 'there is always hope with love.' It did not matter, because no matter how the phrase was turned, the important thing was, there was no beginning and there was no end. It was so beautiful, and it was so like Miguel.

"It was to be your wedding ring. This little gazebo was supposed to be finished before you arrived, but it's Jamaica and things are rarely done on time. But, time is a thing we have a lot of on this island, so no one pays much attention to it. Miguel, he wanted to propose to you here. You know he was always full of romantic plans and he wanted everyone to share in them. So, my job was to be the best man, and I was in charge of getting and keeping the ring until…" He looked down not saying the rest of what he was thinking.

"Rudy, thank you," I said looking down at the precious golden circle. "Thank you."

I looked out over the crystal waters. Miguel had been there all along. He was home with his mother Yemaya in her beautiful sea, an ocean filled with the salt of tears. She had given me all that I had asked for, which was far more than I had ever hoped for. I placed the ring on my finger, rotating it around and around, feeling his words as they turned in my mind. It felt strange, but there were no more tears to be shed and there were no more words to be spoken. There was only a deep and abiding knowing of love, and a new hope emerging from within. Yes Miguel, for as long as there are oceans on this earth, I will know there is love in this world, and with love, there will always be hope.

15

Raising the Dead

I am not sure how long I sat still, flowing in communion with the world around me, when Rudy placed his hand on my shoulder to let me know it was time to leave. I closed my eyes and nodded in agreement. We walked back up the path that led back to the cottages and the car. As we neared the end of the walk, I watched as an attractive young woman in a pale blue pants suit walked towards the burgundy cab.

"Ceil, is that you?" Rudy called out.

"Rudy, I knew it could only be you leavin the car in the middle of the drive and disappearin like a phantom in the night," she scolded.

Rudy smiled, delighted by her acknowledgement. "Ceil I don't know how, but your even more beautiful than I remember."

"Don't be sweet talking me, Mr. Rudy. You know better than to be parkin your car where it don't belong, and it don't belong here. And for that matter, neither do you."

"Now I know you don't mean that Ceil. I know somewhere down in the bottom of your heart you have a little soft place for me."

"I got nothing of the kind for you!"

"Surely you understand Ceil that there were exceptional circumstances at the time. Surely you could find it in your heart to forgive me."

"Mr. Rudy, do you have some business for bein here?" She asked.

"In a manner of speakin," he answered. "I brought Miss Jeanne Marie to see Miguel's gazebo. You remember Jeanne Marie, she was here when…"

"Miss Jeanne Marie," Ceil extended her hand and softened her voice. "I'm afraid I didn't recognize you. I'm so sorry for all the things that happened here. It was a terrible thing for us all. It's good to see you looking so well though."

"Thank you," I said. "I'm afraid I don't remember meeting you though."

"No, I don't suppose you would. We never actually met. I was working here the day it happened though. It was a big investigation. They had everything sealed off, searched the entire area, asked a thousand questions and never found a clue. Rudy got them to allow me to pack your things and I'm sure they went though them after I did. I hope everything was in order when you received it. I wasn't certain I had found all your things to pack. There wasn't a problem was there?"

"No, no everything was fine with my bag. Thank you for your help."

"Oh, of course," she said snapping her fingers. "You came for your mail. I apologize, but we didn't have a forwarding address for you. You know I almost gave it to the authorities, but I know how they are. You would have never gotten it back, everything gets lost over here and I figured you had enough loss as it was. I waited for you to call or send us your address, but I understand with everything that happened. I'm sure it took some time to recuperate. The truth is, I just plain forgot about it until now."

"Mail, for me?" I couldn't imagine who had sent me mail here. No one knew this address. I hadn't even known it before I got here. Miguel had never given it to me.

"Yes, I'm sure it was for you, yours is not a name I was likely to forget. Come on up to the office. I'll get it for you," she said.

I looked at Rudy for some hint of an answer, but there was none. He obediently followed the pretty girl to her office. Ceil opened the door and stepped into the refrigerated air. "I know right where it is," she said opening another door that exposed a small closet. She lifted a white cardboard file box from the floor. "I put it in back of last years files. Here it is."

I reached for the large manila envelope. It was addressed to me! I did not recognize the handwriting, but I was certain it was not Miguel's. There was no return address, but the stamps were clearly Jamaican. My first impulse was to rip it open, but something told me not to. Whatever was inside of me spoke clearly, accept the envelope, quietly, discreetly, and don't open it until you're alone. "Thank you Ceil," I said politely hoping my voice was not shaking. "I appreciate your holding on to it for me so long."

"No problem, I'm glad I could do something for you after all you went through."

"And what about your old friend Rudy? Do you think you might see your way to let me explain just a little Ceil? "Five minutes," he pleaded. "Surely you can spare five minutes for an old friend? I promise I will leave a happy man if you just grant me those few minutes."

"I've got to take a note to the housekeeper," she said picking up an envelope from the desk. You can walk with me, but I'm warnin you now don't get too close."

"I wouldn't think of it Ceil," he said winking at me. "Jeanne Marie I hope you will excuse us for just a few minutes. Some times a man only gets one chance, and if they're lucky maybe two," he said winking again.

"Take all the time you need," I said moving my fingers over the bumps in the envelope for some clue as to what it might contain. The moment the door closed I pulled the tape from flap and unhooked the small tin fastener. It was open. I took a deep breath before reaching inside to pull out its contents. There was a smaller sealed envelope, and a note. Two pages folded together, hand written on lined notepaper.

Jeanne Marie,

My nurse is helping me to write this letter, as this illness has all but consumed me. First let me say, that I am so terribly sorry for causing any undue grief to Miguel or to you. You must understand, that I was the one who begged Miguel to bring you to me. Please believe he did not do this to hurt you in any way. If Miguel has one flaw, it is his innocence, and his childish belief in some basic goodness that exists in us all. Poor Miguel, he has never been anything but kind to me. Something I never accepted, and something I never deserved.

Miguel has told me so much about you. I am truly happy that he has finally found someone worthy of his love. I convinced Miguel that you and I had to meet. I told him how much it would mean to me to let you know this, that it was necessary for me do to this before I died. I do not mean to diminish the truth of these words Jeanne Marie but this was not the reason I wished to meet with you.

I know you are aware of my sorted past, and of my dealings with Tiburon. He is perhaps the only evil Miguel has ever known, but the truth is, he only knows only half of the horrific acts committed by his old enemy. Miguel has always been blind to the other half, the half that I was a part of. He has always tried to protect me, but not even a saint can protect the devil from himself, or herself as the case may be. I am older, and a little wiser, but I am still the same woman I have always been. I would like to say that now, I am trying to protect Miguel, that I am doing this for him. In all honestly, I am once again protecting myself. I am protecting the only thing has ever been in my life truly beautiful and purely innocent, Miguel.

I can only hope at this point, when you receive this package you will understand why I could not give it to Miguel. The knowledge would kill him. I am sure of this. Barnes, the DEA agent who came to you is dead and it is only a matter of time now before they come to kill me. But I have cheated them of this pleasure more than once. How sad Tiburon will be when he finds out that I am already dead, that he cannot kill a dead woman. How angry he will be when he learns that that

I placed the evidence in your hands, the hands of a woman, according to Miguel, destined to destroy Tiburon.

I know very little and understand even less of Santeria, or any of those spiritual things. But I do know Miguel, and I know that in spite of what he is told he will try to protect you just as he did me. I have never forgotten the warnings his godfather gave him about protecting "a woman who witnessed death with eyes other than her own." He was told she would bring about his death, a violent and bloody ending to his saintly life. When you see what I have placed in your hands, you will understand. You will understand why you must do this alone, but I am sure you know all this. I have tempted the prediction too many times already.

By the time you receive this letter I will probably be dead. Please don't think for a moment that I am not at peace with this. I have had more than enough time to come to terms with things, and I will die knowing that I have had the last laugh. If there is one thing this contemptible life has taught me, it is that we are not all born to be saints in this world.

Marion

I couldn't believe it. Why, just when I thought I understood. Why were they doing this to me? My mind swirled in confusion. She thought it was her, but it was me. I was the woman who brought about his death. If I hadn't lost my head when I saw Marion. If only I had not been so stupid. She tried to tell me something. If I had only stayed calm and done what I was supposed to do. Miguel would not have had a reason to go back there. Miguel would not be dead, and Tiburon would not plague the world today! How could I delude myself into thinking that the world was filled with only peace and harmony? How could I believe that everything would just magically fall into some divine order when I had broken the very chain of order.

It wasn't over. I could not bring Miguel back, but I could at least give his death a purpose. Tiburon was still alive. Somehow, I had to make destiny right again. I was a part, maybe only a small piece of the puzzle, but I was a part and it was time to stand up and complete it. I would carry out the destiny I had been given.

The sealed envelope, inside I would find the weapon. I knew without looking what it contained. It was thick with photographs, evidence. Somehow I knew it was the sword that would bring the murderous fiend Tiburon to justice. How ironic that it would be Marion who provided me with that sword.

I peeled open the envelope. It was like opening a tomb, something that had been buried and silent for a long time. I flipped through the photos quickly. The first was a shot of two men boarding a yacht. There were several views of the men talking. The second was a young girl in a skimpy bikini sunning herself on the bow. Another was of a dark haired girl sleeping on the deck. Next there was a shot of a man walking on the dock, and the girl in the bikini jumping onto the shore. Several shots were taken in sequence. The man got closer to the girl. It looked like they were arguing. Then he had the girl by the arm, twisted behind her back. He walked back behind a small green building. Next was a picture of the man walking back to the dock. He had something in his hands, maybe a white cloth, a handkerchief maybe. In the next picture, the same man was boarding the boat again. The negatives were in the bottom of the envelope sealed in plastic covers. One of the men had to be Tiburon, but I had no idea what the pictures were actually trying to show me.

I could hear laughter behind the front door. I quickly shoved everything back into the envelope and closed the metal prongs to secure the contents. Rudy and Ceil were both smiling. Ceil a little more smugly than Rudy, but they both looked happy.

"So Miss Jeanne Marie," Rudy said still not taking his eyes off Ceil. "I suppose if we are to get you to the airport we'd better get on our way."

"Yes," I answered hesitating for a moment. "I guess we'd better get going."

"And Miss Ceil," Rudy reached for her hand and kissed it lightly. "Until tomorrow?"

"Rudy, you are incorrigible," Ceil resigned.

In no time we were clear of the entrance drive and on our way. I needed to think about the envelope. Rudy was too love struck to notice the significance of what had just taken place. I hadn't had time to think of the ramifications. Would Tiburon come after me? I hadn't worried about him before. Perhaps he thought I had died from the infection they had injected me with. Perhaps he knew I had retreated, that I did not care what happened to him. For whatever reason, he had not been anymore of a threat to me than I was to him, until now. Everything had changed, in one single instant I knew it had all changed.

I had been given a job to do, and until I completed it, it would come back again and again. Marion had come back from the grave to deliver the weapon. Miguel had died trying to find it for me. I knew in his heart he died for a thousand children whose bodies and souls were poisoned by the demon Tiburon. I also knew that had I not lost my head, had I just spoken to Marion a year ago, he would not be dead. How many others have died tragically, needlessly in this past year. I am a small flame, but I am Chango. Chango who is the consummate spiritual warrior I will do what I was created to do!

I needed time to think, to plan to know what I had in my hands. "Rudy, is there someplace we can stop for a few minutes?"

"There's a place right up the road where the drivers take the tourists on the way to the resorts. It's not much but they have facilities there."

"No, I don't need to use the bathroom. I just need to stop somewhere and think, maybe get something cold to drink or something."

"I'm sure we can get some cold drinks there," he said contorting the muscles in his face forming an uneasy expression.

"That'll work Rudy. I just need to stop," I said. I would have to tell him about the envelope. Could I risk putting him in danger? He was the only one I knew for certain I could trust right now. How could I not? He would help, if not for me then for Miguel I knew he would help.

We pulled up to the small wooden shack with several smaller stands displaying touristy Jamaican trinkets and tee shirts hanging in the open air. Two or three vendors stood up to approach the car as I got out, but Rudy motioned with a strong hand to stay back and they obeyed. Inside the shaded hut there were a few tables and a small snack bar.

"It's not a big selection," Rudy began, "but there are plenty of cold drinks here. What would like to drink Jeanne Marie?"

"Just a bottle of water, cold water would be perfect."

"Nothin to eat? They do have some nice snacks today. A little meat pie wrapped in some nice pastry?"

"No, I'm really not hungry right now."

"All the same, they're worth it just for the taste. Are you sure I can't tempt you now?"

"No, really I'm fine," I said.

"Okay but you don't know what you'll be missin," he smiled trying to lighten the mood. First he set the plastic bottle in front of me and proceeded to place his food and drink on to the table. "That would be one delicious lemon lime soda for me, two delightful Jamaican pies for me and one plain old cold water for you. Tell me now why is it that ladies make it so hard on themselves instead of just enjoin the fruits of the earth?"

"Some of us are just born to be martyrs I guess."

"Now that's no way to begin your journey home. This is time of joy, a time for returnin with a full heart and stomach from the friends you came to visit."

"Rudy you have been a good friend," I said making an effort to smile at him. "And what I am about to share with you is far beyond the boundaries of friendship."

"For a true friend, there are no boundaries Jeanne Marie. Whatever it is you need to say, say it with full knowledge of that."

"It's about the envelope, the mail that Ceil gave me. Rudy it was from Marion!"

"Marion? Now Jeanne Marie, what ever she might have written you can't let it change what was between Miguel and yourself. You can't let it upset you. I've known Marion for a long time. She was who she was, and she was not always exactly truthful if you know what I mean."

"No, no it's not like that. She sent me some kind of evidence. Rudy I think that's what Tiburon was after all along."

Rudy's eyes widened. "All this time, I can't believe it. What kind of evidence did she have?"

"Photographs, I'm not sure what they all mean yet, but I know they are the key to Tiburon's destruction." I looked to Rudy waiting on his response. He slowly pushed the food away and picked up the can of soda.

"Your in danger Jeanne Marie. I never would have taken you back there if I had known. We have to think this through, carefully, very carefully. Come on, we need to drive."

I followed my giant friend to the car. He drove off without a word, and not until we were safely on the road did he finally speak. "You know you have to change your plans, you won't be safe goin home the way you planned. I know enough about the man to know that."

"But I have to get the photographs to the police. I have to get them to Miami."

"Don't you see Jeanne Marie, they think you came back here for just that reason. They'll be waitin on you at the airport. You've seen first hand how they work. My God, I led you right into it. I never meant for this to happen."

"Rudy, thank God you did. Think about it, whether I found the evidence or not, they would have killed me thinking I did. You saved my life!"

"Maybe for the moment, but we've got a long way to go. It's not like I can drive you back to Miami from here."

"Maybe we should take them to the authorities here?" I suggested.

"That may not be such a good idea. There's too much this government doesn't want to know, especially when large amounts of anonymous drug money is involved. You have to remember that, in any country. I'm sure I don't need to tell you what goes on with law in these matters."

"No, your right. Even in Miami I'm not sure who I can trust. There's no room for a mistake here. Rudy I need time to think, to sort out the information and know what it means. Where can I go?"

"Pearl, my aunt Pearl of course. She'll take care of you, and where she lives, no one will find you. I used to stay with her when I was a young boy. I know it may be hard to believe but there was a time or two that I might have been a little difficult for my mother to manage. She had a house full," he said smiling at the thought. "I have nothing but fond memories of stayin there. Aunt Pearl is quite a woman, but you'll see that for yourself."

It was a long drive to Aunt Pearls. I fell asleep somewhere along the ocean stretch. When I woke up we were winding up some narrow and very bumpy mountain path with a long drop to forest below.

"Oh now that we've almost arrived you've decided to come back to join me," Rudy said looking down his nose as if he had been insulted.

"I can't believe I fell asleep. I don't usually do that. It must be all the confidence I have in your highly proficient driving skills."

"Ah yes, well I can certainly understand that now," he said very pleased with himself.

"Rudy the mountains are beautiful here."

"That they are. This is God's land indeed. That's it, he said turning the car off the road. "I almost missed the place."

In front of us was a small wooden house leaning significantly to one side. On the lower side was a crude addition that looked more like a large lean to resting there. Another smaller structure stood beside it, probably a shed. Banana trees grew abundantly in clumps around the little house and several small hens followed by a bantam rooster walked about the yard. Before we got out of the car a heavyset woman in a white kerchief came out the front door.

"Aunt Pearl," Rudy called jumping out of the car heading towards her. "Aunt Pearl you got company comin."

"Rudy, Rudy I been waitin for you come see your old Aunt Pearl, waitin for near two weeks now," she said hugging him as he bent over so her arms could reach. "Glad you come, bout time."

I was out of the car and standing quietly by for Rudy to introduce me to his aunt when she turned her eyes suddenly to me. "Aunt Pearl," Rudy spoke up. "This is my friend Jeanne Marie."

Aunt Pearl looked at me skeptically. "So you the one," she said turning away and walking back into the house.

I looked to him for the answer. "What does she mean Rudy?" I hesitated to follow him into the house. "I don't think she likes me."

"It's not like that," Rudy motioned for me to come closer. "She knows things. It's been a long time since I've been here, but she always knows when I'm comin. And, she always knows before I do. Then when I arrive she gets her back up because I didn't get here on time. It's always been like that. But, she'll get over it, she don't stay mad long."

Luckily I had not had time to think too much along the way. This had to be one of the most remote places on earth, and no one even knew where I was. Right now that was a good thing. I couldn't think past that. I had to stay focused. I needed to remain calm and not lose my head again. I had a second chance to make things right. Things would never be perfect, but at least they would be in order again. I followed Rudy into the little house.

Bahama beds covered in faded green floral prints served as sofas in the single room that served as a living room, dining room and kitchen. Wooden chairs with layers of chipped paint surrounded a heavy wooden table and blue and white china plates hung decoratively on the walls. In the corner of the kitchen stood a black potbellied stove with a pile a wood beside it. A small hand pump was perched on the counter over the sink and above that a small window. There were no appliances, no lights, and no electricity. Aunt Pearl reached up into the yellowed cabinet mounted on the wall and took out three glasses. She lifted a cloth covering a heavy pottery water pitcher and poured the glasses full. Rudy sat down at the table. I followed his lead. Aunt Pearl placed the glasses in front of us and sat down.

"So you'll be needin to stay for a while," she said as she looked past me with her large dark eyes not waiting for a response. "God love em, Rudy's always findin trouble. Don't take much knowin to know that. Lucky for you God take care of fools and children, and I'm not sure he don't count you for both." Then she looked deeply into my eyes, studying them for a moment. "Some people got more eyes than sense in their head but it's too late to be tellin you that. When the man say pick up the sword, he mean the sword of justice. Man up there don't need to tell you twice. Now you finally got it in your hands cause he put it there. Mmm hmmm, little children little problems," she reached over without flinching and smacked the elbow out from under Rudy's chin. His head jerked up and he looked at her first surprised and then apologetically. "You see what happen you grow up too big, you bring back big problems." Rudy lifted both hands surrendering to the old woman's logic.

"Now, what to do, that's what we got to find out. Might have seen old black Vernon on this one."

"Vernon?" I questioned while Rudy closed his eyes waiting for Aunt Pearl's response.

"Yeah old black Vernon, he's old but wise. Not much to look at these days, skins comin off and he don't look too good right now, but he still works when I call on him. And he's still filled with the spirit as he ever was."

"Can I meet him?" I asked.

"Jeanne Marie," Rudy interrupted. "I don't think you want to meet him," he said repeating the sentiment with his eyes.

"Why not?" I asked. "I've met a lot of old spiritualists."

"Not like this one," he said warning me again.

"I don't let too many people meet old Vernon. He don't like most people. Maybe he like you though. Rudy he know you don't like him, so you wait here. Come on with me," Aunt Pearl took my arm and led me out the door.

The sun was just setting and the sky was on fire above the mountains. We walked past the shed, which I now realized was an outhouse. We crossed over a small stream and then came to an abrupt halt. We were dwarfed beneath a gigantic cotton wood tree that appeared to just spring out of the prehistoric forest.

"Got to ask for entrance here," she said reaching into her pocket and pulling out a small dark bottle. She lifted it up to sky and began mumbling a few words. She took a large swig of the liquid and spat it out onto the roots of the tree. Then she reached for a tall stick leaning against the trunk. It was tied at the top with hemp rope and had tiny shells and tarnished brass bells attached to the frayed ends. She hit it on the ground several times and it jingled as she cried out for entrance into the darkening forest. The whole mountain was coming alive with nightlife. Tiny frogs sang out with the echo of giant crickets. The tree branches blew gently in the wind whispering their secrets to the jungles below as we stood, dwarfed in its midst.

Aunt Pearl returned the stick to its resting place and proceeded to walk around the tree carefully stepping over the thick snarled roots covering the ground. I followed closely behind. The trunk itself was the size of a small house. We were about half way when she stopped abruptly. "Time to be still," she said motioning me to stand where I was and not move. I didn't have much problem with that. I thought about Rudy's attempt to warn me not to come. It was getting darker and I hadn't considered the blackness of the night. If Old Black Vernon's skin was coming off and he was truly as frightening as I was now imagining, I knew I was in trouble. There was plenty of room to run, but no place left to go. I would be courageous and strong. I would not lose my head no matter how horrible the sight of Old Vernon might be.

The old woman walked to the foot of the tree and I could see the outline of what looked like a small doghouse. She picked up a lantern from the ground and bent over to light it. I hadn't seen a kerosene lamp in a long time. It was like the old ones they used in the military. Once it was lit she hung it onto a post next to the miniature house. The light gave the whole area an eerie glow. It was something deeply mystical, and magically ancient and just as excitement was beginning to replace fear her hearty voice rang out again into the night. I was not sure what language she was speaking. It was vaguely familiar but I could not make out the words. It had to be African, probably diluted through the generations of verbal passage. I listened intently for a rustle behind me. I hoped old Vernon would not sneak up and surprise me from that direction.

Meanwhile Aunt Pearl lifted the hinged side of the roof on the little house. She carefully folded it over and reached her arm inside. When she pulled it out my knees went weak. In her hand she was clutching a monstrous black snake darting and weaving his head freely into the air. With her other hand she reached in again to free the remaining four or five feet of dark slithering serpent from his innocuous little house. The old woman hadn't lied. The snake's skin was peeling and his eyes were covered with remnants of the fraying milky veil. He looked positively ghastly, like the graying ghost of a giant serpent. His sleek scaly body slowly wound around Aunt Pearl's ample waist and continued to coil around her arm. It was good that my stomach was too empty to heave and it was good that I was too terrified to move. Old Black Vernon had arrived.

"Good thing," she said looking at me. "Good thing indeed, Old Vernon in a good mood tonight. He don't see so good right now, but he hear everything. Old Vernon talk to the mountain and he talk to the wind come across the waters. Old Vernon know a thing or two." The snake's sharp red tongue darted in and out of his mouth as she spoke. "Old Vernon say you come knowin the old ones, you okay, he like you. He say the winds bring bad news. They carry bad people here, bad like the devil himself. Bloodshed, a saint will die and a demon will be caught. You got to go to the sea for a safe journey, but watch out for the sharks. They evil killers, remember sharks don't eat to live, they live to eat! Things backwards here, he say for you, one that's dead but not buried comes alive, then they die. You got all the power you need in this world. Open your eyes and do what you know. That's the power God gave you. The eyes of the dead will tell you what you need to know."

The old woman closed her eyes and pointed her face towards the stars. Tears streamed down her cheeks and glittered in the darkness. Old Vernon slowly lowered his head and rested it on her shoulder. Without another word, the woman lovingly lowered his head into the opened house and he slid in so quickly his movement was all but invisible.

Aunt Pearl closed the roof flap silently and grabbed the lantern to light our way back to the house. I missed a step in the creek and felt the sting of the icy mountain water as it covered my feet. As we passed the little shed Aunt Pearl handed me the lantern. "You better go now, while we got the light." I gratefully accepted the lantern and took my turn in the lavatory.

"Well the witchin women return," Rudy greeted us as we came in. "So," he smiled. "How did you like Old Black Vernon?"

I could not help but to smile back at him. "More important than me liking him, he liked me," I said.

"Oh did he now," Rudy Raised his eyebrows.

"Yes he did at that," Aunt Pearl piped in. "His likes and dislikes are one thing he don't hesitate to let me know. But I don't care to discuss that with the likes of you. Rudy what you been doin while we gone. Nothin on the table? You waitin to be served I suppose, well move out of my way, someone's got to start to cookin or we'll all starve here.

After dinner Aunt Pearl handed us each a sheet and blanket and directed us to our respective beds. She left the door to her room open. The next morning I woke to the crowing of a small but incredibly loud rooster. Aunt Pearl was up dressed and cooking breakfast already. I looked over to see if Rudy was awake yet. "He only wakes up to the smell of food," his aunt said shaking her head. "My Rudy always been that way. Always in trouble, comin to his Aunt Pearl to take care of things, but he's a good boy." She gazed over his large body and her eyes softened. "He's a fine man. Soon enough he gonna marry a fiery little thing who will bear him a son. But he don't know that yet."

The smell of fresh bread wafted through the air and Rudy began to stir. "I know what I say," she smiled confidently.

After breakfast Aunt Pearl went to the forest to 'take care of business' while Rudy and I reviewed the contents of the envelope to figure out what it all meant. I grabbed a pen and a small pad from my bag and began to jot down a few notes.

"What do we have so far?" Rudy asked trying to sneak a peek at my notes.

"Oh this is just to remind me of what Old Vernon told me last night," I said. "I have to write it down before I forget the exact words."

"So now Old Vernon is talking to you too. You understand what that old black snake says?"

"I think so. He may be ugly, but he's not stupid. In fact I thought he is pretty smart," I said.

"Seems like he talks in circles from what I hear. Of course I don't hear him personally, only Aunt Pearl's translation. Don't make much sense to me ever."

"Like I said, I understand some of it, some of it is more like a riddle. I never was good at riddles. Seriously though, listen to this: The winds bring bad news. They carry bad people here, bad like the devil himself. Sound like anybody we know? The winds bring them in, airplanes?"

"Alright go on," he said, still with a hint of skepticism in his voice.

I skipped the next line that there would be bloodshed, that a saint would die but a demon would be caught. The implications were obvious to me. I might fulfill my destiny, but I would die in the process. "You've got to go to the sea for a safe journey, but watch out for the sharks. They're killers, remember sharks don't eat to live, they live to eat!"

"Tiburon is the shark, and his men the killers. You need to take a boat back! Maybe it does make sense. What else did the old serpent have to say?"

"This part is a little cryptic. It said that things were backwards, that for me, one that's dead but not buried comes alive, then they die. Believe it or not it's a familiar saying. The sign I was given in the religion was almost the same. It was the sign of the first burial, and a story about a woman who pretended to die. She went on to live another life until she got caught. Then she was killed and finally put in the ground where she remained. There's a lot more to the story, but that's the gist of it."

"Jeanne Marie, I think you got to beware of a snakes advice. It's not that they lie. I know Aunt Pearl swears by his truth. But truth is just as tricky sometimes."

"What do you mean Rudy? Do you read something different from that?"

"No, I'm just saying that things don't always mean what you think they mean," he said sounding a little confused.

"I know what you mean Rudy. I've sure done that often enough. Sometimes I think we're not suppose to know exactly what it means until we get to the place where we need to know."

"Yeah mon, I guess that's precisely what I mean."

"Anyway," I went on. "The last line said that I had all the power I would need in this world. To open my eyes and do what I know. That's the power God gave me. The eyes of the dead will tell you what you need to know. I'm fairly certain of that one. My power is to look through other people's eyes, the eyes of the dead. That's how we're going to find out what the evidence is that these photographs have captured."

"Now you're talking," he said. "Just how exactly does it work? And please tell me it don't include no snakes."

"Now Rudy, how can you say that after all the information Old Vernon just provided us with?"

"Well I don't mind telling you Jeanne Marie. I don't mean nothing personal to Old Vernon. I'm not fond of reptiles of any color or denomination. I just don't like snakes."

I had to laugh, Rudy he was such a gentle giant. "Well don't worry. I don't even know any snakes, other than Old Vernon that is. This is pretty easy. All I need you to do Rudy is sit across from me here on the floor. When I ask, hand me a photograph, one at a time.

Now, as you hand them to me, I need you to ask about someone in the picture. We don't know any names, so you'll have to just describe them somehow. Like this one," I pulled out a photo and showed it to him. "Just tell me to find out anything I can about the girl in the green bikini. She is running from a man. When I start talking, just keep asking me questions, like who she is running from. Whether I answer or not, keep asking. Sometimes I'm seeing things but I can't talk. You understand?"

"Yeah mon, I can do well at that."

"Perfect, now it takes me a couple of minutes to relax so I can start okay?"

"I'm good here. You take all the time you need," he assured me.

"One more thing, if it looks like I am in too much pain or I start screaming or anything, just tell me to wake up, okay?"

"Screamin and pain, we didn't discuss that part. Maybe we better go over it a little more before we start."

"I trust you Rudy, you'll know what to do." I closed my eyes, and within seconds I could feel my mind begin to spin, a wonderful glorious spinning. The world was going round faster and faster, lights and colors flew by and finally my mind landed gently in that place of oblivion where time stands still. I was deeply relaxed, and my muscles were not cooperating. It was all I could do to move my mouth and drone out the word, now.

I felt him place the picture into my open hand. I could not feel it. I had to move. I had placed my other hand on top of it to feel it. The effort was immense, but I finally managed. I waited for instructions.

"There's a girl in this picture Jeanne Marie. I don't know her name but she's wearin a green bikini and she has long yellow hair. Tell me who she is running from?"

"Mmm..mon...monster."

"A monster," he repeated. I shook my head. Does this monster have a name?" He asked.

"Tiburon," I answered.

"Why is this girl running?"

"He's trying to kill me, hurry. Linda is dead."

Who is Linda?" He asked.

"Linda, on the deck, she's dead. He killed her. I have to run."

"And do you have a name?"

"Mindy, help me, please help me. Too late, it's too late I couldn't run. My arm, breaking, he's breaking my arm, help me please. It's dark, dirty, no don't hurt me, please, please.

"Where are you, where are you now?"

"On the floor, hard, my head is bleeding. He is on top of me, monster, monster!"

"Wake up Jeanne Marie, you gotta wake up!"

My eyes did not immediately open. It took a moment to get back. Rudy watched me but didn't speak right away. My head was still fuzzy, like waking up from a long sleep. I was confused and overcome with too many emotions. I wasn't certain which ones belonged to me and which ones belonged to Mindy. "He killed her Rudy, raped and killed her. She was so scared," I began to cry.

Rudy gently lifted the photo from my hands and put it down on the floor. Then he clasped my shaking hands into his and bent his head down touching them to his forehead. "I'm so sorry Jeanne Marie. I didn't know when to stop. This should not have happened. None of this should have happened. I didn't know what to do."

"No, Rudy, you didn't do anything wrong. It's just how it works. It's not an easy thing. You did great Rudy, really you did." Rudy still didn't speak. "I'm okay. Rudy please tell me you are too?"

He looked at me suspiciously. "Are you sure you're okay?"

"I swear to you I'm fine. It's just that…poor Mindy. What a horrible way to die."

"I don't know if I'm ready for the details," he said.

"It was awful," I said ignoring him. "He raped her, savagely. Then he slit her throat, like a sacrificial animal. He cut her throat," I said still rubbing my own which felt still raw from the experience.

Rudy pulled back and looked towards the stack of remaining photos. "I just don't know if I'm cut out for this Jeanne Marie. Even Old Vernon is soundin, not so bad."

"You're ready to trade me in on a snake already?"

"Nah, now that I'm thinking about it, you're much better looking than Old Vernon."

"Thanks a lot my good friend."

"Well you know he was much more attractive when he was a virile young black snake. He wasn't so ugly before his scales got to grayin and his beady eyes went blind."

I kicked his foot and he smiled. "You know we haven't finished Rudy?"

"Yeah mon, I knew that was comin. Is there anything I can do to make it easier?"

"No, unfortunately not that I can think of, but we need to think this through carefully. We have to figure out what we know so far." I reached over and spread the pictures out on the floor. "We know this is Tiburon, and we know this is a sequence of him chasing and capturing Mindy. This is him returning." The anger began to spew up inside of me, if ever I hated anyone, it was him. I could no longer call him by name. "I can't believe that monster is still alive."

"You know the cloth he is carrying has blood on it. Look closely, you see it?"

"Yeah, your right," I agreed. "Look at the side of his face. It's scratched."

"You think it's his own blood?" He asked.

"Looks like it, there isn't much there. Do you know how much blood there is when someone's throat is slit?" I did not wait for his answer. "A lot, an incredible amount, but he's an expert. He had to be very proficient with the knife. He grew up in the religion. Once he was actually a priest."

I wasn't sure Rudy had actually heard me. His attention was focused on the dark haired girl sleeping on the deck. "She does look peaceful."

"Linda, Mindy said her name was Linda. When I first looked at the picture, I thought she was sleeping." I looked up at Rudy, "She had to have been dead. We have to find out what happened to her."

"Back to the inevitable I suppose. I'll watch you closer this time Jeanne Marie, I promise."

I slid my back up against the sofa bed and tried to get comfortable. Then I closed my eyes and waited once again for the world to spin me back to my place in the timeless abyss. It always seemed the more worn down I was the faster I got there. Perhaps there was simply less resistance on my part. It was easier to surrender when I was emotionally tired. "You can give it to me now Rudy." I stretched out my hand and waited. Speaking came automatic this time. I never knew why my muscles worked one time and not another, but I was glad they worked now.

"Jeanne Marie, I givin you a picture of a young girl named Linda. See what you can find out about her death," he said placing the photo in my hand.

I held the photo with one hand and ran my fingers over the top of it with the other. I called out in my mind for Linda. No one answered.

Perhaps it was not her real name. I called out for the girl in the picture, the young dark haired girl whose face burned into the foreground of my vision. Still nothing, she did not answer. I tried once more, offering to help her, asking her to help us. Still she did not answer. I opened my eyes. "Something's wrong," I said.

"Maybe she really is at peace Jeanne Marie."

"I'm going to pray that she is Rudy. I'm a little afraid that she may be gone though."

"Isn't that what happens when you're at peace after you die?"

"Yes, I mean I guess so. When you die having become who you were born to be, you know, completed your purpose here and filled your destiny. Like Miguel, he became one with the greater part of who he really was. That's being at peace when you die. Somehow I can't imagine this girl being at peace. Tiburon killed her. I remember what Miguel said he did to the women who... worked for him. He said the monster filled their veins with the disease that was in the drugs. He kept the girls alive by feeding them more drugs. Over a period of time, the disease devoured their bodies, and their souls. My God Rudy, she's not just dead. She's gone, permanently. Her soul has died. He killed her soul!"

"I know what you're talking about Jeanne Marie. I had this conversation many a time with Miguel. You got to collect yourself now. You can't help a soul that's not here, but we can try and save the ones are. And that's what we're doing here and now. I should have gone after him myself and saved you from all this, but I was too wrapped up in my own selfish grief to think straight."

"No, you're right Rudy. We're doing the right thing now. We can't go back, but we can start changing things now. Let's get back to our weapon. There is only one other person that we have not identified here. The man boarding the boat, Tiburon's visitor."

"You're right," he said picking up the picture for a closer examination. "The pictures are all in sequence, right?"

"Right, he's in the first few shots," I agreed.

"Wrong," he said. "Look closer at demons face."

"It's scratched. These are the last frames. What do you think that means?" I asked.

"I'm not even sure it's important," he said shrugging his shoulders. It just tells us the sequence of events."

"There's another thing. Marion must have taken the pictures, but where was she when she did?"

"From the view she had," Rudy looked up. "I'd say she was in the crows nest."

"But why was she up there in the first place? Was she hiding because she knew Linda was dead? She couldn't have known what was going to happen to Mindy. So, was her real target the murder or was she trying to photograph the meeting between Tiburon and this guy and just happen to witness the murder by accident?"

"I'm afraid Marion is the only one who can answer that, and Marion is dead," he said.

"So are Linda and Mindy," I said picking up the photo of the two men. "There is something about this guy, he looks familiar. I studied his face, his clothes and his posture. "Ruddy," I yelled excitedly. "It's the DEA guy. This is the man that came to me!"

"Are you certain that's him?"

"I'm sure of it Rudy." I said dropping the picture onto the floor. "The letter, the one Marion wrote. She said his name, and that they had killed him. She said they would soon find her to do the same. I helped him Rudy. I am such an idiot. He was obviously working with Tiburon and I helped him."

"What do you mean you helped him? Start from the beginning Jeanne Marie, I don't know the details of all this intrigue. Miguel and I spoke often, because we were best of friends, but I didn't ask details of his dealins with Marion and the business of Tiburon. You know a man doesn't talk of the likes of that with another man. I only know a part of it all."

"Miguel never told you how we met?" I asked.

"To be sure he did, and he fell in love with you the first time he saw you."

"I don't know if that's exactly true Rudy. Actually, the first time he saw me was when I was doing the same thing we are doing right know. Only I was looking through Marion's eyes, and I was looking at him."

"The night Miguel went and got Marion. It's all comin back to me now. That part I do know," he said slowly shaking his head in acknowledgement.

"Only I didn't know it was Miguel I saw. I mean I only saw his eyes and then she called his name, not Miguel's name," I said trying to clarify. "Tiburon's name, she called out Tiburon. You can understand why I made the mistake. It was stupid, but you understand how this works and sometimes it's wrong because one thing looks like another, or because I jump to conclusions too quickly. Anyway, until I met Marion that day, I had never put Miguel and her together."

He looked at me now in amazement. "You never knew about Marion?"

"Nothing," I resigned. "Not until that day. Miguel tried to explain about her that night. He seemed so surprised that I didn't know about her. But Rudy how could I? It would be like me knowing Mindy's life story. I only know the story of her death. You see what I mean?"

"Clearly, Jeanne Marie. I see that clearly."

"Then why didn't Miguel see that?" I wanted to cry again. Why had he overestimated my knowledge so badly I wondered?

"Did Miguel ever work with you Jeanne Marie? Did he ever see how you looked through other peoples eyes?"

"No," I said simply.

"Well I have to tell you. If I hadn't seen it myself I'd be inclined to do the same thing now. When a person sees you inside of another woman's eyes, he's likely to make that same mistake. I mean the one of jumpin to conclusions. How was he to know what you did or did not know? Woman you were magic in his eyes!"

"I never thought of it like that," I said. "I always thought he was the one that was magic."

"Love can be like that, both of you blind and believing the other one was seein'," he said.

"Makes you wonder if it's all just an illusion doesn't it?"

"Don't you believe it for a minute Jeanne Marie. Love is real. It's all our thinking and jumpin to conclusions that are not real. Don't be questioning love."

I smiled, "Thanks I needed that. Rudy you're a wise man."

"Well make sure you pass that on to my Aunt Pearl when you see her. I could use a few good words in my direction. Speakin of, she won't be out forever and we still have lot's to do."

"Right, back to business. We have two choices. We can either ask Marion or the DEA guy for the rest of the info. I think Marion might be easier because she is the one who chose to help in the first place."

"That sounds reasonable," he said wrapping his arms around his legs and pulling them closer to his body.

I noticed his obvious discomfort with my suggestion. "Rudy I know this has got to be difficult for you. Talking to Marion can't be too easy but it's really the only way."

"It's just that... I have to admit not all my feelins are good one's regardin Marion. And, I'm not all too keen about callin on the dead for their help to begin with. I can't ever forget the time Marion was callin on the spirit of Annie Palmer. I told you something evil came out of the ground that day. Somethin of her lived on in Marion and I don't want to see the same thing happen again with you."

"Rudy it's not the same. Here, read the letter she wrote to me. Marion doesn't want to come back, not in any form. Marion was not a murderer."

He looked at me squarely in the eyes. "And I'm not as certain of that as you seem to be."

I was a little taken aback. He had a point. How could I be so sure? Rudy picked up the letter and began to read. He folded it up and stroked his chin with his fingers as he thought. "I don't suppose we have too much choice but to hope she meant what she said here. She can't be too much more dangerous than the other murderers lurkin about the island."

I wasn't sure why he kept referring to her as a murderer. I thought he might be referring to the warning from the Santeros, but I decided not to pursue it. "You know the procedure," I said.

"But we don't have a picture of her," he protested.

"It's okay. Her face is permanently etched into my mind. I don't need one to find her."

"Then how do I know when to start askin the questions?"

"I'll let you know," I said preparing myself for the decent. I closed my eyes and tried to picture the photos of the beautiful model hanging on her bedroom wall. But the face I saw was the pale scarred one that Miguel had kissed gently on the cheek. The world began its familiar spin, spirally down through time and light to the other level. I moved my head trying to steady myself for the decent. I knew I needed to stay in the center of the speeding cyclone, but it was moving so fast. I stretched my arms out, grasping for something in the middle of nowhere, but it did not slow me down. Then it was over, as suddenly as it had begun. A deafening silence and visionless void, I had arrived. Again I pictured her emaciated face and called out to her by name. She came, first by thought an unspoken acknowledgement to let me know she was there. Then she appeared, full-bodied and radiantly beautiful. She was smiling, no, she was laughing. I retracted a little not knowing what to expect. "Tell Rudy to stop worrying. I didn't like me either."

"Rudy," I responded. "She's saying don't worry, I didn't like me either."

He either did not respond or I could not hear him. I kept my eyes focused on Marion. "I know why you're here," she assured me. "It was Barnes, the DEA Agent. I figured I could use the pictures for money."

"You were going to blackmail him?"

She looked at me like I was an idiot for being surprised and went on. "They discovered Mindy's body several days later locked in a storage room. Barnes was on the investigation. Even he couldn't stomach the site of what he was involved in. I was afraid. It was only a matter of time before Tiburon would kill me. I tried to bargain, my life for the pictures. He was trying to help." Then she was gone and my eyes popped open.

"I'm sorry, Jeanne Marie," Rudy was saying as I woke up. I kept askin you questions, but you didn't answer and I didn't know what else to do."

"It's okay Rudy, I think I found out what we needed to know. Damn, I just wish I had a little more time. I wanted to ask her about Miguel."

"I told you I'm sorry. I just had to call you back," he said.

"No, no it's not your fault. She just left. That was her choice, not ours. I probably wasn't supposed to ask anyway. It's just as well I didn't. I did get the important information. Marion was taking the pictures to blackmail the DEA guy. The murder just happened at that particular time and when they discovered the body a few days later, he was one of the investigators. She said it sickened him. I believe that. I understand now why he left the department. Anyway she intended to blackmail him with the pictures of he and Tiburon meeting together, but after Marion witnessed him kill Mindy..."

"She figured she was next?"

"Exactly," I said. "Only then she decided to use the pictures to bargain with Barnes to save her life."

"Do you think when they killed him, they found out about the pictures. But if he had them, why didn't he just use them as evidence and hang Tiburon for the murder?"

"He was in them Rudy. He was involved in too much, in too deep. I guess by the time he came to me he really was trying to help Marion. Maybe he really was trying to redeem himself somehow." I looked up at Rudy and realized how self-absorbed I was sounding. "I'm sorry.

Truth is I don't know if they actually found the photos, they might have found some correspondence. All I know is that she knew they would find her through him and somehow they know the pictures exist."

"So, what to do now," Rudy thought out loud. "My Aunt Pearl always told me if you want to destroy a dark thing, you shine a light on it."

"Expose him. Rudy I just thought of something. We don't even know his real name!"

"Oh I know his name alright Jeanne Marie. It's not one I'm likely to forget. When they were investigatin the killins last year, I heard someone say his name. 'Juan Carlos Matanza,' he says, 'and he calls himself Tiburon.' The man thought it was quite a joke. A dark sick one, but a joke all the same. In Spanish, Matanza means slaughter. Imagine with a name like that he goes by Tiburon, a slaughterin shark."

"That's really sick," I said. I guess sometimes a name is not just a name after all. Anyway, we have all the information we need. I think it's time to contact the authorities."

"And which authorities do you think we can trust here in Jamaica? Not that they are all bad mind you, but we know there are a few pieces of rotten fruit in every barrel."

"Your right, what if we sent the information and a copy of the photos to Miami? I know a few people there I can trust."

"How many?" He asked.

"At least two, maybe three. I used to work with them on cases. One is a private detective now. One is in homicide and the other, well I don't really know him well, but he's honest and he works with the FBI."

"Hmm, I say we hedge our bet and send it to all three letting them all know who the copies went to," he said.

"That's an idea. How difficult will it be to get copies of the pictures?" I asked.

"Not difficult at all," he smiled. "I have a few friends myself."

"What about mailing them? Do you think it's safe?" I asked.

"I know a way to do that too. You start writin down the things they need to know and I'll go find Aunt Pearl and let her know we'll be leavin this afternoon."

I picked up the pad and began to write down everything I thought might be pertinent to an investigation. At the bottom I wrote copy sent to and the three names I knew. I did not have their addresses with me. I could find them, but I would need a phone. That was a small problem in the scheme of things. I got up and put away the few things I had taken out of my bag. Then I made up the beds and straightened up while I waited for Rudy and Aunt Pearl to return.

Aunt Pearl hugged us both good bye. Then she opened my hand and placed a little red cloth rolled up and bound with a few strands of hemp. "I was just finishin it up," she said. Old Vernon said you be needin it. You keep it with you."

I thanked Aunt Pearl and told her to thank Old Vernon for me and we were off. On our way to the hotel we made our plans. Rudy said we could get everything done fairly quick. Pretty much all I had to do today was check into a hotel. There I would get the addresses and prepare the three Fed Ex envelopes to mail, while Rudy got copies of the photos made. The next day I would leave for the Cayman Islands. There were plenty of charter boats for divers that left from Montego Bay to the Caymans. The scuba divers could not fly right before a deep dive, something about the altitude. So, they all took a charter boat instead. Rudy knew most of the charter boat captains. He took tourists there all the time. One-way, it was a twelve-hour boat ride. The plan was for me to go to the Caymans and safely wait it out. It all sounded very reasonable.

"Now follow my lead when we get there," Rudy said.

"The girl at the desk knows me well, her name is Christine. I'm going to tell her that your purse got stolen and of course you're without a passport and credit cards now. You need to come up with another name now so you won't be stutterin when she asks for it. Do you have any cash?"

"I have a few hundred. I didn't exactly go wild while I was here. I get to pick a name huh? How about Sophia? Sophia...I can't think of a last name that goes with Sophia," I said.

"Just pick a name you can remember. You're going to have to answer to it."

"I got it, Vernon, Sophia Vernon. I kind of like it."

"Well I suppose it's a good name for being sly," he said turning into the hotel driveway.

Rudy opened the door and I waited as he got my bag out of the trunk. It was an older hotel, British colonial, with rich mahogany furniture and polished brass fixtures. I stepped up to the desk and Rudy placed my bag down behind me. A tall girl in a burnt orange silk blouse looked up from her papers. "Christine," Rudy said trying to get her attention.

"Mr. Rudy," she said curtly.

"I've brought Miss Vernon here, I thought you might be able to help her. She was unfortunately robed of her purse while here on holiday. Now she's unable to get home without her plane ticket and passport."

"That is a terrible thing to happen," she shook her head sympathetically. "I wish I could say I hadn't seen that happen before but it's becoming all to frequent here."

"It's a sad thing," I agreed. "But I think it's happening more everywhere these days."

"Well I know you don't have reservations if you were planning on being home today, so let's see what we can do for you." She proceeded to check for an available room. "I don't suppose they left you with a credit card?"

"No, but I did have some cash put away my other bag," I volunteered.

"That's a lucky thing for you. I know you'll be needin to use the phone to get your affairs in order, so I'll wave the deposit on your calls. I'll just need you to sign here. Is there anything else I can help you out with?" She asked handing me a key.

"No, actually I can't thank you enough for this. Between all Rudy's help and now yours, it really helps a lot. Thank you."

"Yes, of course Mr. Rudy can be a very fine man." She said sarcastically looking at Rudy.

"Oh Christine, your not still upset…" I heard Rudy trying to explain as I picked up my bag and walked towards the elevator. I couldn't help but to wonder what he did to provoke these women. It was late afternoon before Rudy returned with the photographs.

"So Christine let you in?" I said.

"Only if I promised to see her later," he smiled and dropped the package on the table.

"What do you do to make the women in your life so angry Rudy?"

"They're not really all that angry Jeanne Marie, I just bring the fire out in em. They may be a little stirred up, but they're hot while they're stirrin and I like the challenge of coolin em down again."

"You are incorrigible Rudy."

"Ahh but you must admit it takes a certain irresistible quality in a man to stir a woman to a passionate feelin, even it is stated a little harshly at times. They're always happy when I leave."

"That I believe," I said.

"Now you know what I am tryin to say here."

"I know Rudy, I'm just kidding with you," I said sealing the last of the envelopes. I need to get down stairs and make sure these get out today."

"I spoke to the charter captain. You got to be up early. The boat leaves at seven thirty. I'll be downstairs to pick you up."

"Where are you going to be tonight?"

"With any luck, I won't be far," he said. "Christine has asked me over for dinner," he said ducking out before I had a chance to respond.

I picked up the Fed Ex envelopes and tucked some money into my pocket. I wanted to walk them down to the desk myself.

16

Ship of Dreams

I sat on the bow of the boat watching the hues of blues and greens run together as we plowed through a million small waves along the watery sea way. The ocean was calm but I knew that something ominous and foreboding lingered, somewhere in the depths beneath us. It was hard to leave Rudy behind. At the last minute he had insisted on coming with me. We both knew how ridiculous that was, but we entertained the thought for a moment anyway. I knew I had to go alone. I had to remain obscure and invisible until it was over. I pulled the cloth talisman out of my pocket and held it close to my heart. Please protect me Chango. If it's my fate to die soon, please let it be quick, and please don't let it hurt too much. I thought of my children, and my family. I prayed they would understand someday that no one really escapes their fate. They might hide from it. Or they may postpone it, maybe even for a long time. Eventually, however destiny would find them, and demand to be served.

It was dark when we arrived into the port. Rudy had arranged for me to stay on the boat for the night. The quarters were the size of a closet with two narrow bunks built in. There were three women on board. I bunked with a college girl from Boston who had come to dive the reefs off the Caymans. She was sweet but talkative and I was not in much of a mood to talk. She finally fell asleep and left me in silence if not in peace.

I did not want to wake up early the next morning, but there was not much choice. I heard the sounds of the others getting ready for the dive and I knew it was my cue to get off the boat before it left with me on it.

I surveyed the docks for a phone and a place to eat. There was a small restaurant within walking distance. I grabbed my bag and began to walk towards it. I had barely reached the end of the dock when I heard a woman's voice behind me. "Jeanne Marie, I don't believe it. It is you!"

I froze first then stiffly turned around, "Michelle!" I cried. "I can't believe it. What are you doing here?"

"You know me. One of my clients is divorcing her husband and, naturally hiding all his money here in the Caymans so...I had to depo a couple of people. Ah but that's not the best part. Look at this!"

I looked around to see what she was talking about. "The yacht Jeanne Marie," she looked at me incredulously. "It's big enough you should be able to see it."

"Oh, yeah that is a really big boat," I said.

"Not a boat," she corrected, "a yacht! And it has been at my disposal for four, count them four glorious days."

"You are amazing Michelle."

"And life is beautiful." Her expression changed abruptly. "But something's wrong here. You're not looking too well Jeanne Marie. What are you doing here anyway? Is everything alright?"

No, nothing at all is right. I am scared and alone. I am after some black hearted, drug dealing, rapist and murderer. The good news is he will be caught. The bad news is I think I'm supposed to die in the process. I wanted to grab her shoulders and cry out all these things but all that came out was a lie. "Oh I'm okay. It's just, well a crazy thing happened. I was in Jamaica and my purse got stolen, my passport and plane tickets. Anyway I was on a dive boat and I got here. So I figured I'd find somewhere to get some coffee and figure out what to do."

"Not a problem. The universe works in mysterious ways. Come on I'll give you a tour of the yacht. We'll go to the galley and get something to eat. I don't know about you, but I'm starved."

"You are incredible," I said. Michelle was a top-notch divorce attorney in Miami. She was deceptively blond and playfully bimboish. But it was that rare combination of beauty and brilliance that had attracted a long list of wealthy international clients.

"I know and I'm so much fun too," she said brushing the hair from her shoulders with the flip of a hand. "This is all going to work out great, you'll see."

We boarded the elegant vessel. It was impressively inlaid with varying shades of polished teak. "Tina," Michelle called out to a young girl in crisp white shorts and a white cotton shirt.

"Hey Miss Michelle," she answered in a decidedly British accent. "How are you this morning?"

"Wonderful, and look I found a friend who's coming to breakfast this morning. Jeanne Marie, this is Tina. She is the first mate on board, and she plays a mean game of cards too."

"Well if you count that as a card game," Tina smiled and I reciprocated, clearly not getting her joke. "Michelle has introduced me to the game 'Sorry' it's hard to miss with the big numbers and color codes and all."

"All right so it's a kiddie game," Michelle said. "But it's totally mindless and you can drink, get as stupid and silly as you want, and still win. What more could you ask of a game."

"That's so you Michelle," I laughed.

"Oh, I have a great idea. Let's play a threesome after breakfast!"

"I'm afraid I have work to do this morning," Tina said. "The boat's pushin off in the morning and I have to make sure all provisions are stocked before I can take my leave."

"You're leaving?" Michelle asked.

"Going home for a couple of weeks," she said. As of five pm today, I am officially on holiday."

"Oh that's too bad," Michelle said.

"No," Tina shot back. "That's a very good thing for me. I've worked hard for my leave and I am looking forward to every minute of it."

"No," Michelle attempted to explain. "Jeanne Marie is stranded here because her passport and plane tickets were stolen. I thought she could ride back with the boat to Key Biscayne. I mean there are no passengers on the boat, and I know Benito won't mind. Benito is another one of my clients," she said turning to me. "He owns the boat, excuse me, yacht." Michelle turned her attention to Tina. "Well, I don't suppose it really makes a difference, except it won't be much fun without you."

"That's true," Tina said bending her head down to whisper the next sentence. "The captain's a bit of stuffed shirt."

"No sense of humor at all," Michelle agreed. "His name is Captain Roberts, I've been calling him Captain Bob. It absolutely infuriates him, but he won't say a word to me."

Tina covered her mouth and laughed. "I'll go get Gustavo and get you girls something to eat. It was nice meeting you Miss Jeanne Marie."

"Same here," I said. "Michelle, are you serious? Can I ride back with you?"

"You may as well go home first class. I mean someone's got to do it. And I would love to come back with you, but I've got to fly back this afternoon. I've got a flight to Miami at five. My office is going crazy and I've got to get back to reality and take care of business. But there is no reason you should not enjoy the fruits of someone else's labor just because I can't."

"You're a Godsend Michelle. You have no idea what this means to me."

"What are friends for?" She said. "Besides, we still have practically the whole day to do something outrageous with. After breakfast we'll finish the tour and I'll give you the low down on the crew."

It was a fabulous yacht, like something from the rich and famous portfolio of castles and dreams for the masses. The living area was done completely in white and textured in pale shades of cream. Dolphins were artfully etched into Lucite panels that led to a sculptured stairway of the same material. The room was accented with a fine balance of polished brass and cut crystal. Vibrant oil paintings of seventeenth century women in heavy gold frames carried the dreamy room back to the opulence of earth. "It's breathtaking Michelle."

"I know. Truth is I would consider putting Benito on my possible candidate for marriage list. He's so cute, and he has a great wit. Good sense of humor and great taste, but he has this thing for mistresses. You know how I feel about that. So, I'll just have to settle for his friendship, and his yacht."

"So, what's the story on the crew?" I said walking down the steps to the master bed room."

"Oh, nothing really. Gustavo is the chef. He's not bad, quiet and a little moody. But you know how chefs are, temperamental. He's from Brazil to boot. Then there's Peter, another Brazilian. He's the engineer. Takes his job very seriously and doesn't talk much. He's usually in the engine room though, so you don't see him much. And I've already told you about Captain Bob, so you see what I mean. Tina is the only life aboard this ship. I'm going to have to talk to Benito about that. I mean this is a man who really enjoys life, with both hands I might add. And he's so much fun, I can't imagine him of all people with a stick in the mud crew like this. Go figure."

"Oh look at this bedroom," I sat on the edge of the bed and fell back into the quilted satin blanket. "I don't mind about the crew," I sighed. "I'll just suffer, silently surrounded by all this luxury."

"I'm glad to see you taking it so well," She said. "Come on help me pack up and then we can relax and find something to do. I know, we can put on our bathing suits have cocktails on the deck and pretend we're bimbos."

"Oh come on Michelle, can't we at least be countesses or something?"

"Oh all right, you be the countess. I'll be duke's mistress," she said reaching for her bikini. "The tactless American one." We both laughed as we changed clothes and identities for the afternoon. It was all such wonderful fun, such a welcome reprieve. Michelle had come in like the morning sun, and the sunny day ended with her gaily leaving for the airport that afternoon.

In the living room there was a large screen TV, a huge assortment of video taped movies to play. In another room downstairs, I found shelves of books and magazines. Most of them were even in English. I would have no problem being alone and entertaining myself on the way back. This was all just too good to be true. By the time I got back, the detectives would have the information about Tiburon. It would take them a little while, to check out the evidence on the murder. It had been a long time, at least seven years, but he had raped her. He had left his seed, the tell tale DNA inside of her. And if that wasn't enough, beneath her nails was his blood and skin. I knew they kept evidence like that for a long time. "The dead will speak Tiburon. And this time, they will bury you!"

Could it really be that easy? Maybe the test was for me just to stand up, to take charge of my power and responsibility for my destiny. That could be true. Maybe I just needed to be grateful now for all their help. Then again, I had not yet crossed the Caribbean Sea. I was right in the middle of the Devils Triangle. Those dark sinister shark infested waters where danger invisibly lurked. I could not think about it. The only thing left to do was wait, and trust.

Three movies and two chapters of Moby Dick later, I crawled under the covers and begged Yemaya to rock me to sleep. Gratefully, she obliged and I slept soundly through the night. The next morning I woke up with a disturbing dream about Marion and Linda. And, Tiburon, he was in the dream too. They had been all around me. It felt like they were in the room with me. It was unsettling, a skin crawling kind of uneasiness. It was probably just thoughts and fears coming to surface in my sleep, an unconscious brain cleansing, I tried to convince myself.

I spent most of the day on the deck, pretending to read. Michelle had been right. The captain was solicitously polite but there was something really standoffish about him. He was insincere. That's what it was. That's why he was so uncomfortable to be around. No wonder

Michelle hadn't liked him. Captain Bob, I smiled. I thought about Rudy and how he would laugh when he found out how I got home, if I made home that was.

It was lunchtime. I found out quickly that meals were the only break in monotonous lazy days aboard ship. I was getting a little bored with myself, so I wondered into Gustavo's territory down in the galley. There were some photos hanging in the hallway leading to the dining room. One was a boat badly charred and the rest were just a series of boat construction pictures. "Are these pictures of this boat?" I asked the chef trying to strike up a conversation.

"Yeah, this boat got hit by lightning, it went up in flames so fast it almost sank. When this owner bought it he had to practically rebuild it. Actually it was the engine room and the hull that got the worst of it."

"Were you on it before? I mean before it burned," I said.

"No." He said letting me know the conversation had ended.

Ignoring his rudeness, I continued to study the photos. There was writing on the mats at the bottom of the photos. Dates had been scribbled down along with a few words. 'The Predator' was printed beneath the burned boat. That must have been the old name. The last photo was of the yacht in all its shinning newness being christened 'La Bella Santa'. What a transformation, I thought, from 'The Predator' to 'The Beautiful Saint'. The small hairs stood up on the back of my neck and I looked once more at the date on the first picture. Seven years ago, it had been struck by lightning and caught fire. No, it couldn't be, that would just be too ironic, even for me. It couldn't be Tiburon's old white slave boat. Please God tell me it's not.

I sat in the dinning room alone, trying to think things through. If it were true, and that was possible, but astronomically improbable, why would they put me here?" There was certainly nothing left to discover on the boat. It had been completely taken apart and put together again. The dreams I had this morning about Marion and Linda. Were their spirits haunting the boat? Did they want my attention? Were they warning me? I had to stop, and think, calmly and rationally.

The boat was owned by a man who named it 'The Beautiful Saint' that has to say something for him right there. And, he is a friend and client of Michelle's. I've known her for a long time. Her reputation is far more valuable to her than money ever would be. Besides, she's far too ethical to take on a client with any kind of a questionable income. Offshore corporations and international banking maybe, but she would never touch drug money. Oh God, what was I thinking. Of course she would never knowing get involved, but what if she didn't know? What if I flew right into the spider's web?

I was suddenly sick to my stomach. I was not hungry anymore. The only thing I could do was retire to the state room and wait. I watched another movie, and looked out the windows for what felt like hours. I longed for the sight of land. The day was prayerfully uneventful and almost over. The sky was beginning to glow with the colors of blooming roses. I stepped outside to watch the heavens fold for the night. It was then that I realized for the first time that it was quiet. The motors were not running, and we were not moving. I leaned over the railing to see if I could see anything. I did not know what I was looking for, maybe to see if we were anchored, but I couldn't see anything. I decided to go up to the captain's station and ask him why we had stopped when I saw a fishing boat heading towards us. I stopped for a minute to watch the boat. The fishermen on the back were trying to untangle their lines. One of them almost fell overboard and the other dropped the giant rod into the water. They must have been drunk, but they looked really comical.

The boat pulled right up and the captain stepped out onto the deck. The two men in the boat started yelling "ahoy, ahoy there captain." and then burst into laughter.

"I suggest you take your party elsewhere gentlemen," the captain called down to them.

"Now, that's not very friendly of you captain," the first one slurred.

"What my friend here means, wait a minute where is my friend?" He looked worried for a minute and then turned around and bumped into his fishing buddy. "Oh, there you are. What I meant capin sir is we traveled a little too far from home today and I don't think we have enough gas to get back. Can we come stay with you?" He asked weaving his body to keep himself standing as the boat rocked.

"I don't have time for this nonsense. I'm going to ask you once more to shove off gentlemen," he said sternly.

The other man spoke up. "Listen, we don't mean to bother nobody, but if we call the Coast Guard right now, we could have a little problem on our hands. You know," he looked both ways as if some one were listening. "They don't like it when you drink and drive around here." His friend broke up and howled with laughter.

The captain walked down the stairs and looked at me as he passed by without saying a word. A few minutes later he returned to his perch and called down to the two drunken fishermen that his engineer would supply them with enough fuel to get them home. One of the men began to cheer then thought better of it and decided just to continue his effort to stand up on the deck of the rocking boat.

It was not a small fishing boat. Actually, it was the kind of boat you saw featured in glitzy magazines where a weekend fishermen always reels in a giant sailfish. The boat had an upper and lower deck with glass doors that opened from the living room onto the lower deck. There were large mountings for the fishing poles on both levels. It looked brand new. I looked at the name on the front, 'Happy Daze', how appropriate.

The boat was filled up, but when they tried to start it sputtered and stalled. The captain was getting increasingly infuriated. "Get on the boat and get the damn thing started," he ordered his engineer.

Peter boarded the boat and disappeared down the stairs along with one of the drunken fishermen. The motor tried to turn over, it sputtered a few times and then quit again. Suddenly the hatch flew open and the fisherman was yelling for help. His friend, startled by the yelling began screaming with him. "What the hell is going on?" The captain called over.

"It's the engineer, he stood up and hit his head. There's blood everywhere. Tom," he yelled to his friend. "You're a doctor, get down here and help him."

"That imbecile's too drunk to even get down the stairs," the captain said lowering himself down to board the boat himself. "Just stay where you are," he yelled out angrily to the doctor. But the doctor followed him down anyway.

I waited to see what had happened. It had been ten or fifteen minutes already. It must have been bad. My God what if he bled to death down there. Maybe they were calling the Coast Guard from their boat. I watched for the captain to come up spitting mad, but now no one came out. Something was wrong here. What if they were not drunks at all? What if they were pirates? I had heard about that, maybe I read about it somewhere. I had no idea what to do. Gustavo, I had to find the chef. We were the only ones left on board.

I ran to the galley, past the photos on the wall but he wasn't there. I checked the crew's quarters and saw one of the doors closed. "Gustavo," I called pounding on the door. "Gustavo, something has happened, you need to come out here." He waited a minute and then opened the door. He looked at me oddly, "Gustavo," I said. "The engineer had an accident, and the captain went to help him but some things wrong. You've got do something."

Gustavo closed the door carefully and looked at me again like he didn't understand the language or something.

"Gustavo what's wrong with you?" I demanded. Then I saw it in his eyes, he was high. Too drugged to know what I was yelling about and too far into oblivion to even care. "Oh this is great! What am I going to do now?" I screamed running as best I could back up the narrow winding stairway. The radio, I had no clue how it worked, but I had to try.

When I reached the wheel room my heart sank. I knew it was him, before he even turned around I knew it was him. I tried to say his name, but nothing came out. My knees went weak and I knew I was falling, but I couldn't make it stop, "Miguel!"

I opened my eyes, and his face was in front of me. Perhaps I was dead. Maybe it all happened so quickly that I didn't remember and here he was with me. Death was good. "Jeanne Marie, Jeanne Marie can you hear me?" He called.

"Yes, Yes Miguel I can hear you now," I answered. "Am I really dead?" I asked.

"No," he said kissing my hands. "No, you are not dead."

"Why are you here then?" My vision was getting clearer, the doctor, Tom was standing behind him. I jerked back pulling my hands away from him. "What's going on? You're not dead..."

"He reached over and tried to gently restrain me from jumping up. This is Tom. He is with the FBI. The other man on the boat is also an FBI agent. I know this is a shock, but it was the only way. I couldn't let anyone know I was alive, not even you."

"And Rudy?" I asked still too stunned to think straight.

"No, Rudy does not know either."

"Why, why did you do this?" I begged for an answer that would appease me. "Miguel, can you even imagine..."

"I know," he nuzzled his face into my neck. "A thousand times, I know."

I'm not sure how long it was before I could actually locate my muscles and move. When I did I folded my arms around his shoulders and felt his face touching my skin. It was real, he was real and I didn't care how or why anymore.

"Jeanne Marie," he said lifting his head and kissing my cheek. "It's not over. You're still in danger. You have to get on the other boat and let them take you back."

"Are you crazy? Do you think I'm leaving you now?"

"I don't have time to explain everything. The captain was delivering a shipment of drugs tonight. That's why he is anchored out here. Tiburon will be here. He knows you are on board."

"But you have to come with me. He'll kill you Miguel!"

"No, Jeanne Marie. We all have a job to do and this one is mine," he said. "You have to go now."

"I'm not going without you," I demanded.

"Yes, you will," he said sternly. "You will get on the boat and you will wait for me in Miami. I love you, and I will see you when I get there."

"No, you don't understand Miguel," I was crying and struggling as I tried to explain but the agent's strong arms were pulling me out the door and Miguel would no longer look at me.

I struggled with the agent until the boat pulled away. It wasn't long before the yacht was nothing more than a small match, a tiny flame in the middle of the ocean. I watched until it went out, gone from sight, swallowed by the sea. Not again God, please don't let it happen again.

The captain, his engineer and Gustavo were in handcuffs down below. Tom drove the fishing boat back. Two other agents were with Miguel waiting on Tiburon to make his appearance. I was nervous. I couldn't just sit and think anymore, so I sat next to Tom and hoped he would speak to me. "I'm sorry about the struggle," I began.

"Don't worry about it," he said. I guess you had more than you're share of surprises tonight."

"That would be a gross understatement," I agreed. "I'm not sure who's dead or alive anymore. And I have no idea what's going on or what to believe."

"Well if there's anything I can do to help," he said. "Feel free to ask."

"I know I have at least a thousand unanswered questions, but the only one that matters right now is about Miguel. What is he doing back there? He's a doctor, not an agent."

"Right now he's both." He started to look at me while he spoke, then thought better of it and kept his eyes on the instruments. "Don't worry. We've had everything under surveillance for months now.

Miguel has been well trained and the other two agents with him are the best we've got."

I thought of asking him about the photos I had sent. They seemed so petty in the scheme of things, but I thought I should tell him. "I had some evidence," I volunteered. "Photographs, they were in my bag. I sent copies of them to the FBI."

"Yeah, we know. Like I said, we've been tracking this guy for a while now."

"Did they help at all?" I asked.

"Well they certainly sped things up," he said. "Now it's my turn. What ever possessed you to go back there anyway?"

"Love," I said. "Rudy was right. In the end it all boils down to love somehow." Tom shook his head at my gibberish and steered straight ahead. I could see the halo of lights from the shore. Before long there was a perfect florescent outline of the city of Miami. It was all like a dream on fast forward after that. I was shuffled into an empty office downtown. There I would wait for word from Miguel. It wouldn't come until at least one or two Tom assured me. They didn't expect the rendezvous before midnight, "and you know how Latins are, they are never on time. Lay down on the sofa, rest, we'll let you know the moment we hear." I watched the clock raise both hands and salute midnight, still no word of Miguel.

It was twelve after three. I knew because the clock and I had become intimate by then, sharing every precious moment throughout the night. Tom came over and sat down beside me. It was over. I knew the look. I screamed until I heard the sound fill the room bounce off the walls and double back again. Words were spoken. "Miguel was a brave man. It was a terrible tragedy, a dark victory. It was a great loss. It would be shared by all."

Yes, yes, and now he is officially a saint. He is dead. Shot, they said. Shot and this time he would not heal. They airlifted him to Jackson Memorial, but it was too late. They could not make him live. Did I want to see him they asked, yes, yes I needed to see him still.

Lights whirled by, as we sped through darkness and empty streets. Bright white lights and red flashing ones lit the entrance to the hospital. Sirens screamed in the background. Excited voices and hurried people rushed around me in a surreal blur. An unfamiliar voice spoke to me but I couldn't hear them. Someone guided me into a pale blue room. A woman lowered a white blanket exposing his pale face, the face of a sleeping angel. It was Miguel. A few strands of dark hair had fallen over his forehead. I pushed them from his face, and gently kissed him there.

Someone took me home. I do not remember leaving the hospital. I do not remember arriving at my house. I open my eyes once again. I am here, and I am alive. I reconcile myself to the fact that it is the living who must bury their dead. The dead can no longer touch the earth. They cannot dig a hole. They cannot pickup a single handful of dirt to cover themselves. It is up to the living to fill the empty space death leaves behind. If left to the dead, it will not be done. Today I told myself I must bury the dead.

There had been a Catholic church service attended by many people. Miguel was honored for his bravery, and his dedication and service to humanity. My grief felt small and selfish next to the brilliance of his life.

It was not a good day for boating the sky was gray and a cold February rain came down like a liquid veil separating the heavens from the earth. But it was the day that had been chosen and somehow it seemed appropriate that the heavens too should morn. The agency had provided a boat for the occasion and three agents came along to pay their respects to a fallen colleague.

I looked out over the dark waters and thought of the first odu that had been taught to me when I was learning to read the shells, the oracles of divination. "The first mouth speaks a proverb," she said. "If there is no bad, there can never be anything good. The first lesson of a Santera is to understand that the world is neither good nor bad, it simply is. This letter explains that two eyes see but one thing and two legs carry us in one direction, but this is not a sign of balance. It is the sign of the struggle for balance. It is an energy filled with turbulence. In this first letter, we are to remember the story of Chango.

Chango began as a warrior, a great and victorious warrior who had united two opposing kingdoms. His reputation was legendary and everyone recognized him for this great deed. But as time went on he became more and more arrogant. He began to fight, for the glory that came from winning and so he became abusive of his power. It was through his own shame and guilt that the warrior Chango was transformed into the Orisha Chango. His weapons became the tools of growth and change. This is a sign that speaks of the transformation of tragedy and crisis, the transformation of guilt and shame into purpose.

Of course, his weapons were wood. They were the tools of growth, of transition and change, the tools he had exchanged for his weapons. All this time, I thought, through all these things, how was it that I was still struggling with my first lesson? I thought of the words Miguel, spoke to me on the first night we met. "Everyone has a story that brings them to the place they are in this world," and so this one has become mine. The boat rocked fiercely and I opened the urn to pour his ashes into the water. But just as I leaned over the rail, a huge wave came crashing into the boat and the jar slipped from my cold wet hands. There was nothing more to be done. I could only watch, as the urn sank slowly down to its watery grave at the bottom of the sea.

"How many more words need to be said? Your body and blood have been reduced to ashes, cleansed of the violence that defiled your life. A saint dies and a woman weeps. I have returned you to the sea Miguel, where your mother Yemaya is waiting to carry you home. Your destiny was written for this reunion. We are *okana oni*, of one heart you and I. Somewhere inside you knew it all the while. Somewhere inside I knew this too. A flame cannot live in the ocean, and the living cannot walk with the dead. Goodbye Miguel my love."

About the Author

If you have read this book, I can assure you that you already know more about the author than she ever intended to reveal. I can tell you that *'When Angels Die'* was finally completed, I cried. They were not tears of happiness, nor of sorrow, they were tears of pure gratitude. I was so incredibly grateful, that somehow the process of writing had transformed this portion of my life into a journal of memories, allowing me to begin anew.

Three years later I wrote *'Circle of Tears'*. As the events in that story began to unfold I found myself in the midst of a phenomenon with worldwide implications. I knew then, *'Circle of Tears'* was a story much greater than my own. It was the book that would begin a new form of work for me, the work of writing.

It has been nearly five years since my new work began, and I am happily living the third episode of what appears to be an unlimited number of adventures into the mysteries of this world. I am not sure how or when, this next venture aptly named *'Flowers are Forever'* will end. When it does, I can only be certain that another will soon begin. My destiny it seems is to live eternally a series of beginnings and endings. Someday perhaps, I will truly understand this path of living death unending. Until then I will continue to learn the ways of the saints, and in gratitude I will write what I live.

Jeanne Marie

www.jmarieAntoinette.com

0-595-21486-X